# COMMON CALLING

# COMMON CALLING

## The Laity and Governance of the Catholic Church

Stephen J. Pope

Editor

Georgetown University Press/Washington, D.C.

Georgetown University Press, Washington, D.C.
© 2004 by Georgetown University Press. All rights reserved.
Printed in the United States of America

10 9 8 7 6 5 4 3 2 1                                2004

This book is printed on acid-free paper meeting
the requirements of the American National Standard
for Permanence in Paper for Printed Library Materials.

Library of Congress Cataloging-in-Publication Data

Common calling : the laity and governance of the Catholic Church / Stephen J. Pope,
editor.
     p. cm.
   Includes bibliographical references and index.
   ISBN 1-58901-027-2 (pbk. : alk. paper)
   1. Catholic Church—Government. 2. Laity—Catholic Church. I. Pope, Stephen J.,
1955–
   BX1920.C578 2004
   262′.152—dc22

                                                          2004005621

To the Catholic Theological Society of America,
in this time of difficulty, for its integrity, dedication,
and theological leadership

# Contents

# Introduction:
# The Laity and the Governance of the Church Today

## Stephen J. Pope

The recent sexual abuse crisis has led many Catholics to ask how the current system of ecclesial governance within the Catholic Church might be improved and made more responsive to the needs of believers. This chapter examines reasons for expanding the role of the laity within the governance of the church and provides a general context for the other chapters in this book. The first section of this chapter sets the issue of governance in the context of the recent crisis of sexual abuse in the church. Since this crisis was largely the result of a failure of governance, the response of the church to it naturally has to include an examination of how to improve governance. The second section of the chapter examines ambiguities in the laity-clergy distinction, particularly with regard to the power of governance in the church as it exists today. The third section explores the theological interpretation of clergy-laity relations and governance in the teachings, and especially the ecclesiology, of the Second Vatican Council. The fourth section examines the dominant paradigm used today by church authorities for interpreting the role of the laity in the governance of the church. It gives special attention to some of the weaknesses of this paradigm. The fifth section proposes that the church can improve governance generally and enhance the role of the laity in it by promoting three goods: dialogue, participation, and authority. The final section offers a brief indication of how the components of this book take up some of the key themes pertaining to our topic. This book will play a helpful role if it contributes some insights of value for the ongoing conversation within the Christian community about this important issue.

## Crisis in the Church

The immediate context for this book is presented by the crisis of sexual abuse in the United States. As of fall 2003, at least 325 of the 46,000

1

priests in the United States have either resigned or been removed from their posts in the wake of allegations of abuse. The public has been inundated with story after story, some of them depicted in graphic detail, of child molestation, sexual assaults, and unimaginable sexual perversions. Media reports and legal proceedings have drawn attention not only to abusive priests but also to negligent bishops. As public awareness of the dimensions of the scandal grew, it became increasingly apparent that the heart of the problem was not only a matter of sexual ethics but also, and above all, a systematic misuse of institutional authority. Recent polls examining the opinions of the Catholic laity found that decision making by clergy alone, along with an excessive concern to avoid scandal, were the two most frequently cited factors leading to the crisis.[1] As moral theologian James F. Keenan points out, the sexual abuse itself and the misdeeds and negligence of certain supervising bishops were both species of the same evil: the abuse of power.[2] This means that, as journalist David Gibson put it, "The crisis in Catholicism is a crisis of governance rather than a crisis in faith."[3]

There are of course a variety of reasons for reflecting on the role of the laity in the church. Prior to the scandal, demographic trends concerning the falloff of vocations and the rise of immigrant populations of Catholics had already led to increased reflection on this topic. Sociologist James D. Davidson reports that the ratio of laypeople to priests in the United States climbed from 875:1 in 1981, to 1,113:1 in 1991, and to 1,429:1 in 2001, a 63 percent increase over this period. In the summer of 2003, 16 percent of parishes were without a resident pastor.[4] Sociologist Dean Hoge predicts that parish structures will change if ordination rates persist at their current replacement level of roughly 35 percent.[5] For this reason alone, the laity has been assuming more and more responsibilities for governance, especially in parishes and schools.

The scandal, of course, provides a new and even more morally urgent incentive for undertaking serious and extended reflection on the role of the laity in the church. The abuse of power by individual bishops was, for many Catholics, the most disturbing and discouraging aspect of the scandal. Sexual sins and crimes by priests are one thing; a pattern of cover-ups, deception, and denial by prominent church authorities claiming to be moral leaders is another. The laity was absent from episcopal decision making in these cases. By definition, none of the powerful men who made disciplinary decisions about priests who abuse children are themselves parents. These prelates showed much more solicitude for their priests and the public image of the church than for the abused children, some of whom have been irreparably damaged.[6]

As the stream of news about the scandal became an overwhelming flood, Catholics who had previously deferred to clerical leadership began to question the moral appropriateness of a system of institutional power that is so isolated, secretive, and unaccountable.[7] Of course, bishops sometimes consulted selected laymen and -women—physicians, lawyers, and therapists—but ultimately their decisions were made behind closed doors on their own authority. The fact that the timing of the crisis coincided with a number of other major scandals of financial and business institutions in the United States helped to underscore the many problems of accountability, management practices, and governance structures that pervade the institution (see chapter 12 of this volume). Historian Scott Appleby voiced the view of many Catholics when he said to the American bishops at their June 2002 meeting in Dallas: "I do not exaggerate by saying that the future of the church in this country depends upon your sharing authority with the laity."[8]

Though guilty clergymen have been at the center of public attention, it would be a mistake to divide the current situation into "bad" clergy against "good" laypeople. Most members of the hierarchy would never think of harming anyone, let alone commit crimes of sexual abuse. The vast majority of priests have not been sexually abusive, and the vast majority of bishops have not been criticized for moral negligence.[9] Conversely, most perpetrators of sexual abuse in the wider society are laypeople, and, indeed, relatives of their victims. Moreover, certainly some laypeople knew about the sexually abusive conduct of priests and yet, for one reason or another, did nothing.

The laity also needs to recognize its role in the shaping of the culture of the church. The unreflective deference and passivity of the majority of Catholic churchgoers contributed, albeit unintentionally, to the kind of religious culture that would make such unthinkable exploitation possible. I say this neither to suggest moral equivalence between abusive priests and complacent laity nor to lessen the blame due to powerful churchmen who allowed terrible crimes to be perpetrated with impunity. But it serves as a reminder to avoid the temptation to shift all responsibility and to attribute all guilt to the clergy.

## Laity, Clergy, and Governance

The adjective "lay" comes from the Greek *laikos*, which in antiquity signified a person of the common as opposed to the elite social and political classes. The *Oxford English Dictionary* offers three definitions of "laity": (1) the state of being a layman; the not ordained; (2) the body of people not in orders, as opposed to the clergy; laymen collectively;

and (3) unprofessional people, as opposed to those who follow some learned profession.

The earliest strata of the New Testament do not distinguish "clergy" from the "laity" (see chapters 1 and 3 of this volume).[10] The second century saw the emergence of an important distinction between bishops and other Christians and then the development of the threefold ordained offices of bishop, priest, and deacon. The "clergy" has come to designate all those people who are ordained to "holy orders." Though at one time it included all individuals who had received tonsure and therefore all those in the so-called "minor orders" (such as lectors and acolytes), today the ranks of the clergy include only deacons, priests, and bishops.

While the laity–clergy distinction seems on the surface to be clear-cut, it also carries certain ambiguities in practice. *Lumen Gentium*, the Dogmatic Constitution on the Church, follows a threefold distinction between clergy, vowed religious, and the laity (no. 31). Religiously vowed nuns and sisters are usually associated with the clergy by ordinary Catholics, but they often think of themselves as existing in the lay state because they are not ordained. Conversely, since they typically have regular jobs and careers, wives, and children, and do not wear clerical garb, deacons are assumed to be members of the laity. Yet since they are ordained to the deaconate, they are members of the clergy. A similar blurring of the lines exists in cases of lay ministry: lay Eucharistic ministers, directors of religious education, chaplains and campus ministers, etc.

The issue of governance within the church also carries certain ambiguities. The church, like any other large community, needs a system of governance to serve its communal life. Among other things, the church is a society—a group of people who routinely gather as companions to share some important goods, goals, standards, and commitments. The root of this association lies in a shared and existentially vital faith in Jesus Christ. The public expression of this association lies in the forms of communal organization that comprise the church's "body politic."

The Latin term *gubernare* means "to steer," as in a vessel, and so to direct, to rule, to govern.[11] Among the ten meanings of "to govern" in the *Oxford English Dictionary* one finds: to command inferiors or subordinates, to regulate behavior, to exercise authoritative control over a political unit, and to manage affairs of state. Government involves primarily the making of policy and, secondarily, the administration of policies.

The governance structures of the Catholic Church seem clear and straightforward, but in fact in some important ways they are very complex and ambiguous. In a narrow sense, of course, priests and bishops govern by possessing the "power of jurisdiction" within the institution.[12] But if we recognize that governance also involves, more broadly, the kinds of influence exerted over action and policy by different leadership positions, then considerable power is held by laypeople. Sisters run hospitals and, with laymen and -women, administer schools, colleges, and universities. They also function more pervasively to administer parishes and pastoral programs.

There are at least two ways to think about the development of lay leadership in the church. One way, which can be described as a sort of "clergy–laity dualism," understands the blurring of the clergy–lay distinction, and the blurring of the lines of authority in governance, as a necessary lesser evil accepted for the sake of addressing the crisis caused by declining vocations at this point in time. Ideally, however, it holds that the clergy ought to hold and exercise the power of governing the church in all its ministries and that the laity ought to focus on "temporal affairs." The laity can assist the clergy via deputation on an ad hoc basis, but this delegation of power can only be accepted as a temporary remedy for a shortage of priests.

The proximate historical roots of this clergy laity dualism are clear. An observer of the pre-Vatican II Catholic Church might well have described it as a religious community governed by the clergy, where the domain of the clergy lay within ecclesiastical society and the domain of the laity in civil society. The role of the clergy was to govern the body politic of the church—i.e., to organize structures, shape practices, create laws, set policies, enforce norms, judge difficult cases, and, in general, issue authoritative commands. The responsibility of the laity was to follow the lead of the clergy, at least when it came to religion: to adhere to normative practices, conform to regulations, and, in general, obey authoritative commands.

An alternative view regards both clergy and laity as called to serve *both* the church and the world. This view begins not with the clergy-laity distinction but with the equal dignity of baptism, which grounds the common mission of all the Christian faithful to build up the Body of Christ and to transform the world. Sacramental ordination gives priests and bishops a special responsibility of pastoral leadership, a leadership most profoundly symbolized in their presiding at the Eucharist. But ordination does not mean that the concern of the clergy ought to be focused on the church to the exclusion of the world. Conversely, the laity is immersed in the world and charged with its "consecration to Christ," but this responsibility does not obviate their responsibility for the good of the church. On the contrary, devotion to the objects of concern increases in direct rather than inverse proportion to one another: love for the Body of Christ increases rather than diminishes love for the world.

## The Second Vatican Council

Each of these two views of the clergy–laity relation, and of the nature of governance, claims its basis in an interpretation of the teachings of Vatican II. The former perspective, however, has its deepest roots in the preconciliar theology that continues to be expressed in the documents of the Council. The generalization made by historian Giuseppe Alberigo in 1987 continues to hold true today: "At present, the postconciliar period is marked largely by a continuation of the tension experienced at the Council itself; nor is it an accident that almost all the leading figures on all sides today attended the Council."[13] Properly understanding the relation between clergy and laity in the governance of the church, then, depends on how we respond to the ambiguities left by the Council and continued in subsequent teachings of the magisterium.

The First Vatican Council was concerned with the role of the pope in the life of the church, and the Second Vatican Council with bishops and laity. The dominant model of the role of the laity prior to the Second Vatican Council was Catholic Action: "the participation and the collaboration of the laity with the Apostolic Hierarchy."[14] The architects of Catholic Action held that the clergy governed the laity within the life of the church. According to Pope Pius X, for example, "the one duty of the multitude is to allow themselves to be led, and like a docile flock, to follow the Pastors."[15] The pattern is that of an inferior being instructed by a superior. Members of the laity in this view are allowed to "participate" in the mission of the clergy, but they do not have their own distinctive mission.

Important strands of the teaching of Vatican II offer an alternative vision of the laity and its relations to the clergy based on a new way of thinking about the identity of the church. The key document, *Lumen Gentium*, describes the church as a "mystery" or "sacrament," thus emphasizing its spiritual, grace-filled, and symbolic significance as a complement to the First Vatican Council's concern with visible structures. *Lumen Gentium* begins by describing the church as a "sacrament or instrumental sign" of the "intimate union with God and of the unity of all humanity."[16] The church, according to this vision, is a sacrament of *communio*. The overall structure of *Lumen Gentium* highlights the *communio* of the church as prior to its differentiation: it speaks first of the church as a "mystery" or "sacrament" (nos. 1–10) and as the "People of God" (nos. 9–17) before it distinguishes between the hierarchy (nos. 18–29) and the laity (nos. 30–38). This emphasis, complementing and correcting the one-sided institutional and centralizing emphasis of the First Vatican Council (see chapter 13 of this volume), supports collegiality among bishops and cooperation between the clergy and the laity.

The image of "People of God" (see chapter 1) accented the inclusive character of the church, and particularly the significance of the laity within its life. This imagery not only acknowledges that the church includes all the people (and not just members of the hierarchy, as is often taken for granted when average Catholics refer to "the church"), but also emphasizes the universal equality of Christian dignity and discipleship. Correcting the older dualism that identifies the clergy with the church and the laity with temporal affairs, the Second Vatican Council taught that, in virtue of the sacrament of baptism, the entire People of God shares a common call to holiness and responsibility for the church and the world.

The Council's explicit treatment of the laity builds on these themes. *Lumen Gentium* (nos. 30–38) and the *Decree on the Apostolate of the Laity* taught that laymen and -women, in virtue of the sacraments of initiation, are full members of the People of God who share directly in the mission of the church. As Edward Schillebeeckx put it: "By their incorporation into the Church, that is, by their baptism, the laity consequently receive a share in this real function of the Church: they receive, namely, the charge to give visible stature to the faithful communion with Christ in grace, in and through their whole life."[17] The sacraments of initiation place the laity in "union with Christ the Head." "They are brought into the mystical body of Christ by baptism, strengthened by the power of the Spirit at confirmation, and assigned to apostleship by the Lord himself."[18] The laity thus has its own apostolate, one not delegated by the clergy.[19] Individual members of the laity can also have, in addition to their general Christian calling, special apostolates to serve the church in particular ways.

The Second Vatican Council provides a basis for correcting the clergy-laity dualism. For one thing, the clergy is not to be indifferent to the good of the social order. Members of the laity bear the primary responsibility for taking initiatives to transform the temporal order,[20] but the Council did not teach that the clergy should stand aloof from the world.

On the contrary, because core Christian identity is rooted in the sacraments of initiation, each and every Christian, clergy as well as laity, must be committed to the transformation of the social order. Only in this way can the church as such, rather than the laity, function as a "sacrament." "The ordained do not cease being members of the People of God after ordination," ecclesiologist Richard R. Gaillardetz points out, "and the obligations that are theirs by virtue of baptism and confirmation remain the same."[21] Tracing the Council's subtle shift in the use of the metaphor of "leaven" in the world from the laity to the entire church, Gaillardetz shows that the documents challenge all Christians to view themselves as charged with transforming the world.

The second component of this preconciliar dualism that assigns responsibility for the internal life of the church entirely to the clergy is also corrected by the Council. *Lumen Gentium*, following St. Paul (1 Cor 12:1–11), notes early on that the Holy Spirit empowers and enlivens the entire community of the church.[22] The Second Vatican Council recognized that the Holy Spirit distributes gifts and charisms directly to individual laymen and -women, and it is their duty to use these gifts and charisms for the benefit of the community.[23] Indeed, the Holy Spirit "apportions his gifts 'to each individual as he wills' (1 Cor 12, 11), and among the faithful of every rank he distributes special graces by which he renders them fit and ready to undertake the various tasks and offices which help the renewal and the building up of the church."[24] Pastors, conversely, are not to inculcate passivity by leading their parishes as monarchs or treating their parishioners as if they were children. Pastors at their best evoke and coordinate the talents, gifts, and ministries that exist in their local churches so that "all may cooperate unanimously, each in his or her own way, in the common task."[25] The *Decree of the Laity* suggests that the lay apostolate is not merely a matter of completing peripheral tasks that lie beneath the hierarchy.[26] The Holy Spirit works for the holiness of God's people by imparting "special gifts to the faithful." By possessing these charisms, "every one of the faithful has the right and duty to exercise them in the church and in the world for the good of humanity and for the building up of the church."[27]

In one of its most foundational and frequently cited claims, the Council teaches that the laity shares equally with the clergy in the priestly, prophetic, and kingly dignity of Christ.[28] Correcting the preconciliar position, *Lumen Gentium* extends this threefold office to include the laity as well as the clergy. The laity shares in the priesthood of Christ when participating in the offering of the Eucharist, manifesting a Christian life in "prayer and thanksgiving, through the witness of a holy life, by self-denial, and by active charity,"[29] and consecrating the world to God through its activities.[30] The laity shares in the "prophetic" office of Christ when giving a witness to faith and love. Rather than be restricted to "temporal affairs," the laity has the valuable task of evangelizing the world.[31] Finally, the laity shares in the "kingly" office of Christ when it orders the world to the kingdom of God and penetrates it with the values of the gospel, particularly justice and peace.[32]

The threefold office of Christ regards the laity as charged with a profound responsibility for the good of the church as well as the world. The laity has not only a right but even a duty to communicate with the clergy. According to *Lumen Gentium*, every layperson "should make known to these pastors their needs and desires with that freedom and confidence which befits children of God and brothers and sisters in Christ."[33] Indeed, laymen and -women, in "accordance with the knowledge, competence or authority they possess, . . . have the right and even sometimes the duty to make known their opinion on matters which concern the good of the church."[34] This should be done if possible through mechanisms provided by the church.[35] The clergy, in turn, have a responsibility to acknowledge the dignity and responsibility of the laity, put their talents to use for the good of the church, and encourage the laity to "undertake works on their own initiative."[36]

## Laity in Contemporary Governance

This ecclesiology provides the context for specific teachings regarding the relation between clergy and laity in the governance of the church. As I have already noted, canon law teaches that the clergy holds the divinely instituted power of governance in the church.[37] The documents of Vatican II, however, do not regard the hierarchy as holding an *exclusive* role in teaching, sanctifying, and governing the church. The laity can "participate" in these functions (see chapters 9 and 13 of this volume).[38] They can assist in the exercise of governance by the clergy through "consultation," and can exercise governance through "collaboration," "delegation," "deputation," and "cooperation." The language of "cooperation" is especially vague. It seems easier to know what the Council Fathers wanted to exclude in its use than what they desired to allow or encourage: they did not endorse strictly equal partnership, but neither did they mean to promote merely passive compliance or attribute a "second-class" status to the laity.

Paternalism persists, but in an obviously more muted form than what pertained in the dominant preconciliar paradigm. The Council speaks of the clergy as listening to the needs and ideas of the laity as a patient and loving father listens to his children. The laity, in turn, bear the obligation of obedience: they should be "prompt to accept in a spirit of Christian obedience those decisions that the sacred pastors make as teachers and governors of the church and as representatives of Christ."[39]

Clergymen, then, can decide to share their right to exercise the power of governance with qualified lay individuals. Laymen and -women receive the power of governance when appointed to an ecclesiastical office that involves its use—for example, when a person is appointed to a finance council. This form of participation is warranted by the 1983 Code of Canon Law, which holds that while "those who have received sacred orders are capable of the power of governance, which exists in the church by divine institution . . . lay members of the Christian faithful can cooperate in the exercise of this power in accord with the norm of law."[40] Members of the laity also, and more often, exercise an informal kind of governance power simply in the course of fulfilling routine duties they have been assigned within the church—for example, as parish administrators.

Having said this, I should note that John Paul II has taken pains to show that cooperation is based on the maintenance, not the elimination, of distinctive roles. As he explained in *Christifideles Laici* (1988): "When necessity and expediency in the Church require it, the Pastors . . . can entrust to the lay faithful certain offices and roles that are connected to their pastoral ministry but do not require the character of Orders." Yet the pope also made it clear that the exercise of certain tasks within the church "does not make Pastors of the lay faithful: in fact, a person is not a minister simply in performing a task but through sacramental ordination."[41]

Individual laymen and -women are sometimes in supervisory roles over clergy. The Holy See has not condemned these kinds of arrangements, but it has made it clear that members of the laity are not to be in a supervisory position over bishops. This resistance was illustrated recently in the negative response of the Vatican to the American bishops' proposal that a national lay board review diocesan sexual abuse policies and report on the compliance of ordinaries.

Several inadequacies mark the currently dominant way of conceiving of the role of the laity in the governance of the church.

First, the dominant paradigm insufficiently acknowledges the degree of dignity and responsibility of the laity found in conciliar documents. The Second Vatican Council supported levels of coresponsibility that are, at the very least, underutilized in the church today. Recall the teachings of *Lumen Gentium* 37, for example: pastors are to promote the responsibility of the laity in the church, make use of their counsel, entrust to them offices in the church, and leave them freedom to act. Some pastors of local churches, sometimes purely as a practical necessity, have implemented these directives in a variety of ways. Yet there seems to be a disparity between different dioceses and archdioceses in this regard. The principles of *Lumen Gentium* 37 work well with an ordinary who happens to be motivated to apply them, but they are not normatively binding on those who wish to ignore them. To what extent, for example, do members of the laity have a genuine opportunity to express their concerns to their bishops? What mechanisms allow such communication to occur regularly?

Second, the dominant paradigm does not adequately reflect the de facto exercise of governance by the laity in the church today, and especially those forms of governance that result from the explosion of lay ministries.[42] As canon lawyer James Coriden points out:

> There are thousands of parishes and other local Catholic congregations throughout the world led by non-priests. Deacons, religious, lay women and men are actually "in charge" of the pastoral ministry exercised within such communities. These ministers, the vast majority of whom are non-ordained, have been assigned to or chosen by these communities, and they direct or coordinate the ministry within them. This is undeniably an exercise of the power of governance.[43]

Coriden lists a variety of ways in which lay ministers exercise the power of governance: as "judges, defenders of the bond, promoters of justice, auditors, advocates, and notaries in diocesan tribunals, chancellors, finance officers of dioceses and parishes, superintendents and principals of schools, directors of social services and health care facilities, superiors and council members in lay religious institutes."[44] Examples from history also abound, including the early "house churches" of the New Testament (see chapter 1), the imperial convocation of ecumenical councils, the appointment of clergy by landlords, etc. (see chapters 2 and 3).[45]

One can ask whether the key distinction between the "possession" and "exercise" of power is not drawn too sharply and abstractly to fit the actual experience of governance in the contemporary church. Even if the distinction remains useful, the fact remains that members of the laity often employ the power of governance in the church. This power, moreover, is sometimes even exercised over clerics: when an ordained hospital chaplain reports to a sister, for example, or when a priest-professor reports to the lay academic dean of his seminary faculty. Coriden explains that the dominant paradigm is based on a "pragmatic compromise to paper over a gap" between the de jure restriction of possession of power to the clergy and the much broader de facto extension of the possession and use of power to laypeople in various forms of nonordained ministry. It is not unusual for formulations of canon law and theology to lag behind practice, but such gaps indicate the need to reconsider current theory and teachings. Coriden himself argues that canon law ought to be revised to grant laypeople the power of governance in addition to the right to exercise it.[46]

Finally, and most poignantly, the dominant paradigm of clergy-laity relations in governance is consistent—in its letter if not in its spirit—with the framework of power that created conditions that led to the crisis of sexual abuse. This paradigm continues to allow the clergy to be the primary decision makers who are accountable only to other (and usually only more powerful) members of the hierarchy. The relevance of the laity to the governance of the church, particularly regarding oversight and accountability, is left entirely up to the discretion and personal predilections of a local ordinary. A bishop or archbishop is free, if he so chooses, to give significant responsibilities to individual members of the laity for certain institutional functions of the church, but others are equally free not to do so.

## Toward Governance Based on *Communio*: Dialogue, Participation, and Authority

The church can begin to correct these and similar deficiencies by pursuing three goods: genuine dialogue, participation, and authority. The third section of this chapter noted the centrality of *communio* in the ecclesiology of Vatican II. This section proposes that a more adequate implementation of *communio* depends on a proper understanding and promotion of these three goods.

First, the term "dialogue" has been used frequently in official church documents since the Council. It is used in an unambiguously good sense to mean a communication of views for the sake of mutual understanding based on a shared commitment to truth. At present, however, the need to engage in dialogue often goes unmet in the church. If the bishops want to take steps to overcome some of the alienation within the church, they will have to develop structures and habits of mind that facilitate dialogue with the laity. This means, above all, that all of the interlocutors must engage in real listening based on mutual respect and good will.

Second, the term "participation" provides a more helpful avenue for thinking about the role of the laity within the governance of the church—especially when it comes to an increasingly educated and professionally accomplished laity—than do the terms "obedience," "subjection," or "subordination." This is not to say that the latter terms are always illegitimate; on the contrary, under the right conditions, every Christian has a moral obligation to display proper obedience, subjection, and subordination to genuine authority (properly understood, of course, within the limits of justice and self-respect).[47] The term "participation," however, stresses community more than ecclesial rank and signals a sense of cooperation between individuals of equal dignity, relative to the work that needs to be done. Right now, genuine "participation" and "collaboration" are less common than "delegation" and "consultation."[48]

Mary Jo Bane (see chapter 10) identifies three problems that tend to make it difficult for the clergy to value the role of the laity in the governance of the church at the present time. First, the clergy, like everyone else, does not appear eager to give up power. Second, the clergy has never been trained to exercise power collaboratively. Third, some people fear that collaboration will lead to a populist diminishment or watering-down of Christianity.[49] One way to address these concerns restricts lay participation to financial, investment, and budgetary matters and leaves faith and morals to the clergy. Yet, as Bane points out, the laity often wants to participate in decisions regarding the life of the local parish and the wider diocese or archdiocese. The core lay constituency of parishes increasingly wants a voice not only in staff appointments but also in the selection of their pastors. They want some influence on the life of their own parishes beyond making financial donations, teaching religious education, and organizing Friday evening bingo games. They want to be involved in the moral reflection that goes on in their parishes, or at least ought to go on in them. The theme of "participation," then, inevitably includes and depends upon actualizing the previous theme, dialogue.

One of the significant obstacles presented to those who want to increase participation lies in the passivity and apathy of most Catholics. Parishes are too often not the scene of serious ongoing religious and moral reflection but rather just a "place to go to Mass." The term "participation" can be a slogan; it is certainly not an all-purpose answer to the church's problems. Pastors have a right to reject "participation" if it means—as it does to some people in our current political culture—that parishioners simply vote on issues in terms of their perceived self-interest. The church is not a democracy, but Bane suggests that a better model for "participation" than voting can be taken from the practice of "deliberative democracy" in which, she writes, participants "work together to discover or create the best outcome for the polity as a whole . . . through a process of analysis, reflection, and respectful deliberation."[50] Another more identifiably religious language for this kind of participation is "communal discernment"—a process of reflective and prayerful deliberation intended to arrive at a workable consensus based on an enhanced understanding of the will of God regarding a particular area of concern. Some religious orders have practiced communal discernment for centuries.[51] Pope John XXIII, and Vatican II after him, stated that the task of the church was to "read the signs of the times" and interpret them in light of the gospel. This is in fact what every genuine Christian does in his or her life. The challenge of governance requires that it be extended to the context of an ongoing dialogue within local parish and diocesan or archdiocesan communities.

This kind of "participation" works best among a small group of face-to-face interlocutors rather than in large organizations, but even the latter can be influenced by what happens in small groups at the "grass roots" level. The bishops of the United States, for example, engaged in this kind of decision making during the process of writing their pastorals on peace and on economic justice in the 1980s.

Consensus is an ideal. There is, of course, a danger that consensus-seeking will be confused with mere political accommodation. We face the danger, as Francis Davis puts it, that "consensus-building in what we might term the polity of the church becomes the thinnest point of agreement between all the competing images that Catholic organizations and individuals proclaim about the Church."[52] We need "to hear why and discover more about how a theological consensus may or may not be merely a political accommodation rather than the discovery of a deeper metaphysical reality formed around a common conception of the telos of the Church."[53]

Finally, the themes of dialogue and participation are inevitably connected to the issue of ecclesial authority. The term "authority" has a notoriously wide range of meanings, but we usually assume that it refers to the power of command—telling someone what to do or not to do— and the ability to elicit obedience.[54] The coach has authority over his players, the general over his troops, and the teacher over her students. This use of authority, however, identifies all forms of authority with one of its components, the term "governance"[55] or, even more narrowly, the term "jurisdiction."

Authority, however, can be understood in terms of "participatory hierarchy" rather than only "command hierarchy" (see chapter 6). Authority in its deeper sense includes the *ability to evoke trust* on the basis of credibility and perceived wisdom. Trust is as important for the church as it is for contemporary social relations in general. Sociologist Michael P. Hornsby-Smith explains that "trust in authority relationships, in the modern world, depends more and more not only on perceived competence but also on forms of participation in dialogue and decision-making which appear to respect the dignity, competence and autonomy of those whose lives are affected."[56]

The issue of governance needs to be interpreted from within a more fundamental theology of authority that encourages broad participation in the life of the church. The explicit teachings of Paul and Jesus contrasted the way in which disciples ought to exercise authority as a form of humble service with the arrogant and condescending conduct of some of the religious leaders of their day (see chapters 1 and 7).[57]

A more balanced understanding of authority is promoted by ecclesiological positions that acknowledge the nonidentity as well as the close bond between Christ and the church. Theologian Aloys Grillmeier, for instance, held that *Lumen Gentium* 7 employs the image of the bride and bridegroom to indicate the *difference* between Christ and the church in the relation of head and body.[58] A view of authority based on a vision of the church as the entire People of God, and acknowledging the nonidentity of Christ and the church, frames a different place for the laity in governance than does an ecclesiology that practically identifies the church with the hierarchy and that stresses the identity of Christ and the church. Theologian Joseph Komonchak regards the need to integrate statements about the divine and human dimensions of the church to be one of the major challenges left to theologians by the Council. He warns of the dangers presented by what he calls a "new monophysitism" in ecclesiology that so focuses on the transcendent dimensions of the church that it neglects its constitutively human elements. Komonchak urges us to keep in mind that while the church exists in communion with the divine life, it is not itself God.[59]

Proper authority, then, should not be confused with authoritarianism. Christian authority is best based on trustworthiness and reason-giving; authoritarianism expects commands to be obeyed without reflection or internal conviction. Genuine authority engages in respectful dialogue and moves toward conclusions after listening to all the relevant sources; authoritarianism does not. Genuine authority is essentially a form of teaching, and forms of governance follow from its primarily educational task—a notion communicated in the word *magisterium*, which means "teaching authority."[60] Governance is, or ought to be, exercised in the service of genuine authority in the church.

There are a variety of ways in which the laity can have a greater voice in this kind of governance. The Holy See has taken pains to make it clear that, according to current canon law, diocesan and parish pastoral councils and parochial finance councils possess only consultative status and "cannot in any way become deliberative structures."[61] Yet this reservation does not gainsay the Council's call for lay participation (see chapter 11). Church law regarding ecclesial practices, moreover, could be modified to give more weight to lay participation in decision making.

If pastoral councils are to promote lay participation, they must be made genuinely representative and not simply committees composed of "safe" and compliant appointees. Laymen and -women could be given some role in decision making in the selection of parish priests and pastors, greater responsibility in the staffing of parish, diocesan, and curial positions that do not require holy orders, and a stronger consultative voice in diocesan synods and diocesan and parish councils. The laity already has a deliberative voice in finance committees, and steps could be taken to allow for deliberative voice in other domains as well.[62]

Canon law could be changed to give the laity a voice in ecumenical councils. Catholic writers from a variety of theological positions, for example, have called for involvement of the laity in the selection of bishops (see chapters 3 and 4).[63] There are precedents in the early tradition for involving the laity in electing bishops, appointing clergy, making conciliar decisions, and reconciling repentant sinners (see chapter 2). Greater power in these areas would bring greater oversight and accountability than obtains today and would do so without compromising the liturgical and pastoral responsibilities of the clergy.

Something can be learned from the kind of initiative, oversight, and responsibility exercised by the laity in parishes under the "lay trustee" system earlier in American history (see chapter 5). This system allowed lay boards to hold and manage church property and at times involved them in the selection of pastors and bishops. Its focus was on "temporal affairs," but it employed a system of "checks and balances" that might have allowed the church to avoid the secretive practices that contributed so powerfully to the sexual abuse scandal (see also chapter 10).

Since all of these roles would be open to women, expanding the role of the laity would contribute significantly to gender equality within the church as well. As Lisa Sowle Cahill points out: "There may be no real reason, as far as even present church law is concerned, that women cannot be involved in the higher administration of local dioceses, or even of the Vatican and its offices."[64] And of course, since present restrictions on the power of the laity in the governance of the church are the result of positive ecclesiastical law rather than revelation, there seems to be no reason in principle why innovations cannot be proposed to extend opportunities for laywomen beyond those that are currently allowed.

Involvement in these modes of governance would in all likelihood have the effect of *building up*, rather than challenging, genuine ecclesial authority and institutional loyalty. Moreover, lay initiatives from Catholics working outside the institutional structures of the church can play a supportive role (see chapter 12). The exercise of lay responsibility both within and outside official channels of governance can enable the church better to function as the sacrament of the love that is said to characterize the inner life of the Body of Christ.

## The Purpose of This Book

This book is intended to contribute to ongoing reflection on the contribution of the laity to the governance of the church. It seeks to address the question: What has been, is, and can be the role of the laity in the governance of the church?

The chapters in part I of this volume provide important historical precedents regarding the status and roles of the laity in the first millennium, but they discuss these precedents in light of the needs of the contemporary church. The chapters in part II address the contemporary scene, but always with an eye to relevant historical contexts. They consider fundamental theological and moral issues relating to the role of the laity in church governance, including the just-mentioned themes of dialogue, participation, gender equality, and loyalty. Their authors examine these themes from a variety of disciplinary perspectives, including systematic theology, sacramental theology, canon law, political science, moral theology, pastoral theology, and management. They speak from dual backgrounds as active believers and academic specialists in their own fields, as both existentially concerned people of faith and learned scholars. It is hoped that the contribution of authors from a variety of relevant disciplines will help to deepen and broaden the ongoing and vitally important discussion about how the laity might be of service to the church. If canon lawyer Ladislas Orsy is correct when he claims (in chapter 13) that we are entering into a new era in the history of the church, then there can be no topic of greater import for Catholics than the one addressed in these pages.

## Notes

1. The conclusions of the study conducted by Zogby International, "Views of American Catholics and Opinion Leaders on Issues Regarding the Catholic Church," were reported by Alan Cooperman, "Bishops Get Low Ratings in Poll of Catholics," *Washington Post*, 14 November 2003. For the study, see the Ethics and Public Policy website, www.eppc.org/conferences/eventid.65/confdetail.asp (accessed 8 December 2003).

2. See James Keenan, "Sex Abuse, Power Abuse," *The Tablet*, 11 May 2002, 9–10.

3. David Gibson, *The Coming Catholic Church: How the Faithful Are Shaping a New American Catholicism* (San Francisco: HarperSanFrancisco, 2003), 14.

4. James D. Davidson, "Fewer and Fewer: Is the Clergy Shortage Unique to the Catholic Church?" *America*, 1 December 2003, 10–13.

5. See Dean Hoge, *The First Five Years of Priesthood: A Study of Newly Ordained Catholic Priests* (Collegeville, Minn.: Liturgical Press, 2002).

6. See The Investigative Staff of the Boston Globe, *Betrayal: The Crisis in the Catholic Church* (New York: Little, Brown, 2002).

7. See Peter Steinfels, *A People Adrift: The Crisis of the Roman Catholic Church in America* (New York: Simon and Schuster, 2003).

8. R. Scott Appleby, "What Is at Stake in the Present Crisis?" *Origins* 32 (27 June 2002): 114. Also available at www.usccb.org/bishops/appleby.htm (accessed 8 December 2003).

9. Psychologist Thomas Plante holds that about 2 to 5 percent of priests have had at least one sexual experience with a minor. He also maintains that this percentage is consistent with male clergy from other religious traditions and that male clergy have lower rates of abuse than members of the general male population, which he estimates have an abuse rate of about 8 percent. See Thomas G. Plante, "Priests Behaving Badly: What Do We Know about Priest Sex Offenders?" *Journal of Sexual Addiction and Compulsivity*, 9 (2003): 93–97, and Thomas G. Plante, ed., *Bless Me Father for I Have Sinned: Perspectives on Sexual Abuse Committed by Roman Catholic Priests* (Westport, Conn.: Praeger/Greenwood, 1999).

10. On the clergy–lay distinction, see Richard R. Gaillardetz, "Shifting Meanings in the Lay-Clergy Distinction," *Irish Theological Quarterly* 64 (1999): 115–39.

11. James A. Coriden, "Lay Persons and the Power of Governance," *The Jurist* 59 (1999): 335.

12. *Code of Canon Law*, English translation by the Canon Law Society of America (Washington, D.C.: Canon Law Society of America, 1983), canon 129.

13. Giuseppe Alberigo, Jean-Pierre Jossua, and Joseph A. Komonchak, eds., *The Reception of Vatican II*, trans. Matthew J. O'Connell (Kent, England: Burns and Oates, 1987), 8.

14. The encyclical by Pope Pius XI, *Non Abbiamo Bisogno*, "On Catholic Action in Italy," promulgated on 29 June 1931, no. 22.

15. Pope Pius X, *Vehementer Nos* (On the French Law of Separation), 11 February 1906, no. 8.

16. *Lumen Gentium* 1 (hereafter *LG*): English translation taken from *Decrees of the Ecumenical Councils*, ed. Norman Tanner, 2 vols. (London/Washington, D.C.: Sheed and Ward/Georgetown University Press, 1990), 2: 849.

17. E. H. Schillebeeckx, O.P., *The Layman in the Church and Other Essays* (Staten Island: Alba House, 1963), 40.

18. *Apostolicam Actuositatem* 3 (hereafter *AA*), Decree on the Apostolate of the Laity, in Tanner, ed., *Decrees*, 2: 982.

19. See *AA* 1–4, and *LG* 30, 33, in Tanner, ed., *Decrees*, 2: 981–85, 873–75, and 876, 877, respectively.

20. See *LG* 31 and *Gaudium et Spes*, The Pastoral Constitution on the Church in the Modern World, in Tanner, ed., *Decrees*, 2: 875 and 1096–98, respectively.

21. Gaillardetz, "Shifting Meanings," 124.

22. See *LG* 8, in Tanner, ed., *Decrees*, 2: 854–856.

23. See *LG* 12, in Tanner, ed., *Decrees*, 2: 862–863; see also *AA* 3.

24. *LG* 12, in Tanner, ed., *Decrees*, 2: 858.

25. *LG* 30, in Tanner, ed., *Decrees*, 2: 875.

26. See *LG* 33, in Tanner, ed., *Decrees*, 2: 875–77.

27. *AA* 3, in Tanner, ed., *Decrees*, 2: 983.

28. See *LG* 7 and 34–36, in Tanner, ed., *Decrees*, 2: 853–54, 877–79.

29. *LG* 10, in Tanner, ed., *Decrees*, 2: 857; see Gaillardetz, "Shifting Meanings," 128.

30. See *LG* 34, in Tanner, ed., *Decrees*, 2: 877.

31. See *LG* 35, in Tanner, ed., *Decrees*, 2: 877.

32. See *LG* 36, in Tanner, ed., *Decrees*, 2: 879.

33. *LG* 37, in Tanner, ed., *Decrees*, 2: 879.

34. Ibid.

35. Ibid.

36. Ibid.

37. Canon 129, par. 1; see Coriden, "Lay Persons and the Power of Governance."

38. Canon 129, par. 2, drawing from *LG* 33, and *AA* 24.

39. *LG* 37, in Tanner, ed., *Decrees*, 2: 879.

40. Canon 129.

41. John Paul II's postsynodal exhortation *Christifideles Laici*, 23, emphasis in original. See *Origins* 18, no. 35 (13 February 1989): 561–95.

42. See Thomas O'Meara, O.P., *Theology of Ministry* (New York: Paulist Press, 1999), 139–224.

43. Coriden, "Lay Persons and the Power of Governance," 336.

44. Ibid.

45. Ibid., 337.

46. Ibid.

47. See Leo Jozef Cardinal Suenens, "Obedience and Faithfulness," in *Obedience and the Church*, ed. Karl Rahner, S.J., et al. (Washington, D.C., and Cleveland: Corpus Books, 1968), 190–96, and, similarly, the mutual interdependence of obedience and freedom in Bernard Häring, *Free and Faithful in Christ* (New York: Seabury Press, 1978–81).

48. An analogous set of issues concerns the bishops in relation to the Holy See. Archbishop John Quinn's address at Campion Hall, Oxford, in June 1996 identified some of the key issues. See John R. Quinn, *The Exercise of the Primacy: Continuing the Dialogue*, ed. Phyllis Zagano and Terrence W. Tilley (New York: Crossroad, 1998). The archbishop took up the challenge issued by John Paul II's 1995 encyclical on ecumenism, *Ut Unum Sint*, requesting "patient and fraternal dialogue" regarding "how the gift which is the papacy can become more credible and speak more effectively to the contemporary world" (Quinn, *The Exercise of the Primacy*, 3); the archbishop's address was a response "to the Pope's invitation to rethink with him the style and manner of exercising the papal ministry 'open to a new situation' " (5). Quinn called for more discussion of the meaning of episcopal collegiality, International Synods, the principle of subsidiarity, reforming the curia, the process used in the appointment of bishops, consultation with local churches, and what he called "the tension between the political model and the ecclesial model at work in the church" (26). Quinn argued that the political concern with order and control should not undercut the proper role of the ecclesial model with its focus on "communion and therefore discernment in faith in the diversity of gifts and works of the Spirit" (ibid.). A healthy church requires that the two components be kept in balance and fruitful tension, but Quinn worries that the "claims of discernment" are "all but eliminated in favor of the claims of order, thereby making control and the political model the supreme good" (ibid.).

49. See Mary Jo Bane, "Exit, Voice, and Loyalty in the Church," *America Magazine*, 3 June 2002.

50. Bane, chapter 10 of this volume.

51. See William Spohn, *Go and Do Likewise* (New York: Continuum, 1999).

52. Francis Davis, "A Political Economy of Catholicism," in Noel Timms and Kenneth Wilson, eds., *Governance and Authority in the Roman Catholic Church: Beginning a Conversation* (London: SPCK, 2000), 112.

53. Ibid.

54. See Max Weber, *The Theory of Social and Economic Organization*, ed. Talcott Parsons (London: Collier-Macmillan, 1964), 152.

55. See Nicholas Lash, "Authors, Authority, and Authorization," in *Authority in the Roman Catholic Church: Theory and Practice*, ed. Bernard Hoose (London: Ashgate, 2002), 59–71.

56. Michael P. Hornsby-Smith, "Sociological Reflections on Power and Authority," in Timms and Wilson, eds., *Governance and Authority in the Roman Catholic Church*, 29. Hornsby-Smith relies on the work of Anthony Giddens, particularly *The Consequences of Modernity* (Cambridge: Polity Press, 1990) and *Modernity and Self-Identity: Self and Society in the Late Modern Age* (Cambridge: Polity Press, 1991).

57. Christians often cite the Sermon on the Mount when they discuss the Christian meaning of authority: "When Jesus finished these words, the crowds were astonished at his teaching, for he taught them as one having authority and not as their scribes" (Matthew 7:28). Casual auditors often interpret this passage to mean that Jesus was a great public speaker or very sincere, but biblical scholars tell us that the crowds were "astonished" because Jesus taught as if he had his own direct commission from God, rather than by repeating and interpreting the received teachings of the tradition. The striking, "You have heard it said     but I say unto you . . ." of the Sermon on the Mount signaled Jesus' explicit and unambiguous willingness to depart from received traditions in discerning the will of God—and this was possible because Jesus held an "authority by commission" given by God himself. See John L. McKenzie, "The Gospel According to Matthew," in *The Jerome Biblical Commentary*, 2 vols., ed. Raymond E. Brown, S.S., Joseph A. Fitzmyer, S.J., and Roland E. Murphy, O.Carm. (Englewood Cliffs, N.J.: Prentice-Hall, 1968), 2: 76.

58. See Alloys Grillmeier, "Chapter 1: The Mystery of the Church," in *Commentary on the Documents of Vatican II*, 3 vols., ed. Herbert Vorgrimler (New York: Crossroad, 1989), 1: 145.

59. See Joseph A. Komonchak, "Ecclesiology of Vatican II," delivered at The Catholic University of America, 27 March 1999, and available at http://publicaffairs.cua.edu/speeches/ecclesiology99.htm (8 December 2003).

60. See Lash, "Authors, Authority, and Authorization."

61. "Instruction on Certain Questions Regarding the Collaboration of the Non-Ordained Faithful in the Sacred Ministry of the Priest," 13 August 1997, article 5, par. 3.

62. See Robert Ombres, O.P., "What Future for the Laity? Law and History," in Timms and Wilson, eds., *Governance and Authority in the Roman Catholic Church*, 91–102.

63. On this issue, see "Electing Our Bishops," *Concilium: International Journal for Theology* 7 (Glen Rock, N.J.: Paulist Press, 1980).

64. Cahill, chapter 7 of this volume.

# Part I

# Historical Perspectives

# ONE

## "Being of One Mind": Apostolic Authority, Persuasion, and *Koinonia* in New Testament Christianity

### PHEME PERKINS

Accustomed to the authoritarianism of today's hierarchy, most Catholics presume that Paul exercised apostolic authority in the same way. Imprisoned and uncertain of his own fate as he writes his letter to the Philippians, the apostle is concerned about rivalry and division among those preaching the gospel, a group that included two women, Euodia and Syntyche (Phil 4:2–3).[1] When Paul asks his audience for unanimity, "that you think the same, having the same love, united in spirit, thinking as one" (Phil 2:2), we often assume that he intends apostolic authority to clamp down on debate. He goes on to invoke the self-sacrificing death of Christ on the cross as a warrant for the desired attitude: "think among yourselves in the same way as in Christ Jesus" (Phil 2:5–11).[2] In today's church, women have good reason to suspect that when ecclesiastical authorities use lofty Christological metaphors, the images are a rhetorical covering for exclusion and subordination. Even within the Pauline tradition, scholars have observed a shift from the communal patterns of missionary fellowship presumed in Philippians—a form of association that includes both women and men as deacons, fellow laborers, and apostles—to the late-first-century model of the church as a hierarchically ordered household. Good order in that context both silences and subordinates women.[3] This transition becomes canonized as authentic Pauline tradition in the deutero-Pauline Pastoral epistles (e.g., 1 Tim 2:9–15; 5:3–16).[4]

Honest historical scrutiny and exegesis, sensitized by feminist and liberation theology, make it impossible to give unambiguous answers to such questions as "What does the New Testament say about church leadership?" On the one hand, we can find in the New Testament striking examples of resistance to first-century cultural patterns of authoritative domination and elitist leadership.[5] On the other hand, we can also find a shirking of responsibility and even a drawing back from essential insights. Paul's formulation of bodily holiness in 1 Cor 6:12–20 effectively excludes Christian slaves, both women and men, from the fullness of being in Christ's body because they are the sexual property of their masters, whom they are encouraged to obey. Paul's assurances that "in Christ" one's status as slave or free makes no difference, which follows in 1 Cor 7:20–24, stands in tension with his words on sexuality and holiness.[6] Exegetes today draw on increasingly detailed and nuanced studies of Roman social history to understand how people lived in the first century C.E.[7] Consequently, we find ourselves engaged in a more complicated conversation with our sources. To simply repeat grand theological insights or elements of religious poetry that seem timeless, as is the case with selections of scripture used in worship or in theological writing uninformed by biblical scholarship, undercuts the critical questions one ought to ask about the text. What did this language mean to those who used it and those who heard them? Did it illuminate and transform? Or did it reinforce and reflect inherited religious or social patterns?

## The Meaning of "Governance"

The subject of this book is the role of the laity in the governance of the church. What might "governance" mean to a first-century Christian? Given the sociological realities of small, face-to-face assemblies that met in the houses of wealthier members, all relationships were personal, not anonymous or distant.[8] Seth Schwartz has assembled a considerable body of evidence that common assumptions about the synagogue and its authorities as the central organizing element of Jewish communities are anachronistic. There was no fixed pattern for organization and/or authority in such private religious gatherings.[9] Consequently, various social models could be invoked in regulating a particular community. Prominent examples involve patronage relationships between benefactor and clients, the household religious functions of the "father of a family,"[10] as well as gatherings to hear the oratory or teaching of traveling rhetoricians or philosophers.[11]

Of course, our first-century C.E. auditor might assume that we mean by "governance" something more abstract than the practical organization of religious associations. Philosophers of that period debated the true nature of "kingship." By the second century c.e., sophists in the Greek East often contrasted "educated" Greek theories of rule and social harmony to the imperial projection of power that the Roman empire had brought to the region.[12] Imperial power masked the harsh reality of subjection to foreign rule by projecting its greatness in elaborate civic ceremonies and speeches alleging enlightened concern. Tim Whitmarsh comments: "The idea that the philosopher exerts some authority in the household and the language of self-restraint and equality are all for show, dissimulating the workings of hierarchical power."[13] If the issue of "governance" is code for power exercised in the imperial mode, then one might anticipate that early Christians—at least insofar as Christian opposition to cultural mores was confused with the cultural criticism of popular Cynic philosophers—would employ the familiar rhetoric of opposition to the authoritarian exercise of power.[14]

## Power and the Rhetoric of Reversal

Anyone who reads the gospel narratives will be familiar with images of status and power being overturned by God or Jesus. The accepted cultural and social forms of domination are not representative of God's order. Catholics are familiar with Mary's Magnificat (Luke 1:46b–55), which sets this theme in the grand style of biblical poetry:

My soul magnifies the Lord,

And my spirit rejoices in God, my savior,

Because He has regarded the low estate of his servant [cf. 1 Sam 1:11]. For behold, from now on, all generations will call me blessed,

For the Mighty One [cf. Zeph 3:17; Ps 8:9] has done great things for me [cf. Deut 10:21], and holy is his name,

And his mercy from generation to generation toward those who fear him.

He has shown strength with his arm, he has scattered the proud [cf. Isa 2:12; 13:11] in the imagination of their heart;

He has cast down the mighty [cf. Job 12:19; 1 Sam 2:7] from their thrones and exalted the lowly [cf. Job 5:11],

He has filled the hungry with good things [cf. Ps 107:9; 1 Sam 2:5] and sent the rich away empty [cf. Job 22:9; 15:29; 1 Sam 2:7].

> He has helped his child [or: servant] Israel, mindful of his mercy
>   [cf. Ps 98:3],
> As he promised our fathers, Abraham and his descendants forever.

This rich pastiche of allusions to the Hebrew Bible celebrates Israel's God as the one who can exalt and defend the lowly righteous ones and bring down the arrogant—whether they be great nations that oppress God's people or wealthy sinners who trample on the poor. Most scholars agree that Luke has placed an earlier Jewish or Jewish-Christian hymn in the mouth of Mary because she is the mother of God's messiah.[15]

This vision of salvation as God's powerful "no" to all forms of human domination, arrogance, injustice, and self-assertion shapes Luke's version of the Beatitudes as well (Luke 6:20–26). Jesus had already used Isaiah 61:1–2 to announce himself as the agent of salvation for the lowly, suffering, and oppressed in his inaugural sermon (Luke 4:18). Luke combines that theme in the Beatitudes with a series of "Woe oracles" against the rich and privileged:[16]

> Woe to you who are rich, you have received your consolation.
>
> Woe to you who are full now, you will go hungry. Woe to you
>   who laugh now, you will mourn and weep.
>
> Woe to you when everyone speaks well of you, for their fathers
>   did the same for the false prophets. (Luke 6:24–26)

Luke develops this theme of God's judgment against the rich who have no regard for the poor in such familiar parables as the Rich Fool (Luke 12:13–21) and the Rich Man and Lazarus (Luke 16:19–31). But the final Woe saying departs from the others in its form and content and comes as a bit of a shock. It is possible to have social approval and a good reputation and yet be condemned as false to the gospel. The Hebrew prophets confronted false advisors and prophets who enjoyed the kind of popular esteem that God's spokesmen were often denied (Isa 30:10–11; Jer 5:31; 6:14; 23:16–17).[17] Social approbation is a more subtle form of power than wealth or imperial rule, perhaps, but such approval is certainly necessary in leaders. In 1 Timothy 3:7, Paul insists that churches should choose men who are well thought of by outsiders as bishops. Once again we confront a dilemma: leaders need the respect and esteem of others, yet such approval can be dangerous for disciples of Jesus.

The stories in the Gospels that emphasize the difficulty that Jesus' disciples had with his predictions of suffering indicate a reason for this caution against seeking power and popular approval. Mark's narrative links the disciples' confusion about power with their inability to accept Jesus' words about the cross. For example, James and John assume that when Jesus arrives in Jerusalem, there will be a reversal of status that will mean throwing the leadership out and putting Jesus in charge of God's people. They make a secretive request for the highest administrative posts (Mark 10:35–45), a move that enrages the other disciples. Jesus not only reminds his followers that discipleship requires suffering in this world, but also enunciates a principle of greatness that is the reverse of ordinary human behavior: "whoever wishes to be first among you must be the slave of all" (v. 44).[18] This saying cannot be enacted by a simple trick of naming leaders "servants" while at the same time leaving them with all the social trappings of power and authority. Rather, this phrase serves as shorthand for a more striking image from the prophet Isaiah, that of God's suffering servant (Isa 52:11–53:12). Jesus will enact the role of God's servant as he makes his way to death on the cross. Thus, anyone who would claim to be the "slave of all" must engage in real acts of low status that can only draw scorn and derision from the world's elite.

## Leading from Behind: The Suffering Apostle

When students sit down to read the New Testament as a whole for the first time, they are always surprised to find that all the hard work of coming up with "a church" was left to Jesus' followers. Jesus and his closest followers lived an itinerant life dependent upon the hospitality of others (Luke 9:1–12, 57–62). After Jesus' death and resurrection, Christians had to come up with patterns of community that could be maintained apart from the Jewish community. The process was drawn out, experimental, and even divisive. Even Luke, who has an apologetic interest in showing that God's Spirit guided the emergence of the church, cannot smooth out all the rough patches. Take some familiar examples from the opening chapters of Acts. Summary statements present the Jerusalem community as the model of mutual love, pious devotion, and concern for the poor (Acts 2:43–47; 4:32–37). Suddenly a sharp conflict breaks out over a system of care for widows that discriminated against those of diaspora origins, who were Greek-speaking rather than Aramaic-speaking (Acts 6:1–6). Scrambling for a solution leads Peter to appoint some Greek-speaking converts as deacons. As Fr. Joseph Fitzmyer points out in his commentary, the disciples had no hesitation about restructuring their organization to handle a problem. This solution to an immediate problem later became the basis for a new class of ministers in the church, deacons.[19]

By the time Luke wrote Acts in the last decade of the first century C.E., this Jerusalem-centered Christianity was long gone. It was probably a casualty of two very different events: the great success of evangelization among non-Jews in the diaspora, and the Jewish revolt against Rome (66–70 C.E.), which ended with the destruction of the Temple and consequently the loss of Jerusalem as a religious center with which Jews might identify. In contrast to the more orderly process in Acts, the letters of Paul give us a firsthand glimpse of how turbulent apostolic leadership and authority could be. For example, scholars even disagree over whether or not Paul's efforts to establish his understanding of the gospel in Galatia succeeded.[20] Modern readers often react negatively to Paul's exercise of apostolic authority (e.g., Gal 1:1–8) because they do not recognize that Paul makes such statements in situations where he is under pressure. Paul may have no standing in a church that he has never visited but that he hopes will aid his future mission, as in Rome. Or a church that owes its very existence to his personal missionary efforts is in danger of defecting, as in Galatia and Corinth. In all cases, the crucial issue for Paul is the alleged "gospel" being preached by others.[21] In the Corinthian letters, Paul depicts the opposition as purchasing status, the approval of others, and even a reputation as "religious" at the expense of both the gospel message and the well-being of the church.

Paul insists that apostolic authority is always constrained by the gospel. Consequently, he publicly attacks Peter's compromise with Jewish Christians from Jerusalem in Antioch. The church cannot be divided into a Eucharist for Jewish members separated from that for Gentiles (Gal 2:11–14). If an apostle is in conflict with the gospel, his authority alone cannot carry the day.[22] Paul probably lost the immediate argument with Peter in Antioch.[23] But his principle remains fundamental to authority within the Christian churches: there must be a discernable "fit" or coherence between the concrete words and deeds of leaders (apostles, preachers, teachers) and the gospel they proclaim.

Paul clearly understands this coherent lifestyle to involve two elements: a parental care and self-sacrificing love for believers whose faith he brought into being and must now nourish, and a willing imitation, even visible portrayal, of the suffering Christ.[24] Paul repeatedly insists that his conduct toward his churches never gained him even such advantages as he might have rightly expected (see 1 Cor 9:1–23). His acceptance of harsh physical labor, hunger, imprisonments, and beatings, and his avoidance of wealthy patrons led opposing missionaries to depict him as "lowly" (Greek: *tapeinos*; 2 Cor 10:1–2).[25] Paul mocked the social and religious pretensions of those in Corinth who took pride in rhetorical skill, alleged religious wisdom, and their association with prominent apostles. He refused to use sophistic methods in defense of the gospel, since such forms of persuasion were antithetical to the gospel of Christ crucified (1 Cor 2:1–5).[26] The true apostle was not to be found in the royal entourage of a triumphal parade, but among the condemned captives at its end, mere garbage in the world's estimation:

> Already you have been filled! Already you have become rich! Without us you have become kings! And would that you did reign so that we might share the rule with you! For I think God has exhibited us apostles as last of all, like those sentenced to death, that we have become a spectacle to the world, both angels and human beings. We are fools for Christ, but you are clever in Christ; we are weak, but you are strong; you are honored, but we are dishonored. Right to the present time we hunger and thirst, we are naked and beaten and homeless, and we labor, working with our own hands; when reviled, we bless; when persecuted, we endure; when slandered, we respond in a friendly manner; so that we have become rubbish of the world, scum up to the present. (1 Cor 4:8–13)[27]

Since the Corinthians were familiar with the demand that students of the Sophists imitate their teachers, Paul could reverse that cultural habit by challenging his audience to imitate the crucified Christ modeled in the humiliated apostle (1 Cor 4:16–17).[28]

However, this initial appeal did not stick. The letters patched together in 2 Corinthians evidence further conflict between Paul and the Corinthians over his apostolic leadership. They describe a reconciliation after a disastrous visit in which a member of the church had publicly humiliated Paul (2 Cor 1:23–2:11), and then a further breakdown when traveling missionaries seem about to win the church away from Paul. Paul refers to the outside preachers as "superlative apostles" (2 Cor 12:11) as well as false apostles (2 Cor 11:13–15). They claim to operate on the same basis as Paul himself (2 Cor 11:12).[29] Paul resorts to mock boasting, challenging the opposition to match him on two fronts: the physical hardships he has willingly endured, including opposition from persons within the church; and the pressing anxiety he has for the welfare of everyone in the churches, for the weak and those caused to fall (2 Cor 11:21–33).[30] In the wonderful title of his essay on this passage of 2 Corinthians, Scott Andrews describes Paul's self-presentation as "too weak not to lead."[31]

Paul even converts what might be considered the strongest basis for his preaching, heavenly visions, into an occasion of weakness (2 Cor 12:1–10). The visions do not give him access to special knowledge of God, though they must have confirmed his faith that Christ embodies the glory of God.[32] God leaves the apostle subject to a chronic, debilitating condition—whether illness or the persistent opposition to his mission. God's ability to work through the weakness of his apostle is essential to the gospel: "The same truth also held for the Messiah, who was crucified in weakness and yet lives through the power of God. His ministers are 'weak in him' but likewise live through the power of God with respect to the Christian community (2 Cor 13:4)."[33] Despite the strong language Paul uses in defending his apostolic authority in these churches, he refused to use social mechanisms either to establish his personal power or to prove the gospel through flashy rhetoric (media or marketing savvy). Consequently, even when he appears most dogmatic, regulating the conduct of women prophesying in the assembly (1 Cor 11:3–16), he uses rhetorical formulas that leave the matter open to communal discernment as long as the church is not split over the issue.[34]

## Authority Strengthens the Community of Faith

When Paul refers to his pressing concern for the welfare of all believers (2 Cor 11:28–29) or to his parental relationship with churches he founded (1 Cor 4:14–15), he reflects the deeply personal investment he has made in building up communities of faith. His letters to churches in Thessalonika and Philippi show the apostle engaging churches where the personal bond between the community and the apostle remains strong (Phil 4:1, 14–20; 1 Thess 3:6–10). Both churches are threatened by suffering. Paul writes to Philippi from prison. He cannot be present to the persecuted Christians in Thessalonika (1 Thess 1:6–8) because the apostle had been ejected from the city. In both cases, the letter brought by one of his associates will have to substitute for the encouragement of personal presence. Paul is not using the letter form to demand conformity from those he does not know, as might be the case in an imperial order. Paul acknowledges that all believers can anticipate suffering as Christ did. He must ensure that suffering does not shatter the faith and love of these fledgling churches.

Paul has a particularly close fellowship with the church in Philippi. The word *koinonia* ("fellowship") occurs six times in this short epistle

(1:7; 2:1; 3:10; 4:14, 15). This dynamic association depends upon a three-way bond that unites Paul and his personal missionary associates like Timothy with members of the church, and with the Christ, who is the basis of Christian fellowship.[35] Though Paul avoided dependence upon patronage relationships by working at his trade in Corinth (1 Cor 4:12) and Thessalonika (2 Thess 3:7–10), he did not insist on that practice in Philippi. Paul is concerned about situations in which religious leadership risks being attached to false social structures.[36] Nevertheless, Paul shows himself to be flexible in adapting to different community situations.[37] This principle of adaptability is not simply limited to the needs of evangelizing in different areas. It is a basic pastoral principle that even permits the apostle to depart from the known Jesus tradition and the practice of other apostles like Peter.[38]

Paul's adaptability could be perceived as a lack of stable principles, as an attempt to gain favor with his audience through flattery.[39] Paul defends his dealings with the Corinthians by insisting on his personal, parent-like self-sacrifice and love for those to whom he writes (2 Cor 2:3–4; 11:11; 12:14–15), and the ministerial task of building up and strengthening the faith of the community (2 Cor 12:19–21; 13:8–10). Paul's weaknesses and suffering are demonstrable evidence that he speaks for the crucified Christ (2 Cor 13:3–4). In Thessalonika, Paul's adaptability to the needs of different audiences is described as both a nurse-like gentleness and parental care (1 Thess 2:1–12). These images are characteristic of the ancient tradition of philosophical care of the soul. The philosopher/teacher knows how to heal the ills of human nature by nurturing his students with words.[40] Paul has adapted this tradition by introducing the example of the crucified Lord as the behavioral model to be copied. The goal of such a life is not philosophical wisdom but leading a life worthy of God.[41]

In Paul's case, the imitation of Christ crucified engendered a pastoral practice that acknowledged the need for local flexibility in preaching the gospel and building up the community of faith. By the early second century C.E., one finds Ignatius, the bishop of Antioch, taking the identification between ecclesial authority and Christ quite literally. In letters he writes as he is being taken to Rome for martyrdom, Ignatius insists that Christians not attempt to gain his release.[42] At the same time, Ignatius insists upon obedience to episcopal authority in the churches to which he writes. How does suffering modify the relationship between the bishop and his people? Unlike the false teachers, the bishop shows love and concern for those persons who suffer at the margins of society, the poor, the prisoners, the widows.[43] Thus, Ignatius can make strong statements of hierarchical authority while still modifying the ordinary cultural patterns for exercising power over others.[44]

However, Ignatius uses a language of submission to the bishop that marks a significant departure from the Pauline situation some sixty years earlier. Ignatius considers the local church to be personified in its bishop.[45] Strengthening the faith of the church no longer means, as it did for Paul, calling upon the whole community to engage in mutual exhortation and discernment.[46] Instead, a community is strengthened when its members submit to the local bishop along with his presbyters and deacons. This shift permits those charged with teaching and pastoral care[47] to compel the assent of fellow believers without providing persuasive reasons. Even Paul's own apostolic authority did not carry that level of social compulsion. The local leaders and teachers of Paul's time had no "office" that gave them the right to determine belief or action. Rather, the authority of communal prophets and teachers was a consequence of their activities in the church, encouraging, exhorting, and instructing others.[48]

## Conclusion

The contrast between Paul and Ignatius can be used to illuminate competing views of governance in our own churches. For some, strengthening the community of faith means investing those who hold ecclesiastical offices with an authority that derives from the awe-inspiring divinity of Christ. They read Paul's exhortations to "be of one mind" (Phil 2:2; 2 Cor 13:11) as commanding the faithful to give ready assent to what the magisterium discerns as the mind of Christ.

For others, strengthening the community of faith means adopting the model of Paul's pastoral practice in Philippi and Thessalonika. It requires local churches to develop a Christian maturity that can discern how God is working in their particular contexts and respond accordingly.[49] Even in the extended disputes with the Corinthians, where Paul's authority was challenged both from within the church and by Christian preachers who came from outside, Paul insists that a true apostle shows humility, gentleness, and weakness, not the power of command.[50]

In the final section of Paul's Corinthian correspondence (2 Cor 10–13), there is evidence of his deep disappointment and anger over the persistent challenges to his ministry as an apostle whose life exemplifies Christ crucified. Should we consider Paul's insistence on weakness as the mark of a true apostle to be no more than making a virtue of necessity? The bottom line is that God would not lift the burden of

physical illness and mental suffering over the state of his churches from
the apostle (2 Cor 12:1–10). Paul also presents himself as though he
were the victorious general besieging a city with the authority to "capture
thoughts for Christ, to punish disobedience" (2 Cor 10:5–6). But his
personal weaknesses are such that when he is on the scene, he cannot
deliver the goods (2 Cor 10:8–11). Thus, it may have been easy for
more impressive Christian preachers to wean the minds and hearts of
Christians in Corinth away from the apostle.

To accept Paul's statements as a rhetorical ploy, motivated by the
ongoing challenges that he faced in Corinth, is to side with his opponents.
It also treats the theological insight that Paul had gained from his
sufferings as inconsequential. The cross negates every form of human
self-assertion and domination (2 Cor 13:3–4). Paul cannot endorse the
social norms of his day to single out men who are entitled to the authority
of apostle missionaries. The Corinthians have been swept away by
personal gifts, rhetorical ability, and, perhaps, social prominence. Instead, the Corinthians have to remember that the Christian community
is not a "church" (Greek: *ekklesia*) in the ordinary meaning of the word,
"assembly of citizens." There such marks of excellence would have a
role to play. But the church is the body of Christ. God's Spirit is at
work in and through that body. Therefore, Christians should test their
lives by that criterion. Are those who claim to lead models of the
suffering Christ? Are the relationships among believers consistent with
the presence of Jesus Christ in their midst (2 Cor 13:5–6)? Or—a sad
conclusion after several years of Christian life—is this group still in
need of restoration or basic training (2 Cor 13:9)?

Paul holds out the hope that the Corinthian church will have restored
its vision of the gospel and the Christian way of life before he returns
there (2 Cor 13:11).[51] He makes a subtle change in the final benedic-
tion formula to highlight his hope for a return to communal harmony
(2 Cor 13:13). Ordinarily, he would conclude with the phrase "grace
of Jesus Christ" by itself.[52] Here he adds "love of God" and "fellowship
of the Holy Spirit."[53] Is Paul asserting that the Spirit will restore the
fellowship that has been so badly damaged by factions within the Corinthian church? Study of his use of the word "fellowship" with a genitive
elsewhere suggests a different nuance to this expression. Paul uses the
genitive after "fellowship" to indicate what persons who participate in
it share.[54] Consequently, the Spirit is not external to the church. The
Corinthians enjoy a personal relationship with the Spirit just as much
as they experience grace and love as gifts of the Son and the Father,

respectively.[55] Where then does God's Spirit inform the church? In individuals who hold office at the top of a hierarchical structure, who possess authority to impose faith and practice without regard for particular contexts of faith and communal discernment? Or, rather, as Paul's pastoral practice suggests, in the community as body of Christ—a community whose life may be guided by apostolic service, but one that must be empowered to discern the Spirit working in its midst? Without the Spirit working in the community to inspire love between its members, the church loses its distinctive character as body of Christ and becomes nothing more than a private religious association.

## Notes

1. See Nils A. Dahl, "Euodia and Syntyche and Paul's Letter to the Philippians," in L. Michael White and O. Larry Yarbrough, eds., *The Social World of the First Christians: Essays in Honor of Wayne A. Meeks* (Minneapolis: Fortress Press), 3–15.

2. Gordon D. Fee, *Paul's Letter to the Philippians* (Grand Rapids, Mich.: Eerdmans, 1995), 174–97.

3. David G. Horrell, "From ἀδελφοί to οἶκος θεοῦ: Social Transformation in Pauline Christianity," *Journal of Biblical Literature* 120 (2001): 293–311.

4. Jouette Bassler, "The Widow's Tale: A Fresh Look at 1 Tim 5:3–16," *Journal of Biblical Literature* 103 (1984): 23–41.

5. For example: Paul's challenge to the cultural assumptions of his Corinthian converts. See Andrew D. Clarke, *Secular and Christian Leadership in Corinth: A Socio-Historical and Exegetical Study of 1 Corinthians 1–6* (Leiden: Brill, 1993).

6. Jennifer Glancy, *Slavery in Early Christianity* (Oxford: Oxford University Press, 2002), 39–70.

7. For a discussion of the appropriate methods for doing social history, see Susan Treggiari, *Roman Social History* (London: Routledge, 2002).

8. For an attempt at social demographics of the early Christian movement, see Rodney Stark, *The Rise of Christianity: A Sociologist Reconsiders History* (Princeton: Princeton University Press, 1996).

9. Seth Schwartz, *Imperialism and Jewish Society, 200 B.C.E. to 640 C.E.* (Princeton: Princeton University Press, 2001), 215–28.

10. Treggiari, *Roman Social History*, 102–8.

11. Abraham J. Malherbe, *Paul and the Popular Philosophers* (Minneapolis: Fortress Press, 1989).

12. See Tim Whitmarsh, *Greek Literature and the Roman Empire: The Politics of Imitation* (Oxford: Oxford University Press, 2001), 134–246.

13. Ibid., 289.

14. On Paul's attempt to distinguish himself from these popular, traveling philosophers see Paul Winter, *Philo and Paul among the Sophists: Alexandrian and Corinthian Responses to a Julio-Claudian Movement* (Grand Rapids, Mich.: Eerdmans, 2001), 141–239.

15. See Joseph A. Fitzmyer, *The Gospel According to Luke I–IX* (New York: Doubleday, 1981), 338, 359, 367–69.

16. Ibid., 629–30.

17. Ibid., 637.

18. Craig A. Evans, *Mark 8:27–16:20* (Nashville: Thomas Nelson, 2001), 119–25.

19. Joseph Fitzmyer, *The Acts of the Apostles* (New York: Doubleday, 1998), 343–45.

20. Pheme Perkins, *Abraham's Divided Children: Galatians and the Politics of Faith* (Harrisburg: Trinity Press International, 2001), 16–25, 130–31.

21. James Dunn, *The Theology of Paul* (Grand Rapids, Mich.: Eerdmans, 1998), 571–73.

22. Ibid., 573.

23. After that time, Paul is engaged in missionary efforts on his own, not with Barnabas as representatives of the Antioch community (Perkins, *Abraham's Divided Children*, 55–56).

24. Dunn, *Theology of Paul*, 574.

25. Margaret A. Thrall, *The Second Epistle to the Corinthians, Volume 2: VIII–XIII* (Edinburgh: T. & T. Clark, 2000), 600–603.

26. Winter, *Philo and Paul*, 141–94.

27. Ibid., 196–200.

28. Ibid., 200–201.

29. Thrall, *Second Epistle to the Corinthians*, 667–76.

30. Ibid., 729–57.

31. Scott Andrews, "Too Weak Not to Lead: Form and Function of 2 Cor 11.23b–33," *New Testament Studies* 41 (1995): 263–76.

32. Thrall, *Second Epistle to the Corinthians*, 729.

33. Winter, *Philo and Paul*, 236.

34. Troels Engberg-Pedersen, "1 Corinthians 11:16 and the Character of Pauline Exhortation," *Journal of Biblical Literature* 110 (1991): 679–89.

35. Fee, *Paul's Letter to the Philippians*, 444–45.

36. Dunn, *Theology of Paul*, 570.

37. As he claims, 1 Cor 9:19–23; 10:33–11:1.

38. Dunn, *Theology of Paul*, 576–77.

39. For example, 2 Cor 2:1–3 indicates that a canceled visit to Corinth led to recriminations over the integrity of Paul's word. His refusal to accept Corinthian patronage, while at the same time receiving aid from the

Philippians and soliciting funds for poor Christians in Jerusalem, led opponents to accuse him of fraud (2 Cor 11:7–12; 12:14–18).

40. Abraham Malherbe, *The Letters to the Thessalonians* (New York: Doubleday, 2000), 146–51, 323–24.

41. Ibid., 327.

42. Ignatius, *Romans* 5.2–3; *Smyrneans* 4.2; *Ephesians* 5.1.

43. Ignatius, *Smyrneans* 6.2.

44. Judith Perkins, "The 'Self' as Sufferer," *Harvard Theological Review* 85 (1992): 263–64.

45. Ignatius, *Ephesians* 1.1.

46. As Paul does in 1 Thess 5:16–22, for example (see Malherbe, *Letters to the Thessalonians*, 328).

47. Paul recognizes that communities have persons who are charged with teaching and pastoral care. He encourages Christians to honor and pay such persons (see Gal 6:6; Rom 12:8; 1 Thess 5:12–13). The activities performed by such persons are not clarified in Paul's letters (Malherbe, *Letters to the Thessalonians*, 309–11).

48. See Dunn, *Theology of Paul*, 584.

49. Malherbe points out that nurturing the church in Thessalonika required that Christians be able to withstand opposition and persecution on their own. Paul is not able to return to visit. He is only able to send Timothy, his representative, to see how the church is holding up by special exception (1 Thess 3:2–3). The brief words of ethical exhortation at the letter's conclusion require that Christians themselves undertake the same style of pastoral care that Paul had engaged in when he founded the church (Malherbe, *Letters to the Thessalonians*, 325).

50. 2 Cor 10:1–6; Thrall, *Second Epistle to the Corinthians*, 600–615.

51. Thrall, *Second Epistle to the Corinthians*, 907–8.

52. The genitive, "of Christ," indicates that Jesus is the source of grace (see 2 Cor 8:9; 12:9). For this phrase as Paul's usual final greeting, see 1 Cor 16:23; Rom 16:20; Gal 6:18.

53. Though some exegetes have proposed that this expansion is a later post-Paul modification made to reinforce Trinitarian teaching or as a copy of tripartite pagan religious formula, most agree that Paul is responsible for this shift (see Thrall, *Second Epistle to the Corinthians*, 915–16).

54. As in 1 Cor 1:9; 10:16; Phil 3:10.

55. Thrall, *Second Epistle to the Corinthians*, 919.

# TWO

## St. Cyprian on the Role of the Laity in Decision Making in the Early Church

### Francis A. Sullivan, S.J.

B y the middle of the third century, there were close to one hundred local churches in Roman North Africa, whose bishops were accustomed to meet annually in a council presided over by the bishop of Carthage. While the system of metropolitan sees had not yet fully developed, still the importance of Carthage as one of the four greatest cities of the Roman empire, and of its church as second only to the Church of Rome in the West, made the bishop of Carthage one of the key figures in the life of the Christian Church. St. Cyprian was bishop of Carthage from 248 to 258 c.e., when he died as a martyr in the persecution of the Emperor Valerian. He left behind a collection of eighty-two letters, of which sixty were written by himself, sixteen were those he had received, and six were conciliar letters, informing other churches of decisions taken at the councils of Carthage. This collection is an incomparable source of our knowledge about the life of the church in the third century. It is from this source that I shall draw the information I shall present concerning the role of the laity in decision making in the early church. Cyprian speaks of the participation of the laity in decision making in four different contexts: in the election of a bishop, in appointments to the clergy, in conciliar decisions, and in the reconciliation of repentant sinners. I shall present evidence from Cyprian's letters about the role the laity played in each of these kinds of decisions.

### The Role of the Laity in the Election of a Bishop

In a letter in which he defended the legitimacy of the election of a Spanish bishop named Sabinus, Cyprian argued that the procedure being followed in the choice of bishops was based on "divine teaching and apostolic observance." He found the "divine teaching" in the instruction the Lord gave to Moses as to how he should make Aaron's son Eleazar a priest, and the "apostolic observance" in the way that Matthias was chosen to replace Judas. In the following passage of his letter, we see how Cyprian stressed the participation of the laity in the choice of a bishop:

> Moreover we can see that divine authority is also the source of the practice whereby bishops are chosen in the presence of the laity and before the eyes of all, and they are judged as being suitable and worthy after public scrutiny and testimony. For just so the Lord bids Moses in the Book of Numbers with the words: *Take your brother Aaron and Eleazar his son, and place them on the mountain in the presence of the assembled people. Strip Aaron of his robe and put it upon Eleazar his son, and there let Aaron die and be laid to rest.* Here God directs that His priest is to be invested before all of the assembled people; that is to say, He is instructing and demonstrating to us that priestly appointments are not to be made without the cognizance and attendance of the people, so that in the presence of the laity the iniquities of the wicked can be revealed and the merits of the good proclaimed, and thus an appointment may become right and lawful if it has been examined, judged, and voted upon by all. This rule we find subsequently observed in the Acts of the Apostles following these divine instructions. When Peter addresses the people on the subject of appointing a bishop to replace Judas, we read: *Peter stood up in the midst of the disciples, for a large number was gathered together.* . . . Now the whole congregation was called together and great caution and scrupulousness was here being exercised just so as to avoid that anyone unworthy might sidle his way into the service of the altar or the dignity of bishop. . . .
>
> Hence we should show sedulous care in preserving a practice which is based on divine teaching and apostolic observance, a practice which is indeed faithfully followed among us and in practically every province. And it is this: when an episcopal appointment is to be duly solemnized, all the neighboring bishops in the same province convene for the purpose along with the people for whom the leader is to be appointed; the bishop is then selected in the presence of those people, for they are the ones who are acquainted most intimately with the way each man has lived his life and they have had the opportunity thoroughly to observe his conduct and behavior.

And we note that this procedure was indeed observed in your own case when our colleague Sabinus was being appointed: the office of bishop was conferred upon him and hands were laid upon him in replacement of Basilides, following the verdict of the whole congregation and in conformity with the judgment of the bishops who had there convened with the congregation as well as of those who had written to you about him.[1]

Twice in this passage Cyprian has used the Latin term *suffragio* in describing the role of the whole gathered congregation: *omnium suffragio et iudicio* ("judged and voted upon by all"); and *universae fraternitatis suffragio* ("the verdict of the whole congregation"). Cyprian does not explain exactly how the whole congregation expressed its "vote" or "verdict"; it is thought most likely that it was by acclamation in favor of a candidate of whom they approved. In any case, it is clear from Cyprian's insistence that a bishop had to be chosen in the presence of those who were best acquainted with the character of the candidates, that the role of the laity in the selection of their bishop was an effective one. Cyprian could even express the effectiveness of their role by saying, "The laity have the power of choosing worthy bishops and refusing unworthy ones."[2]

In another letter, Cyprian witnesses to the fact that the procedure he described here was followed in the church of Rome. Defending the legitimacy of the election of Cornelius as bishop of Rome against the charges made against his election by his rival Novatian, Cyprian wrote: "Cornelius was made bishop by the choice of God and of His Christ, by the favorable witness of almost all of the clergy, by the votes of the laity then present, and by the assembly of bishops, men of maturity and integrity."[3] Here again the participation of the laity is expressed by the Latin word *suffragio*.

The most dramatic example of the effective role of the laity in an episcopal election is the case of Cyprian himself. Having been a Christian for only about four years, and a member of the clergy of Carthage for even fewer, his candidacy for the bishop's chair was strongly opposed by five of the presbyters of that church. The deacon who wrote the biography of Cyprian attributed his election "to the judgment of God and the favor of the laity."[4] In a letter that Cyprian wrote to the laity of his church, he referred to himself as "the one whom you made your bishop with such love and zeal,"[5] and he said of his opponents: "They have not lost their old venom against my episcopate, against your vote and the judgment of God."[6] In another letter, he referred to himself as having been chosen "by the vote of the entire congregation."[7] There can be little doubt about the effectiveness of the *suffragium* of the laity when we see that it prevailed over the opposition of five presbyters who could understandably have objected to the choice of a recent convert as their bishop.

## The Role of the Laity in Cyprian's Appointment of Clergy for His Church

About a year after Cyprian had become bishop, the persecution ordered by the Emperor Decius struck in North Africa, and since bishops were especially targeted by it, Cyprian prudently withdrew from the city to a safe place in the country, where he continued to exercise the care of his flock through letters addressed to his clergy and faithful. Several young men who had suffered imprisonment and torture for refusing to offer sacrifice to the gods, but had subsequently been released, found their way to the place where Cyprian was staying. Cyprian decided to enroll these confessors of the faith among the clergy of the church of Carthage, and wrote three letters about it, each of which he addressed to the presbyters, deacons, and all the laity of his church. The first of these letters begins in the following way:

> Dearest brethren, it is our custom when we make appointments to clerical office to consult you beforehand, and in council together with you to weigh the character and qualities of each candidate. But there is no need to wait for evidence from men when already God has cast his vote. Our brother Aurelius is a young man with a splendid record; he has already received the Lord's approbation and is dear to God. Tender in years he may be, but he is far advanced in glory for his faith and courage; though junior in terms of natural age, he is senior in honor. He has striven in a double contest: twice he has made confession and twice he has covered himself with the glory of victorious confession. . . . Such a man deserved higher grades of clerical appointment and greater advancement, judged as he should be not on his years but on his deserts. But it has been decided, for the time being, that he begin with the duties of reader. . . . You should therefore know, dearly beloved brothers, that I and my colleagues who were present have appointed this man to office. I know that you warmly welcome this action just as you are anxious that as many men as possible of this caliber should receive appointments in our church.[8]

While it seems probable that in the appointment of men to the clergy Cyprian would have taken counsel especially with his presbyters and deacons, it is noteworthy that the letters in which he took such care to explain and justify these appointments were all addressed to the laity as well.

## The Role of the Laity in Conciliar Decision Making

The decree of Decius obliging all the inhabitants of the Roman empire to offer sacrifice to the gods to invoke their blessing on his regime followed a half-century of relative peace for the church, and a great many Christians found themselves unprepared to suffer imprisonment, torture, and even death for refusing to offer the sacrifice ordered by the emperor. Many, including some of the clergy, offered the required sacrifice, and others bribed officials to obtain certificates attesting to their having done so. Both of these acts were judged to be grave sins, excluding the guilty from the communion of the church. Even while the persecution was still going on, many Christians who had failed the test were seeking to be reconciled to the church. While Cyprian was still in hiding, some of the presbyters in Carthage began reconciling such penitents, especially on the recommendation of confessors who were in prison or martyrs who had undergone torture. Given the gravity of the sin of apostasy, which some had considered to be unforgivable, along with the complication of deciding whether obtaining a certificate falsely attesting to the offering of sacrifice was equally grave, and the lack of a precedent for dealing with so great a number of cases of apostasy, Cyprian insisted that the reconciliation of the "lapsed" had to be delayed until a uniform policy could be established. He further insisted that this could be done only when peace had been restored and a council could be held. The point on which I wish to focus is the role that he expected the laity to have in such a council. Here are some passages of Cyprian's letters that speak of the coming council and of the part the laity were to have in it.

In the first of these letters, which was addressed to the presbyters and deacons of the church of Carthage, Cyprian seemed to be thinking only of a diocesan council. Referring to the question of the reconciliation of the lapsed, he wrote:

> I can make no reply on my own, for it has been a resolve of mine, right from the beginning of my episcopate, to do nothing on my own private judgment without your counsel and the consent of

the people. But so soon as by God's favour I have come to you, we will then discuss in council together, as the respect we have for each other demands, what has been done or what is to be done.[9]

The next letter is one that Cyprian addressed to the laity of his church. After expressing his concern that some of those who had lapsed were being prematurely reconciled because those who had suffered for the faith had interceded on their behalf, he again insisted that the question had to wait for a conciliar decision. While he now looked to a gathering of bishops, he assured the laity that their views would be heard:

I beg them to pay patient heed to our advice: wait for our return. Then, when, through God's mercy, we have come to you and the bishops have been called together, a large number of us will be able to examine the letter of the blessed martyrs and their requests, acting in conformity with the discipline of the Lord and in the presence of the confessors, and in accordance, also, with your judgment.[10]

Finally, in another letter that Cyprian addressed to the laity of Carthage at a time when he could foresee the end of the persecution, he again spoke of their participation in the council that would meet to settle the question of the lapsed:

This is the latest and the last trial of this persecution; under the Lord's protection even it will soon pass and then we shall be there with you in person after Easter-day, along with my fellow bishops. In the presence of these colleagues we will be able to arrange and determine whatever needs to be done, acting in accordance with your views as well as with the common counsel of us all, just as we have firmly decided to do.[11]

A letter that Cyprian received from the presbyters of Rome while the persecution was still going on shows that in Rome, too, it had been decided that the question of the reconciliation of the lapsed had to wait until peace had been restored and a council could be held. The letter from the presbyters makes it clear that in the council to take place at Rome the laity who had remained steadfast during the persecution would have an active part in the deliberations:

On this major issue we are indeed in agreement with the opinion which you yourself have argued, namely, that we must wait first until the Church has peace, and then, after bishops, presbyters, deacons, confessors and the laity who have remained steadfast have exchanged views in conference together, we can deal with the question of the lapsed.[12]

## The Role of the Laity in the Reconciliation of the Lapsed

When the persecution had ended, the councils that were held both at Carthage and at Rome agreed on a common policy with regard to the lapsed. Those who had fallen were all obliged to do penance, in proportion to the gravity of their sin. Those who had actually offered sacrifice had to do penance indefinitely, but were to be reconciled to the church when in danger of death, or at the onset of another persecution. Those who had obtained certificates falsely attesting that they had offered sacrifice could be reconciled after an appropriate period of penance. In each case, it had to be determined whether a person showed signs of true repentance. The striking feature of Cyprian's practice in the examination of those seeking reconciliation was the role that the laity played in it.

What added to the problem of the administration of penance in the aftermath of the persecution was the fact that some of the clergy had not waited for the issue of the lapsed to be settled by a council, but had adopted their own policy—in Carthage one of excessive laxity, and in Rome one of excessive rigor. Unwilling to accept the moderate decision made by the councils, these clergy, with a following of laity, became truly schismatic. Among them were also people who had lapsed during the persecution. Eventually, a number of such people, guilty of schism as well as apostasy, sought to be reconciled to the church. In a letter he wrote to Cornelius, the bishop of Rome, Cyprian described the difficulty he had overcoming the opposition of faithful laity to the readmission of some such people to the church:

> Oh how I wish, dearly beloved brother, that you could be present here with us when those who make their way back from schism are warped and twisted sinners! Then you would see under what difficulties I labor to persuade our brethren to show forbearance, to stifle their feelings of bitter resentment, and to consent that these evildoers should be let in and given healing treatment. They do indeed show joy and delight when those who come back are good enough people whose sins are less offensive; but, correspondingly, they put up noisy protests and resistance whenever those

who would return to the Church are diehard and shameless sinners, men contaminated with adulteries or pagan sacrifices, and yet, to crown it all, still remaining arrogant, and there is, therefore, every likelihood of their corrupting the well-disposed souls within the Church. It is with enormous difficulty that I manage to persuade my people—I really extort it out of them—that they allow the admission of such sinners. And in fact the resentment our brethren have felt has proved all the more reasonable in that one or two, despite protests and objections from the people, were received in through my leniency and then turned out to be worse than they had been; for they proved incapable of faithfully keeping up their penitence, having come without genuine repentance.[13]

It should be noted that the term "brethren" most likely includes both the clergy and the laity of Carthage, but the term "people" translates the Latin *plebs*, which Cyprian consistently used in referring to the laity. From this letter it is clear that the examination of those seeking readmission to the church was conducted in the presence of clergy and laity, giving them freedom to express their views about the genuineness of the repentance shown by the guilty. While it was Cyprian who ultimately decided whether to admit those guilty of grave sin to the penitential process by which they could be readmitted to communion, it is also clear that in making that decision he sometimes had to override the protests and objections of the laity—objections that, in some cases, he came to realize should have been allowed to prevail.

On the other hand, Cyprian also spoke of the "joy and delight" that the brethren showed when those who came back were guilty of less-offensive sins. There is an interesting example of this in a letter that Cyprian received from Cornelius, the bishop of Rome, which shows that in Rome also the laity participated in the readmission of sinners to the communion of the church. This case involved a Roman presbyter and a group of laypeople who were honored as confessors for having suffered imprisonment during the persecution of Decius, but who had subsequently allied themselves with Novatian and his rigorous policy regarding the lapsed. When they realized that their adherence to Novatian involved them in schism, they repented and sought readmission to communion with the rightful bishop of Rome. In his letter, Cornelius gave Cyprian a full account of the process of their reconciliation. The first step was an interrogation of the penitents by several of the Roman presbyters. When these were satisfied with the genuineness of their repentance, they so informed Cornelius, who gave the following account of the events that followed:

> When word was brought to me of all these proceedings, I decided to call together a meeting of the presbyters. Also attending were five bishops who happened to be in Rome that day. The purpose of the meeting was to form a clear proposal of the manner in which we ought to treat their cases and to ratify it by unanimous agreement. . . . After these transactions there appeared before the assembled presbyters Maximus, Urbanus, Sidonius and a number of other brethren who had allied themselves to them. They beseeched and prayed most earnestly that they would cast into oblivion all their past actions, that henceforth no mention should be made of them just as if nothing whatever had been said or done. . . . Naturally the faithful had to be notified of all these proceedings so that they might see installed in their church the very people whom they had seen, to their grief, wandering and straying away from it for so long. When their feelings on the matter had been ascertained, a great number of our congregation assembled together. With one voice they all gave thanks to God, expressing in tears the joy in their hearts as they welcomed them just as if they had come freed on this very day from the confines of their prison. . . . Accordingly, we gave directions that Maximus was to resume his former position as presbyter. As for the others, amid wildly enthusiastic acclamation from the people, we remitted all their past actions, reserving judgment for God the Almighty to whose power all things are finally subject.[14]

This description makes it clear that as in Carthage, so also in Rome the laity were involved in the process by which repentant sinners were reconciled to the church. The first stage here was conducted by a group of presbyters, followed by a meeting of Cornelius with his whole presbyterium, along with some visiting bishops. After that: "Naturally the faithful had to be notified of all these proceedings." The Latin phrase that is here rendered "naturally" can be translated more literally by the phrase "as was appropriate." Furthermore, the faithful had not only to be notified; their will in the matter had to be ascertained (the Latin word translated "feelings" is *voluntate*). It was only when the will of the faithful in the matter was known that a general gathering of the congregation was held, at which "with one voice they all gave thanks to God." And finally, the "voice of the people" was expressed in the form of "wildly enthusiastic acclamation" when Cornelius absolved these confessors of their past sins. Here again it is useful to know that the Latin phrase that has been rendered "wildly enthusiastic acclamation" is *ingenti populi suffragio*, which literally could be translated: "with an overwhelming vote of the people." The use of the word *suffragium* here throws a good deal of light on the meaning of the word when it was used to describe the role of the people in the choice of a bishop. It suggests that the people expressed their approval of a candidate not by casting ballots, but by acclamation. (No doubt there could be equally vocal expressions of disapproval of other candidates.)

## Conclusion

The letters of St. Cyprian—both those he wrote and those he received—provide incontrovertible evidence of the participation of the laity in decision making in the church of the third century. They make it clear that both at Carthage and at Rome, the laity played an active role in the choice of a bishop, in appointments to the clergy, in conciliar deliberations, and in the reconciliation of repentant sinners.

What conclusions can we draw from these facts of history? Obviously, one cannot simply repeat history; too many factors are different to allow anything like a reproduction of third-century practices in the twenty-first century. However, there is one conclusion that I think can certainly be drawn from this history: it is that genuine participation of the laity in decision making cannot be contrary to the nature of the church.

## Notes

1. Letter 67:4.1–5.2, trans. G. W. Clarke, in *The Letters of St. Cyprian of Carthage*, Ancient Christian Writers, 43, 44, 46, 47 (New York: Newman Press, 1984–89), vol. 4, 23–24.
2. Letter 67:3.2, in Clarke, *Letters*, vol. 4, 23.
3. Letter 55:8.4, in Clarke, *Letters*, vol. 3, 38.
4. Pontus, *Vita Cypriani* 5; *Corpus Scriptorum Ecclesticorum Latinorum* III, 3, ed. G. Hartel (Vienna: C. Geraldi, 1871), xcv.
5. Letter 43:4.1, in Clarke, *Letters*, vol. 2, 63: *sacerdoti quem tanto amore et ardore fecistis*.
6. Letter 43:1.2, in Clarke, *Letters*, vol. 2, 61: *contra suffragium vestrum et Dei iudicium*.
7. Letter 59:6.1, in Clarke, *Letters*, vol. 3, 71: *populi universi suffragio*.
8. Letter 38:1–2, in Clarke, *Letters*, vol. 2, 52–53.

9. Letter 14:4, in Clarke, *Letters*, vol. 1, 89.

10. Letter 17:3.2, in Clarke, *Letters*, vol. 1, 97.

11. Letter 43:7.2, in Clarke, *Letters*, vol. 2, 66–67.

12. Letter 30:5.3, in Clarke, *Letters*, vol. 2, 30.

13. Letter 59:15.3–4, in Clarke, *Letters*, vol. 3, 83–84.

14. Letter 49:2.1–5, in Clarke, *Letters*, vol. 2, 77–79.

# THREE

## Laity and the Development of Doctrine: Perspectives from the Early Church

### FRANCINE CARDMAN

In the mid-nineteenth century, two English Catholic clerics took up the topic this essay addresses. Monsignor George Talbot posed a rhetorical question to himself: "What is the province of the laity?" His response was adamant and to the point: "To hunt, to shoot, to entertain. These matters they understand, but to meddle in ecclesiastical matters they have no right at all." Although his response reflects a worldview common to both the Roman Catholic hierarchy and the British gentry of his day, his contemporary, Father John Henry Newman, responded to a similar query but from a very different perspective. When asked "Who are the laity?" Newman replied with a certain equanimity, "The church would look foolish without them."[1]

Starkly different assessments of who the laity are in relation to the church and the world frame these churchmen's witty assertions, and also underlie many contemporary ecclesiological issues. Exploring the thought and practice of the early church (from the second through the fourth centuries) can clarify differences implicit in Newman's and Talbot's ripostes while also casting light on current questions about laity and the governance of the Roman Catholic Church. To that end, I will consider four aspects of early church history: the evolution of distinctions between laity and clergy; the relationship of prayer and belief; the process of handing on apostolic faith, and the role of the laity during the Arian controversy after the Council of Nicaea. But first a word on perspective.

Catholics have long had a tendency toward a kind of "theological fundamentalism" about the origins of doctrines and practices, especially in regard to the institutional structures of the church. This Catholic literalism assumes that because certain doctrines, practices, and structures are held to be true or authentic, they must always have existed in the history of the church—and existed in the forms we know today. Or to put it more simply: Catholics often assume or assert that the way things are now is the way they must have been then. Reading scripture and history through this lens is like looking through the wrong end of a telescope. From this myopic viewpoint, we can only see ourselves. It's no wonder, then, that we often equate tradition with "what we've always believed, taught, and done"; or that we tend to assume that we can only do now what we have already (and always) done. But this is not the only way—and not the only Catholic way—to understand and appropriate our history as we embody the church for our times.

## "Laity" and "Clergy" in the Early Churches

The concepts "laity" and "clergy" have no place in the earliest churches founded by the apostles and other missionary preachers. The simplest way to demonstrate this point is by noting that, although we read in Paul's letters about celebrations of the Lord's Supper in local Christian communities (most notably at Corinth, where abuses of hospitality on the part of the affluent were a serious problem; see 1 Cor 11:17–34), nowhere in the New Testament is there any mention of who presided at those ritual meals. Whoever they were, they certainly were not "clergy" as we now understand that term. What we know about house-holds and meals in the Greco-Roman world, however, suggests that the person who hosted or presided at such a meal was likely to be the owner of the house where the church community gathered. And we also know, from the lists of believers named in greetings at the beginning and end of Paul's letters (especially Romans 16), that women were the heads of some house churches.[2] What Romans 16 and similar passages make clear is that ministries were fluid and diverse in these early communities, lacking formality and definition; women as well as men exercised these ministries and other charisms.

It is not possible here to recount the development of ministerial offices from the end of the first century (e.g., the Pastoral epistles, the *Didache*, and the letters of Ignatius of Antioch) through the evolving church orders of the late second and third centuries (the *Apostolic Tradition* of Hippolytus, c. 215; the *Didascalia*, c. 230–250), or the rapid elaboration of ecclesiastical structures, offices, and roles in the fourth century.[3] Rather, I can only note in summary fashion some critical points in the process. Offices of bishop and deacon began to be differentiated from other ministries (e.g., apostles and prophets) toward the end of the first century, with Ignatius of Antioch vigorously promoting the role of the bishop early in the second.[4] Over the course of the next century, the threefold offices of bishop, presbyter, and deacon gained definition, becoming fairly common by the time of Irenaeus of Lyon (c. 180). Hippolytus recorded ordination prayers for all three offices early in the third century. Among the eastern churches, the *Didascalia* (c. 230) still labored to urge acceptance and respect for these offices, while in the West they seem to have become more firmly established by the time Cyprian became bishop of Carthage in North Africa in 248. The rapid elaboration of ecclesiastical structures and hierarchy begins in the fourth century during the reign of Constantine, the first Roman emperor to embrace Christianity.[5] Distinctions between "laity" and "clergy" accompany this process: they begin to develop by the end of the second century, become more evident by the middle of the third, and achieve a brittle clarity in the fourth.

Under Constantine (312–37), Christians learned to adjust to a world in which they were no longer persecuted but tolerated and then favored, until Christianity became the established religion of the Roman empire under Theodosius I (379–95). Distinctions of role and status within the church might have developed more gradually and less sharply than they ultimately did had it not been for the momentum generated by social and political forces endemic to the new religious environment. As the empire grew more Christian, the churches, especially those in major cities, became more imperial in their outlook and expression. Over the course of the fourth century, ecclesiastical office took on a sacral cast even as it clothed itself in imperial garb. The liturgy expanded in form and style to fill the new, grand spaces available to it, especially in the imperial cities; theological understandings of priesthood (by which was usually meant the episcopacy) and eucharist developed apace. The divide between laity and clergy widened dramatically. In time, the church emerged as the dominant institution in the West as the Roman empire declined and then disintegrated across the western Mediterranean from the late fourth century through the fifth. The rising power of bishops, particularly the Roman bishop, in the West in late antiquity and the early Middle Ages owed as much to the effects of geopolitics and demographics as to any internal logic or ecclesiological necessity.[6]

We know that Christian communities had chosen leaders from their midst at least since the time of the Pastorals (see 1 Tim 3:1–13, on bishops and deacons). Church orders such as the *Apostolic Tradition* of Hippolytus and the *Didascalia* confirm and continue the practice of laypeople and clergy selecting their bishop and other ministers, although these documents do not specify the processes that were followed. Even the late-fourth-century compilation of church orders and directives for church organization known as the *Apostolic Constitutions* bears witness to the participation of laity in the selection of clergy. By the end of that century, circumstances that had hastened the institutional development of the church also gave rise to conflicting interests and impulses in recruitment and appointment of clergy, especially bishops. Ambrose of Milan and Augustine of Hippo are but the best known of prominent men propelled (even compelled) into church office by the insistence of a crowd of Christians, lay and clerical. Ambrose was only a catechumen, recently finished serving as provincial governor in northern Italy, when he was spontaneously acclaimed as the new bishop of Milan in 374 by a cheering crowd that had taken up a chant issuing from the fringe of the gathering: "Ambrose for bishop, Ambrose for bishop!" Similarly, Augustine, who had long made it a practice not to enter North African cities where the bishop had recently died, was surprised one day in Hippo and pressed into accepting ordination as a presbyter, much against his will; a few years later, in 396, he would become bishop there. At the other end of the spectrum of what might be called "lay participation" in church governance, there was, throughout the fourth century, increasing imperial influence in the appointment and advancement of bishops, and even their deposition and exile during times of controversy. The imperial hand was strongest in Constantinople, but could be felt in other major cities as well, especially in the eastern empire.

Distinctions and divisions between laity and clergy, then, are long-standing but neither absolute nor uniform across the history of the church, whether in the early centuries or later ones. It would be a mistake to attach post-Tridentine and post-Vatican I meanings and expectations to these distinctions as if they had existed forever in the same form as we know them today. A similar caveat applies to understanding the form and function of episcopal office, whether that of local ordinary or bishop of Rome. Taking these cautions into account, however, allows us to learn from the early church as we grapple with questions of authority and participation in the Roman Catholic Church of the twenty-first century.

To that end, I want to shift focus from immediate questions of governance and decision making as such and look instead at the way in which "the laity" constituted the sine qua non for the development of doctrine in the first four centuries of the church's existence. By changing the lens as well as the focus, I hope to open up the contemporary discussion while also reframing our view of this aspect of early church history and its import. In what follows, I will consider the general development of a *sensus fidelium* (sense of the faithful) by the end of the second century, the emerging theological understanding of how the churches' faith was handed on, and the critical role of laypeople in the doctrinal controversies of the fourth century.

## Lex Orandi, Lex Credendi

Liturgists and others who study the early church are fond of quoting an aphorism about the relationship of prayer to belief: *lex orandi, lex credendi*, the law of praying is the law of believing.[7] Or, as we pray, so we believe. Articulation of belief follows the movement of faith as it finds expression in prayer. Individuals come to faith, but they do so in the context of or in relation to a community living that faith and making it known; community shapes prayer and thereby gives rise to more explicit proclamations of belief. Reflection on faith that has been articulated in kerygmatic statements is the stuff of theology, which thematizes these foundational experiences; theology in turn shapes the contours of doctrine, the formal and formally ritualized statements of the community's beliefs. Prayer—liturgical prayer and personal prayer—is the middle term in the dynamic interaction of experience and reflection, communities and individuals of faith. Prayer is the province of all believers, forming and simultaneously being formed by all. Even when given formal expression in liturgies and professions of faith, prayer and belief are continually subject to subtle reformulation through shifting nuances of meaning and practice. The *lex orandi* defies precise definition, and thus the *lex credendi* does as well. Prayer warms and animates the body of Christ through the centuries, and is in turn formed and nurtured by that living, changing body. *Lex orandi* is the life-breath of embodied faith. We do well to listen for and to its susurrations—both from the past and in our own times.

The second century C.E. was a time of enormous diversity of belief and practice as church communities took root in cities of the Roman empire. Competing centrifugal forces within local churches and among the loosely knit network of churches threatened to sunder the growing Christian movement even before it could assemble much of an infrastructure to support its nascent and still quite fragile superstructure. It is probably difficult for most of us to imagine, from the vantage point of the early twenty-first century, the ad hoc nature of life in Christian churches of the second century: no centralized authority or authorities, no uniform structures of ministry, no formally recognized canon of Christian scripture, no official commissions to write or approve liturgical texts and rites, no mechanisms for decision making beyond local communities. Yet over the course of the century, an informal, rough consensus began to emerge in eastern and western churches in regard to basic beliefs and practices, as well as to some ecclesial structures necessary to sustain these developments.

At least two aspects of the process through which this consensus came into being require attention here. The first is the development of a ritual of baptism and accompanying profession of faith that was fairly similar among churches within broad regions; the second is the appearance toward the end of the second century of summary statements of belief known generically as the Rule of Faith. In both instances there was no formal or official mechanism for approving and adopting these developments beyond their acceptance in practice by the faithful—the women and men who constituted the churches.

By the 60s of the first century, Paul's letters drew on earlier traditions as well as his own experience to exhort his readers in regard to practical and theological implications of baptism for their life together in the church. The well-known baptismal fragment in Gal 3:28 ff. (for all baptized in Christ, "there is no longer Jew or Greek, slave or free, male or female") is the most obvious example of liturgical prayer (*lex orandi*) influencing not only belief (*lex credendi*) but behavior (what might be called *lex vivendi*). The representation of Paul's missionary work in Acts contains another instance of baptismal practice that does not usually receive much attention, perhaps because of its apparently anomalous character. But the account is worth closer inspection. When Paul arrives in Ephesus, he finds disciples of Jesus there already (Acts 19:1–7) and asks them if they had received the Holy Spirit when they became believers. Their reply is startling: "No, we have not even heard that there is a Holy Spirit"! Once Paul ascertains that they were baptized into John's baptism, he baptizes them in the name of the Lord Jesus and lays hands on them to call down the Holy Spirit; they immediately begin speaking in tongues and prophesying. The episode reveals great diversity in missionary preaching and practice in the first century, while also suggesting movement toward a minimal kind of coherence among groups of Christians. No one directed Paul to impose his practice—the tradition he himself had learned—and he had no inherent authority over those isolated believers. There was no de facto (much less de jure) necessity for the few Ephesian followers of Jesus to accept Paul's ministrations in place of the baptism they had already received. Instead, they considered his arguments, were persuaded, and chose to act accordingly. In time, the memory of Paul became important enough to the Christians of Ephesus that they preserved the letter that he, or someone writing in his name, later sent them.

The practice of baptism in the name of Father, Son, and Holy Spirit was becoming commonplace by the end of the first century (see Mt 28:19 ff.). Sometime before the middle of the second century, instructions for how to administer the rite had begun to circulate among some churches in Syria or Palestine in a document known as the *Didache*. That early compilation of moral instruction and incipient church order gives considerable latitude for adaptation to circumstances. For instance, it directs that baptism should be performed in running water or some other; in cold water or hot; if no body of water is nearby, then water should be poured three times over the head of the one being baptized; regardless of the kind of water available, however, baptism should be done in the name of Father, Son, and Holy Spirit (*Did* 11). We do not know who the author/compiler of the *Didache* was, nor why he took on the task of producing this document, nor what authority he hoped it would carry. We likewise lack much information about the process by which the rite of baptism and other liturgical actions took form in this early period or how they came to be adopted in the churches and achieved a degree of regional standardization.[8] What we can surmise, nevertheless, is that liturgical rites came to be accepted through the very act of using them. That is to say, they arose from practice and were recognized or received in practice. In the first and early second centuries, then, it was laypeople who created, used, and adopted these rites.

Professions of faith developed in relation to the evolving rites of baptism.[9] These declarations took two basic forms, both following the tripartite structure familiar to us today. Interrogatory creeds such as that preserved in the *Apostolic Tradition* of Hippolytus (c. 215) questioned those being baptized, asking whether they believed in the Father, the all-governing (*pantokrator*); in Jesus Christ, the Son of God (details of his birth, death, and resurrection followed); in the Holy Spirit and the church (resurrection of the body was sometimes included in the list as well). Declaratory creeds took the form of affirmative statements such as those in the old Roman Symbol and the profession of faith that came to be known as the Apostles' Creed: I believe in God the Father, the all-governing, and so forth. By about 250 in the west and a century later in the east, Christians were calling these declaratory creeds "symbols" of faith, perhaps because they served as tokens by which believers could recognize one another. As with other parts of the baptismal rite, professions of faith developed through use and acceptance by the community as a whole. Again, it is laypeople who must be seen as the primary agents in this process.

Roughly contemporaneous with the development of baptismal creeds was the appearance of summary statements of faith that came to be known generically as the Rule of Faith. Irenaeus and Tertullian in the west preserved several versions of the Rule of Faith (c. 180–200); some fifty years later in the east, Origen offered a précis of Christian teachings that functions much like the Rule, but he did not call it such. What is striking about these summaries is, on the one hand, their apparently independent appearance in churches of several regions (southern France, North Africa, and Egypt, respectively) from the late second century to the middle of the third century; on the other hand, there is a surprising degree of fluidity and variability within a generally similar structure (usually tripartite).[10] Neither Irenaeus, nor Tertullian, nor Origen are apt to have composed their versions of the Rule of Faith de novo; rather, they most likely worked with and sometimes reworked material that had been handed on to them, perhaps in catechetical contexts. Irenaeus was a bishop when he composed the treatise *Against Heresies* that contains several versions of the Rule; Tertullian, learned, acerbic, and theologically astute, most likely was a layman; Origen, after some difficulties in finding a bishop to ordain him, eventually became a presbyter in Caesarea (in Roman Palestine) and a brilliant speculative theologian. None of the three can be thought to have worked in isolation from a community of believers in and through which the faith and traditions of earlier Christians were handed on. Even when these three theologians (and others) made advances or innovations in the conceptualization and understanding of Christian faith, they wrote for churches (predominantly laypeople) that read, received, preserved, and passed on their writings.

## Handing on Apostolic Faith

The Rule of Faith emerged from a process of tradition—of handing on (the root meaning of the word) the faith experienced and shared in communities of Christians over several generations and across the Roman world. The process involved both laypeople and, as ministerial offices began to develop, clergy; both simple believers and emerging theologians. Common to all participants in the process was a belief that, to use Origen's words, "grace and truth came by Jesus Christ, and that Christ is the truth."[11] Likewise, most of them also believed that the truth brought by Jesus was handed down by the apostles and preserved in the churches from their time to the present. Connection to the apostles and, through them, to Jesus was taken as a guarantee of the authenticity of Christian faith. During the late-second and third centuries, "apostolicity" became a marker of identity, a norm of faith, and an expression of unity among believers across time as well as space. Because it continues to function this way in the Roman Catholic Church today, it is important to understand the origins of the concept, changes in its meanings, and the role of laypeople in giving rise to apostolic faith and identity.

Irenaeus was a major exponent of the norm of apostolicity and the process of handing on the church's faith. As he described it in his treatise *Against Heresies*, this faith was characterized by continuity and unanimity:

> Having received this preaching and this faith, the church, though scattered in the whole world, carefully preserves it, as if living in one house. She believes these things [everywhere] alike, as if she had but one heart and one soul, and preaches them harmoniously, teaches them, and hands them down, as if she had but one mouth.[12]

This glowing picture is colored by a mythic view of Christian origins and history, but it expresses a sense of Christian identity that was becoming more widely accepted in the late-second and third centuries, just as increasing disagreements among Christians made it ever more necessary. The immediate context of Irenaeus's work was the challenge presented by gnostic interpretations of Christian faith that claimed a secret tradition of saving *gnosis* (knowledge). Such knowledge was different from the public faith of the churches and available only to a spiritual elite.[13] To counter the growing appeal of gnostic teachers, Irenaeus was eager to establish a public and unbroken tradition of faith and teaching that reached back to Jesus and the apostles. That tradition, as we have seen, was established and preserved in the churches through the faith of believers, which was nurtured and handed on in ritual (baptism and eucharist) as well as in preaching and teaching (homilies and catechesis). Irenaeus brought a new emphasis to understanding the traditioning process by giving heightened symbolic and practical importance to bishops as the essential link between the apostles and contemporary Christians. The bishop in each church is, in turn, linked to his predecessors and successors in an unbroken chain of faith, teaching, and office. Against the recent and secret tradition of gnostic teachers, Irenaeus counterposed a public and (for the most part) historical succession of teachers, the bishops. His argument warrants quoting at length:

> The tradition of the apostles, made clear in all the world, can be clearly seen in every church by those who wish to behold the truth. We can enumerate those who were established by the apostles as bishops in the churches, and their successors down to our time. . . . But since it would be very long in such a volume as this to enumerate the successions of all the churches, I can by pointing out the tradition which that very great, oldest, and well-known church, founded and established at Rome by those two most glorious apostles Peter and Paul, received from the apostles, and its faith known among men, which comes down to us through the successions of bishops, put to shame . . . all those who gather as they should not. For every church must be in harmony with this church, because of its outstanding pre-eminence, that is, the faithful from everywhere, since the apostolic tradition is preserved in it by those from everywhere.[14]

There follows a list of Roman bishops that is familiar, at least in part, to countless later generations of Catholics through the old Roman canon (eucharistic prayer) of the Mass.[15]

Like the earlier passage on apostolic faith, this one is a narrative of origins. Taking Rome as paradigmatic of all the churches, Irenaeus seeks to validate its faith—and that of the other churches as well—by demonstrating Rome's historical succession of bishops. His accomplishment can be measured by the fact that this is essentially the same foundational myth that many Roman Catholics appeal to today. The narrative is mythical not in the sense that it is untrue, but in what can be termed its ideological purposes and its anachronistic treatment of ostensibly historical material. For instance, we know that there was a church community in Rome well before either Peter or Paul arrived there—otherwise, to whom was Paul writing in his letter to the Romans? Similarly, we know that Clement played an important role in the Roman church when (c. 96) he wrote a letter on its behalf to the Corinthian Christians urging them to end divisions within their community; but whether Clement held any formal office and, if he did, just what it was and whether it can be equated with that of bishop as it later developed are questions open to debate. Despite Irenaeus's tendency to read later structures back into earlier ones, his account nevertheless remains important for understanding the process by which faith was articulated and handed on in this formative period.

Acknowledging the kaleidoscopic blend of myth and history in Irenaeus's narrative allows us to discern more clearly the logical and historical priority he attaches to succession of faith and teaching over succession of episcopal office. If there is in the churches continuity of faith with the preaching and witness of the apostles, that continuity can only have been generated by the prayer and praxis of believers—by laypeople. Faith and its handing on within Christian communities existed long before the emergence of episcopal office. As institutional structures developed during the second century, the role of bishop took on increasing significance as a focus of unity and teaching, especially in light of conflicting interpretations of Christian belief. Irenaeus and others began to see episcopal succession as the means or mechanism that preserved the continuity of apostolic faith. Emphasis started to shift from the entire church (all believers) as preserving and passing on faith, to the bishops as the specially designated successors of the apostles and the teachers of apostolic faith. Nearly exclusive concentration on the mechanical—and mythical—unbroken historical succession of bishops, however, developed in the polemical contexts of the sixteenth-century reformations, distorting the meaning of both apostolic faith and apostolic succession. Because an overly literal understanding of apostolic succession eclipsed the more encompassing and participative process of handing on apostolic faith, Catholics have long tended to equate the apostles with bishops, who were regarded as their successors. Recognizing the priority of apostolic faith over episcopal succession, however, allows us to recover the identity of the apostles as *lay*people standing at the head of a long succession of laypeople handing on the grace and truth of Jesus Christ in the churches.

## Keeping the Faith during the Arian Controversy

The first theological controversy to engage a large number of churches and to issue, eventually, in decisions meant for all of them arose early in the fourth century.[16] Known as the Arian controversy for one of its vanquished protagonists, the conflict centered around the question of the divinity of the Word (*Logos*) of God made present or known in Jesus. Since the theological issues themselves are not the point of this essay, I will try to summarize a very complicated controversy as briefly and accurately as possible here in order to move on to the ecclesiological point at hand. Put simply, Arius argued that the Word (also called the Son) could not be divine and equal to God the Father, but must be derivative from and subordinate to God; Alexander, bishop of Alexandria where Arius was a presbyter, insisted that the Word was equal to the Father in both divinity and eternity. From 318 on, sides were quickly chosen and the debate rapidly spread through the eastern churches. For the most part, these questions received only minimal notice among the western churches. But the disturbance caught the attention of the emperor Constantine, who had been instrumental in granting religious toleration to Christians in 313 and now considered himself a friend of the church. Displeased with the disorder among the churches and the resultant lack of concord in his empire, he directed that all the bishops be called together in council to resolve the controversy and restore both ecclesiastical and political peace. Constantine paid for the council, which met at Nicaea, near Constantinople, in 325; he also provided imperial conveyance for the bishops attending the proceedings (only a few western bishops were present, along with two presbyters sent by bishop Sylvester of Rome), presided at many council sessions, and feasted the bishops at the gathering's conclusion. It is worth noting that the first of what we now call the ecumenical councils was summoned by the emperor—who was not only a layman, but an unbaptized layman at that.

The Council of Nicaea decided in favor of Alexander's position and excommunicated Arius and his followers. All but two of the bishops present signed the council's decrees, which included a creed affirming that the Son or Word was "of one substance" (*homoousios*) with the Father and was "begotten not made." (That creed is a prototype for the one we know today as the Nicene creed.)[17] And there the matter rested—or so they thought. In the years after Nicaea, however, ecclesiastical and imperial politics grew ever more intricately entwined. Toward the end of his life, Constantine had wearied of the continued bickering between pro-Nicene and Arian Christians, and, influenced by Arian-leaning bishops around the imperial court, had begun to tilt his policies toward moderate Arianism. Among the pro-Nicenes, Athanasius, bishop of Alexandria, stood out for his defiance of Constantine and, later, Constantius II, his son and successor. Five times an exile, Athanasius became a rallying symbol of the Nicene faith, garnering for himself the nickname *Athanasius contra mundum*—"Athanasius against the world." In addition to resisting imperial pressures, the Nicene party still needed to do serious theological work in order to reach agreement on just what the council had decided so expeditiously and with such ambiguity in its key term, *homoousios*, as to garner nearly unanimous support from the bishops at Nicaea.

Tracing the shifting political and theological alliances in the years after Nicaea is well beyond the scope of this essay. Councils held in 359 and 360, however, require some consideration. Called by the emperor Constantius II and attended by a large number of bishops, the councils attempted to put an end to the ongoing controversy by issuing decisions that were increasingly Arian in nature. The Council of Sirmium in 359 had forbidden use of the term *ousia* (substance, essence) or its compounds (of which the Nicene *homoousios* was one) to describe the relation of the Word/Son to the Father. In response to this decree, Jerome wrote: "The world groaned and was amazed to find itself Arian."[18] Throughout the 360s and well into the next decade, most bishops were at least nominally Arian. By the standard of Nicaea itself as well as of later orthodoxy, those bishops, representing the majority of the churches (the conflict had little play in the west at the time), were heretical in their beliefs about the nature of the Word/Son of God. Some bishops, however, resisted the trend toward Arianism. They began to engage the unresolved theological issues while also attending to the political work of forging a pro-Nicene coalition of bishops. By themselves, however, neither the "orthodox" nor the "heretical" bishops would have been able to stand, much less bring the long-running conflict to a resolution.

For nearly twenty years Arianism held sway. The faith of Nicaea, once judged by the bishops gathered there in council to be consonant with the ancient traditions of Christian belief and teaching, was maintained largely by laypeople, "the faithful," and some staunch and astute pro-Nicene bishops. So fierce was the debate by the early 380s that Gregory of Nyssa, in a witty and often-quoted passage, observed in regard to the city of Constantinople:

> The whole city is full of it, the squares, the market places, the cross-roads, the alleyways; old-clothes men, money changers, food sellers: they are all busy arguing. If you ask someone to give you change, he philosophizes about the Begotten and Unbegotten; if you inquire about the price of a loaf, you are told by way of reply that the Father is greater and the Son inferior; if you ask "Is my

bath ready?" the attendant answers that the Son was made out of nothing.[19]

In 381, the Council of Constantinople, called by the emperor Theodosius I, met in the imperial capitol to affirm and complete the work of Nicaea and bring more than fifty years of conflict closer to a conclusion. The council also dealt with new questions that had arisen in the interim: the divinity of the Holy Spirit, which had been debated since the 360s, and issues about the way in which the divine Word/Son was joined with the humanity of Jesus, a topic that would lead to the christological controversies of the fifth century. The creed written at Constantinople was similar to that of Nicaea, with a few additions and clarifications; it is this creed that we today call the "Nicene creed." For all practical purposes, Arianism was eliminated within the Roman empire after the Council of Constantinople. But by a quirk of fate, some of the Germanic peoples outside the empire had been evangelized in the 340s by Arian missionaries. Thus, Arianism would continue among the "barbarians" and return to haunt the disintegrating western empire during the late-fifth and sixth centuries as these peoples made their way across its frontiers during the so-called "barbarian invasions."

As Gregory of Nyssa had seen, somewhat to his dismay, doctrine comes from and belongs to the people as much as or more than the bishops. The Arian councils of 359 and 360 were no longer recognized as authoritative after the Council of Constantinople because, ultimately, the people had not recognized them as such, despite the leading of their bishops. Modern-day ecclesiologists are fond of pointing out that a council's teaching must be *received* before it becomes authoritative: the mere fact of claiming authority is not sufficient in itself for obtaining it. Reception of a council (or other teaching, for that matter) depends not only on the approval of bishops or other hierarchs but especially, and perhaps more importantly, on acceptance by the "faithful," that is to say, the laity, the people who are the church.

John Henry Newman made precisely this point about the Arian controversy after Nicaea. In an appendix to his long monograph *The Arians of the Fourth Century*, Newman reprinted an earlier essay in which he had argued that it was the laity who had preserved the faith during those parlous times between Nicaea and Constantinople:

The episcopate, whose action was so prompt and concordant at Nicaea on the rise of Arianism, did not, as a class or order of men, play a good part in the troubles consequent upon the Council; and the laity did. The Catholic people, in the length and breadth of Christendom, were the obstinate champions of Catholic truth, and the bishops were not. . . . [O]n the whole, taking a wide view of the history, we are obliged to say that the governing body of the Church came short, and the governed were pre-eminent in faith, zeal, courage and constancy.[20]

Newman cites numerous examples from fourth- and fifth-century sources of the failures of bishops as well as the support of laypeople for Athanasius and other pro-Nicene leaders. Two stories already mentioned or alluded to here—of Ambrose in Milan and Athanasius in Alexandria—further illustrate his argument. First, it was the death of the Arian bishop of Milan, Auxentius, that occasioned the popular acclamation of Ambrose as bishop; soon thereafter, Ambrose had the backing of a virtual mob of Christians in refusing to grant a church for the use of the widowed empress Justina and Arian Gothic soldiers stationed in Milan. Second, Egyptian monks (laymen, it should be noted) from the desert outside Alexandria enthusiastically and, at times, force fully protected and supported Athanasius during his clashes with the emperor Constantius II. When imperial soldiers attempted in 356 to exile Athanasius from his episcopal see, the monks successfully hid him in the desert for five years. Constantius had installed in his place an Arian bishop, George, who was so disliked by the majority of Alexandrian Christians that they offered no resistance when, after Constantius's death, a pagan mob lynched George in 361 because of his disparagement of the temple dedicated to the *Genius* (or spirit) of the city. Shortly thereafter, Athanasius returned triumphantly to his see.

Stories like these may not be entirely edifying examples of lay participation in church governance, but neither is the behavior of bishops in that period an argument against it. For Newman, it was the laity's preservation of the faith despite most bishops' denial of it during the ascendency of Arianism that eventually persuaded him that this faith could still be found in its fullness in the Roman Catholic Church. Although this conviction led him from Anglicanism to Roman Catholicism, it is not necessary to accept Newman's theological assessment of Rome over Canterbury, or his particular theory of doctrinal development, in order to appreciate his insight into the vital role of the laity, "the faithful" who constitute the church and preserve its faith.

## Toward the Future

The loose association of churches in the early centuries is, of course, vastly different from the centrally organized, global institution that is the

Roman Catholic Church today. Yet there is much from that seemingly simpler era that speaks to present-day needs for structural change and reform of ecclesial ethos. In the context of reframing the way we look at "laity" in the early church, I have argued for a much broader understanding of the crucial role that laypeople played in developing, handing on, and preserving Christian faith and teaching in those centuries. As both second-century doctrinal developments and fourth-century doctrinal conflicts show, apostolicity is an attribute of the whole church—of all believers, not just the bishops. The faith that "comes to us from the apostles" comes from laywomen and -men as much as (or perhaps more than) from clergy.

That laypeople played such an important part in the development of doctrine in these early centuries argues for once again trusting their participation in the processes of decision making, selecting bishops, and teaching. It even suggests that such participation is a necessity if the church is to be truly apostolic (faithful) and truly catholic (embodied and inclusive). In matters of doctrine as well as in theories and practices of church governance that require reform in our own day, we would do well to acknowledge along with Newman that the church would indeed look foolish without the faith, participation, and perseverance of the laity.

## Notes

1. Talbot's remarks are quoted in Charles Stephen Dessain, *John Henry Newman* (London: Thomas Nelson and Sons, 1966), 117; Newman's are quoted in John Coulson, *Newman and the Common Tradition* (Oxford: Clarendon Press, 1970), 112 (from a memorandum of Newman's). On the occasion of the twentieth anniversary of Vatican II, I used these contrasting views to examine the role of women and laity in the church since the council. Now on the fortieth anniversary of the council, they are more apt than ever. See Francine Cardman, " 'The Church Would Look Foolish without Them': Women and Laity since Vatican II," in *Vatican II: Open Questions and New Horizons*, ed. Gerald M. Fagin, S.J., Theology and Life Series 8 (Wilmington, Del.: Michael Glazier, 1984), 105–33.

2. Bernadette Brooten analyzes one of the names in this list: see Brooten, " 'Junia . . . Outstanding among the Apostles' (Romans 16:7)," in *Women Priests: A Catholic Commentary on the Vatican Declaration*, ed. Leonard Swidler and Arlene Swidler (New York: Paulist Press, 1977), 141–44. For more detailed consideration of women in the Pauline churches, see Margaret Y. MacDonald, "Reading Real Women through the Undisputed Letters of Paul," in *Women and Christian Origins*, ed. Ross Shepard

Kraemer and Mary Rose D'Angelo (New York: Oxford University Press, 1999), 199–220. Note the importance of Phoebe, whom Paul commends as "our sister, who is a minister [*diakonos*] of the church at Cenchreae" (Rom 16:1–2).

3. See Francis A. Sullivan, S.J., *From Apostles to Bishops: The Development of the Episcopacy in the Early Church* (New York: The Newman Press, 2001). I have traced these developments with a particular regard to the ministry of women: see Francine Cardman, "Women, Ministry, and Church Order in Early Christianity," in Kraemer and D'Angelo, eds., *Women and Christian Origins*, 300–329.

4. There is scholarly debate, some of it still confessional and polemical, about whether the offices of bishop, presbyter, and deacon as witnessed in Ignatius's letters represent a widespread practice (an interpretation often taken as supporting the early appearance and acceptance of the "monepiscopate") or a local development in which Ignatius may have been at the forefront even among the churches in Asia Minor. See William R. Schoedel, *Ignatius of Antioch: A Commentary on the Letters of Ignatius of Antioch* (Philadelphia: Fortress Press, 1985), 22–23 (introduction) and commentary for these issues.

5. Despite his interest and later involvement in the church, Constantine was not baptized until just before his death in 337.

6. For a popular introduction to the history of the papacy and the lives of the popes, see Richard P. McBrien, *Lives of the Popes: Pontiffs from St. Peter to John Paul II* (San Francisco: HarperSanFrancisco, 1997); for more detailed information, see *The Papacy: An Encyclopedia*, ed. Philippe Levillain (New York: Routledge, 2002).

7. This is the popular form of the expression; the origin of the principle dates to the fifth century, in a document known as the *Indiculus*, mistakenly attributed to Celestine I of Rome: *ut legem credendi lex statuat supplicandi* (so that the law of praying may establish the law of believing).

8. For study of the early liturgy, see Paul F. Bradshaw, *The Search for the Origins of Christian Worship: Sources and Methods for the Study of Early Liturgy*, 2d ed. (New York: Oxford University Press, 2002). See also Theodor Klauser, *A Short History of the Western Liturgy: An Account and Some Reflections*, 2d ed. (Oxford: Oxford University Press, 1979). For particular topics, see *The New Dictionary of Sacramental Worship*, ed. Peter E. Fink (Collegeville, Minn.: Liturgical Press, 1990).

9. Frances Young, *The Making of the Creeds* (Philadelphia: Trinity Press International, 1991), is a brief but solid presentation of creedal development; chapter 1 covers this early period.

10. Versions of the Rule can be found in Irenaeus, *Against Heresies* I.10.1–2; III.4.2; III.11.1 (does not include the Holy Spirit). Tertullian often refers

to the Rule in a general way in his works, citing its contents with some variations in *The Veiling of Virgins* 1 (no mention of Holy Spirit), *Prescriptions against the Heretics* 13, and *Against Praxeas* 2. Origen's summary of Christian belief is found in *On First Principles* I.3–5.

11. Origen, *On First Principles* I.1 (preface), trans. G. W. Butterworth (New York: Harper Torchbooks, 1966; originally published 1936).

12. Irenaeus, *Against Heresies* I.10.2; cf. Tertullian, *Prescriptions* 37, speaking of the rule [of faith] "which the church has handed down from the apostles, the apostles from Christ, and Christ from God." Translations of Irenaeus from *Early Christian Fathers*, ed. Cyril C. Richardson (New York: Macmillan, 1970); of Tertullian from *Early Latin Theology*, ed. S. L. Greenslade (Philadelphia: Westminster Press, 1956).

13. "Gnosticism" is a catch-all term for a variety of religious beliefs and groups in this period. In addition to secret knowledge, gnosticism is usually characterized in part by dualism, a spiritualized view of salvation, and (sometimes) elaborate cosmological myths. Gnostic teachers offered an interpretation of Christian faith and scriptures that was sufficiently attractive to Christians to be a cause of alarm for Irenaeus and others. Until the discovery of gnostic scriptures at Nag Hammadi in Egypt in 1945, nearly all information about these groups came from their opponents. Some recent scholarship has begun to question the usefulness of the term "gnosticism" as an interpretive or historical category. For a critical study of the conceptualization of "gnosticism" and the function it served in the formation of Christian identity in the early centuries, see Karen L. King, *What Is Gnosticism?* (Cambridge, Mass.: The Belknap Press at Harvard University Press, 2003).

14. Irenaeus, *Against Heresies* III.3.1–2.

15. *Linus, Cletus, Clement*, Evarestus, Alexander, *Xystus [Sixtus]*, Telesphorus, Hyginus, Pius, Anicetus, Soter, and Eleutherus, bishop in Irenaeus's day. Names in italics are found in the Roman canon, now Eucharistic Prayer I in the post–Vatican II sacramentary.

16. Decision making at a regional level developed in the third century, with synods of bishops addressing questions of practice and teaching for their churches. Presbyters and laypeople, however, continued to play a role in decision making in this period: see, e.g., the essay by Francis A. Sullivan, S.J., in this volume. Bishops and their churches within a region (e.g., North Africa) were in communion with each other and with bishops and churches in other regions; differences between regions were generally tolerated, though occasionally they led to conflicts.

17. See Young, *The Making of the Creeds*, ch. 3.

18. Jerome makes this observation in his treatise *Against the Luciferians* 19, in *St. Jerome, Letters and Select Works*, trans. W. H. Fremantle, Nicene

and Post-Nicene Fathers, second series, vol. 19, Philip Schaff and Henry Wace, series editors (Grand Rapids, Mich.: Wm. B. Eerdmans, 1954; reprint of 1892 edition).

19. Gregory of Nyssa, *On the Deity of the Son, and the Holy Spirit*, PG xlvi, 557B, as quoted in Timothy Ware, *The Orthodox Church* (Harmondsworth: Penguin Books, 1963, rev. 1967), 43–44.

20. John Henry Newman, *The Arians of the Fourth Century*, with introduction and notes by Rowan Williams (Notre Dame, Ind.: University of Notre Dame Press, 2001), appendix 5, "The Orthodoxy of the Body of the Faithful during the Supremacy of Arianism," 445. The first edition of the book was published in 1833, when Newman was still an Anglican and an important figure in the Oxford Movement promoting High Church theology and practice. Newman became a Roman Catholic in 1845, was ordained in 1847, and was made cardinal in 1879. He added appendices to the third edition of the book, published in 1871; the appendix on Arianism was originally an essay published in *The Rambler*, a liberal, English Catholic periodical, in 1859.

# FOUR

## Resources for Reform from the First Millennium

### Michael J. Buckley, S.J.

A llow me to introduce my discussion by specifying briefly both the problematic situation out of which it arises and the question it attempts to address.[1] The problematic situation I should like to explore in this chapter is not directly the horror and scandals of clerical sexual abuse, but what has emerged as its consequence: a crisis of confidence in the government of the church, a crisis whose full dimensions remain to be assessed and whose character entails a far-reaching diminishment of the effective authority of the bishops and of the Holy See. We are dealing with a diminishment in credibility that is unparalleled, I believe, in the history of the church in the United States.[2]

Out of this situation comes the particular question I will explore: What resources does the first millennium of the church offer to address this crisis about leadership, especially as it involves the laity and the governance of the church? What norms and practices of those centuries might we retrieve—however analogically—in order to redress the damage suffered by the church in our time and to obviate its reoccurrence? Obviously such a question encompasses a field far too vast and events far too intricate for a single response. But allow me—without naively canonizing the first thousand years of the church (it was certainly no utopian society!)—to formulate four suggestions for consideration whose lineage derives from the convictions and normative practices of the first millennium. I emphasize the phrase "suggestions for consideration," because the following discussion makes a claim not to an apodictic assessment, but only to the judgment that these suggestions seem worth considering. Finally, the issue before the church in the United States is not precisely to restore confidence in our time; that sounds too much like public relations. The issue is to have structures and leadership in the church that warrant this confidence.

## The Selection of Bishops

My first suggestion is that we must restore to the local church—and hence to the laity—a decisive voice in the selection of its own bishop. "Decisive" can obviously mean many different things and can be realized in many different ways, but in general it indicates that the selection of the local bishop should ordinarily be made by the local church and the regional bishops.[3] This was certainly the practice of the church over much of its first millennium.

Some of the earliest documents of the church characterize the election of bishops as a grave and essential responsibility for all the members of the local church. The *Didache*, dating from the early second century, addresses all of those who participate in the Eucharist: "Therefore, elect/appoint [*cheirotonesate*] for yourselves bishops and deacons worthy of the Lord, meek men and not lovers of money, and truthful, for they also minister to you the ministry of the prophets and teachers."[4] In the third century, this responsibility dictated that three different groups collaborate in the selection of bishops: the laity of the local church, the clergy of the local church, and the bishops of the region, especially the metropolitan bishop. This was done in different manners, but all three components were present and vitally influential within an episcopal election.[5] *The Apostolic Tradition*, a work attributed to the redoubtable Hippolytus—the most prolific theological writer in Rome of the third century and both an antipope and a martyr—insisted that the bishop is to be chosen *first* by *all* of the people [*hypo pantos tou laou*] and *then* that this initial election is to be approved subsequently by the assembled bishops and presbyters.[6] One can find a similar double election in the third-century *Life of St. Polycarp*.[7] Cyprian, the magisterial third-century African bishop and martyr, recognized the election of Cornelius as bishop of Rome because he had been "made bishop by the judgment of God and of His Christ, by the testimony of almost all of the clergy, by the vote of the people who were then present, [and] by the college of venerable bishops and good men."[8] This combination was crucial for Cyprian, for "he stated emphatically that the *entire community—clergy, laity, and neighboring bishops*—should participate in the selection of episcopal leaders."[9] In the same period, Origen, possibly the greatest theologian of that century in the church, insisted that "the presence of the laity was essential in episcopal elections."[10] An imperial variation in this process was recorded by the ecclesiastical historian Sozomen, writing of the appointment of John Chrysostom at the end of the fourth century to the see of Constantinople: "John was adjudged worthy, in word and in deed, by all the subjects of the Roman empire, to preside over the church of Constantinople. The clergy and people were unanimous in electing him; *their choice* was approved by the emperor; messengers were dispatched for John."[11]

The shifting of the popular suffrage to an acclamation or a rejection by the laity of the choice of the local priests or bishops seems to have evolved over the centuries that followed and found its spare articulation in the *Decretum* of Gratian in the eleventh century: "Election belongs to clerics; consent [to this election], to the people."[12] But in the centuries before Gratian, this acclamation of the laity had exercised a "constitutive power."[13] One must not exaggerate the regularity over these centuries nor discount the problems of civil unrest, rivalries, factions, and ambition that this mode of episcopal selection sometimes unleashed, as Augustine recorded.[14] Moreover, the chaos of history played out as the lines of development afforded increased power to the local clergy. Despite the heightened clericalization of the process, however, it is important to underline that in the first millennium the local church—the laity together with the local clergy and bishops—had or was expected to have, in one way or another, a decisive voice in the selection of its bishop.

Nor was this simply a usage into which the church fell. On the contrary, this universal practice was founded on a principle taught and stated starkly by Pope Leo the Great in the fifth century: "Let the one who is going to rule over all be elected by all [*qui praefuturus est omnibus, ab omnibus eligatur*]." Leo concretized this maxim, as Robert L. Benson notes, by insisting that a "proper election needs not only the will of the clergy, but also of the more eminent laymen and of the common people."[15] But this fifth-century papal maxim of Leo did little more than render in lapidary form what Pope Celestine I had stipulated more than a century before: "A bishop should not be given to those who are unwilling [to receive him]. The consent and the wishes of the clergy, the people, and the nobility are required."[16] Note that it is the Roman See—not simply some provincial church—that is insisting so strongly on the freedom of the local church to elect its own bishop. Benson states that this dictum of Celestine I underlay the electoral theory throughout the early Middle Ages. Even the preference of the bishops of the province was not of itself decisive. The laity and the local clergy had to be consulted.[17] For centuries, the Roman See viewed its primatial powers as a support of the freedom of the local church in times of great crisis. As late as the Council of Reims (1049)—the end of the first millennium—presided over by Pope Leo IX, this Gregorian formula appeared and was to reappear again and again in the centuries that followed: "the bishop had to be 'chosen by the clergy and the people.' "[18] Even in the great lay investiture struggles between Gregory VII and Henry IV in the next millennium (eleventh century), the effort of the papacy was not to transfer power from the secular lords to the Apostolic See but "to win the freedom of the local church in selecting their bishops."[19]

Now, let me explain why I give this particular retrieval of the past pride of place. Very simply, I think that if we were to follow this practice, we would get better bishops in greater numbers. I do not mean this as an anti-episcopal jab. My experience with the American bishops convinces me that so very many of them are deeply dedicated men, doggedly attempting to meet the responsibilities of their office in a very difficult time. The church in the United States has much to admire among its bishops, but I think that the church can do still better, and, in some cases, much better. I think that the committed Catholic laity and the clergy of a locale—working possibly through a diocesan pastoral council and priests' senate—would obviously be in a position to judge both the serious needs of the diocese and the religious capacities of the candidates, especially for religious leadership, far better than a papal nuncio under the influence of those he has chosen to consult.

It is simply scandalous to hear in diocese after diocese the local clergy voice their fears about who will be imposed upon them because he is well connected in Rome or recommended by a restorationist theology. It is scandalous to listen to their aching discouragement that so-and-so has been appointed bishop of their diocese because of his close identification with powerful ecclesiastical figures that he has assiduously cultivated over the years. "Testimony from all over the world," wrote Archbishop John Quinn some four years ago, "points to a widespread dissatisfaction with the present procedure for the appointment of bishops."[20] James O'Toole, the distinguished historian of the church in Boston, cites precisely these contemporary procedures for the selection of a bishop as bringing about the scandals and political struggles for power that have ridden the church in Boston: "At the heart of the problem was the procedure by which Catholic bishops were chosen during the O'Connell Century [i.e., the twentieth century]."[21]

Professor O'Toole finds the present procedures for the selection of bishops hopelessly compromised because "ambitious prelates could lobby advancement and succeed, because they only needed to persuade a handful of officials in Rome to obtain the prize."[22] He recalls William

O'Connell's "actively campaigning for promotion to Boston, funneling large contributions to various Vatican causes and loudly protesting that he was more loyal to the papacy than anyone else." And O'Toole added: "others followed his example."[23] John Quinn criticizes this procedure on the grounds that it "choos[es] candidates who can be trusted to be safe. . . . But the problem is that 'orthodoxy' can be confused with integralism. Integralism may be described as a kind of narrowness and intolerance, raising private opinions and viewpoints to the level of dogma."[24]

It is not simply the present crisis in the United States that has raised the question of the adequacy of this protocol of episcopal selection. One hears the same growing alienation in country after country throughout the world, as Archbishop Quinn has stated. One is reminded of the statement of Augustine that was so crucially important in the life of John Henry Newman: "*Securus judicat orbis terrarum* [The judgment of the entire world is certain]."[25] The church must find its way back to a better way of selecting and appointing bishops, and it is here—it seems to me—that the normative practices of the church in its first millennium offer some very promising suggestions.

One should obviously not become rhapsodic about a retrieval of something like this earlier protocol of the first millennium. Those centuries sometimes saw great problems in attempts at political control, manipulation, and civic disturbance in the selection of a bishop. The church would have to learn from that history, and these dangers would have to be guarded against, as is done in the selection of a college president, a superior of a religious community, an administrator of a major health facility, or a Benedictine abbot. There are many different ways in which the local church could be given substantive electoral responsibility and work out in practice a decisive voice in the selection of its bishop. The procedures need not be uniform from one local church to another; each would have to be adapted to the culture of the locale.

There is nothing in the first thousand years of the history of the church to suggest that the primacy of the Roman See should entitle or require its occupant to determine who is to be the bishop of every see in the church. There may have been many good reasons that have led to this present settlement as the church struggled for its freedom from the political control and the hegemony of the absolute state. But one must recognize that—in much of the world—those days are, for the most part, gone, and that the church would profit immensely from retrieving something of the freedom and self-direction of the local churches of the first millennium. I fear it is necessary to state this more emphatically: if the present system for the selection of bishops is not redressed, all other attempts at serious reform will founder, and greater and greater numbers of Catholics will move toward alienation, disinterest, and affective schism. I believe that the situation is that serious.

## The Bishop's Commitment to His See

The second suggestion I submit for consideration is this: The church should restore the *enduring* commitment of the bishop to his see. The church should reaffirm strongly and effectively the ancient canonical prohibition that forbids a bishop's leaving one see to obtain another. The fifteenth canon of the Council of Nicaea, the fifth canon of Chalcedon, and many regional councils insistently enjoined bishops—or priests and deacons—from moving from one see to another. The bishop was considered bound to his people by a mystical union that was "expressed as being akin to the marriage bond." Thus, the Council of Alexandria (338) went so far as to call a bishop who had moved from one see to another an adulterer.[26] Translations from one see to another did occur in the first millennium, but it required something like a claim of divine revelation or an action by an episcopal synod to justify it in terms of the urgent needs of another church; and even then, as Hamilton Hess has remarked, "we find that nearly all proposed and effected translations were regarded with a degree of suspicion."[27] The church in the west was far stricter in this matter than in the east. Paradoxically perhaps, no see in the first millennium was more faithful to these canonical prohibitions than Rome itself. The Roman church never elected a bishop from another see to become bishop of Rome until late in the ninth century (882), with Marinus I, originally bishop of Caere (Cerveteri), whose pontificate was followed by the horrors of the papacy of the end of the ninth century and most of the tenth.[28]

Why such an insistence? Because the early church saw quite practically in this effort to move from one see to another an endless source of clerical ambition, rivalry, and self-promotion, as well as, more theologically, the violation of the union that should exist between the bishop and the people of his diocese. Sarcastically, the first canon of the Council of Sardica (342) noted: "Almost no bishop is found who will move from a large city to a small one . . . whence it appears that they are inflamed by the heat of avarice to serve ambition."[29]

These concerns of the church for centuries were not trivial. Ambition and its correlative fears can tempt one to a time-serving careerism in which one adjusts his statements and positions in order to cultivate a higher authority who can advance his career from one see to a greater one. This would have been impossible in much of the first millennium. This is not to condemn those who quite legitimately have followed the protocols of our own time. If one looks at the major sees in the United States, very many of their bishops have advanced from lesser dioceses to greater. But I think, finally, that the normative usages of an earlier time were much better.

One cannot but ask honestly whether the contemporary system does not effectively turn these lesser sees into farm teams to prepare men for the big leagues—rather than viewing the people of each of these sees as a holy people in whom the bishop has, in a sacred and irrefragable bond, invested his life permanently. This procedure denigrates the sacred importance of the diocese if it is small, encourages regressive ambitions and even competition within the episcopate, and seriously damages the bishop's effective and affective union with the local presbyterate and laity—a union that takes years to develop.

It is heartening to note that voices in the Holy See, such as those of Cardinal Bernardin Gantin and Cardinal Joseph Ratzinger, have so strongly and so recently condemned this translation from one see to another. In May 1999, Cardinal Gantin, prefect emeritus of the Congregation of Bishops and then dean of the College of Cardinals, spoke of the need to restore the ancient canonical prohibitions against the advancement of bishop from see to see in order to eliminate, he said, "social climbing and 'careerism.' " His remarks occasioned, as you might expect, strong protest from some, Cardinal Camillo Ruini among them, but they evoked an even stronger agreement from Cardinal Ratzinger the following month: "I totally agree with Cardinal Gantin. In the Church, above all, there should be no sense of careerism. . . . There can be exceptional cases. . . . [A] very large See where experience of episcopal ministry is necessary, *could* be an exception. But it should not be common practice; it should happen only in the *most exceptional cases.*"[30]

My first suggestion, then, urges that the local church, clerics and laity, should have a critically determinative voice in the selection of its bishop. The second suggestion urges the restoration of the permanent, mutual commitment of the bishop to his clergy and to his people until the bishop leaves the active ministry. Both of these were normative in the first millennium. Their retrieval is suggested here in order to counter problematic settlements in the contemporary church that most

Christians of the first millennium would have considered illegitimate and corrupting.

## Restoring Regional Gatherings

My third suggestion is that the church needs to restore or strengthen episcopal conferences and regional gatherings of local bishops. The history of the first centuries of the church bears witness to innumerable regional gatherings of the bishops of local churches in Asia, Africa, and Spain. This was simply how the church was governed. "Over four hundred synods and meetings of bishops, Eastern and Western, [are] known to have been held between the mid-second century and the pontificate of Gregory the Great. . . . Most were local or provincial gatherings; others included all the bishops of a larger political region or 'diocese.' "[31] They could and did legislate, with a majority—ideally a consensus—constituting their collective judgment. The purposes of these local meetings were many, but all of them bore upon the responsibility of the region to settle its own serious problems, whether of doctrine or of order or of discipline. There is an amusing remark by the pagan historian Ammianus Marcellinus that "the public transportation system, during the reign of Constantius II [337–61] was paralyzed by Christian bishops traveling to and from their [numerous] synods at the imperial expense."[32] But by means of these regional meetings, the local churches could and did govern themselves. If massive and intractable internal contradictions occurred, then the issue could be referred to the Apostolic See. This relatively rare practice itself was susceptible of great variety, however. The historical situation was very complex, but by and large, Rome did not interfere in the life of the churches in Africa, Asia, and Spain or attempt to govern them. On the contrary, it often acted to protect the integrity and freedom of the local church. It was Pope Julius I who intervened to protest the deposition of Athanasius from the see of Alexandria. It was Pope Innocent I who came to the defense of John Chrysostom in Constantinople.[33] The Council of Nicaea had legislated that the local bishops were to gather twice a year, and "the efforts of the popes—especially those with a strong sense of universal leadership like Leo and Gregory—were often directed towards encouraging bishops to observe the canonical requirement of regular provincial and regional meetings."[34] As I have noted, even the massive claims of Gregory VII were introduced to safeguard the freedom of the local churches.

The contrast with the present situation of the church could hardly be greater. I think it is fair to say that the church has never been so centralized as it has become today, a centralization abetted by modern means of communication. International synods of bishops are fixed as little more than consultative meetings, advising the pope in his government—not *their* government—of the church and awaiting the definitive action of the Holy See. There is widespread belief that even the agenda is carefully controlled by the Roman Curia. Local episcopal conferences have been crippled in their practices and deprived of much of their authority by the most recent provisions set by the Holy See. To pass something as a teaching act of the conference, the Holy See has imposed upon these conferences as a necessary condition a unanimity of judgment that no synod or provincial council ever had to meet in the first millennium—or even now. Failing this, the decision must now be referred to the determination of the Holy See. The Curia's treatment of the International Commission on English in the Liturgy has been sharply criticized by Bishops Donald Trautman and Maurice Taylor, while virtually unanimous judgments of national hierarchies have been set aside by Roman congregations acting with the authority of the pope.[35]

Almost everything in the church is ruled finally by Roman prescriptions or Roman officials, despite the increasing anger that this denial of local authority is awakening. There is a growing restiveness in the Catholic Church in the United States that is unprecedented. And I wonder if very neuralgic and delicate issues such as presently divide the church would not have been handled more successfully if they had made their way through open, careful conversations among regional gatherings of bishops—as was done in the early church—before being considered by the Holy See. In such local and regional gatherings, the voice, the experience, and the concerns of the laity have a much greater chance of an effective presence.

That Rome should encourage and support strong regional and national episcopal conferences, which would incorporate the experience of the members of the local churches, would not set a course contrary to the primacy of Roman See. On the contrary, it would realize much of the fraternal ministry of the primacy—the strengthening and unification of the bishops that the First Vatican Council in *Pastor aeternus* gave as the purpose of the primacy.[36]

## Reconsidering Some of the Institutions of the Church

My fourth and final suggestion: To counter the present excessive centralization within the church, certain institutions that may at one time have served a useful purpose need to be reconsidered and perhaps even abolished. They were either entirely absent from the church of the first millennium or far more modest in their presence. I think of such institutions, for example, as the College of Cardinals, the office of papal nuncio, the appointment as "bishops" in the Roman Curia of those who have no local church they administer, and even such honorific attachments to the papal court as "monsignor."

Theologically or sacramentally, the "Sacred College" is not the College of Cardinals, but the college of bishops. The origins of the College of Cardinals are obscure, but for all of its variations it bespeaks four functions within the Roman Church: to advise the pope, to elect the pope, to execute various papal offices, and to govern the church when there is no pope. But de facto cardinals are given precedence even over bishops and patriarchs, whose function is not primarily to advise the pope but to govern and lead the church with the pope.[37] It might make better ecclesial sense—especially with the growing international position of the papacy—to have the pope elected in some way by the Church of Rome and by representatives of various episcopal conferences. The present settlement—that the cardinalate provides for election of the pope by the Church of Rome—seems little more than a legal fiction.

One wonders further if the papal nuncio is a novelty that should be reconsidered—a permanent representative of the Apostolic See or ambassador to a secular government. It makes a good deal of sense to have an apostolic delegate represent the Holy Father to the church in the United States, but the representation of the church in the United States to the American body politic should be through its bishops and its own officials. What is sacramentally important is that the college of bishops with the pope as its head—and in vital, effective contact with the people who constitute the church—actually govern and represent the church.

## A Final Word

These are the four suggestions I submit for consideration. I will close by noting that the Catholic Church is still very young—only two thousand years old. It is still growing and has been sent into a world that may well last for hundreds of thousands of centuries. There is nothing in these suggestions that a very ordinary theology of the church could not sanction, but one must recognize that to effect anything like the changes suggested here, the primatial leadership of the pope would be of critical importance.

The only single influence now that could lead the church to the restoration of the structures, to the freedoms and the self-direction the individual churches enjoyed in the first millennium, is papal. Even conciliar leadership would be dependent upon the pope's initiative or confirmation. These four suggestions that the first thousand years could offer to the present crisis are both ordinary and radical. They are ordinary in the sense that for this period many of them were normative practices, followed in usage and taught in theory throughout the church; they are radical in that they indicate a correction, even a reversal, to the excessive centralization of the present church's governance. If these suggestions are found to be sound, it is still true that only the pope, exercising his primacy with and within the college of bishops, would have both the ecclesial credibility and the international position to restore—possibly working with another ecumenical council—to the local and regional churches what was once unquestionably theirs and what seems so needed now to address the present crisis in leadership.

It was precisely the structures of the first millennium that John Paul II praised so strongly in his encyclical *Ut Unum Sint* and urged as a guide to the present church in its dealings with the Orthodox: "The structures of the Church in the East and in the West evolved in reference to that Apostolic heritage. Her unity during the first millennium was maintained within those same structures through the Bishops, Successors of the Apostles, in communion with the Bishop of Rome. If today at the end of the second millennium we are seeking to restore full communion, it is to that unity, *thus structured*, which we must look."[38] And even more strongly: "The structures of unity which existed before the separation are a heritage of experience that guides our common path towards the re-establishment of full communion."[39] It is precisely those structures of the first millennium that gave the local church and its laity far greater and more effective presence in the church's government.

In that same remarkable encyclical, the pope recognized his responsibility "to find a way of exercising the primacy which, while in no way renouncing what is essential to its mission, is none the less open to a new situation." He asked the pastors and theologians of the church to seek for contemporary "forms in which this [papal] ministry may accomplish a service of love recognized by all concerned."[40] One wonders if leadership in the retrieval of these forms and structures, which I have suggested above and by which the local church existed in the first millennium, could not be part of that papal ministry.

It may seem to some that these four suggestions evince restless discontent. That is not the case. They hold in great reverence the church as the People of God and as the body of Christ. Viewing it in this way, they experience it as holy—whatever its history also of sins, defects, and failures. But it is this very demanding vocation to holiness that dictates the need for continual self-examination and reform. And to meet that need, I think we have much to learn from our first thousand years.

## Notes

My reflections in this chapter were in formation for some time and were delivered in part in Rome (December 1996) and as a unit initially at a panel discussion at Boston College (30 September 2002) and then at a conference in Kansas City, Missouri (31 May 2003). The Roman edition was published in *Il primato del successore di Pietro: Atti del simposio teologico, Roma, dicembre 1996* (Vatican City: Liberia Editrice Vaticana, 1997), and in Michael J. Buckley, S.J., *Papal Primacy and the Episcopate: Towards a Relational Understanding* (New York: Crossroad Publishing Co., 1998). The lectures in Boston and Kansas City were recorded, and tapes from the latter meeting were distributed. After each of these presentations, the text was modified and augmented as suggestions and corrections were received and won agreement. An earlier version of this chapter was published by Liguori Press.

1. For this understanding of the problematic situation and the problem that is articulated as a question and gives some order and character to the indeterminate as a preparation for inquiry, see John Dewey, *Logic: The Theory of Inquiry* (New York: Holt, Rinehart, and Winston, 1938), 101–12.

2. See the Contemporary Catholic Trends poll conducted by LeMoyne College and Zogby International. "The number of American Catholics who think their bishops are doing a good job has fallen nearly 25 percentage points in the past eighteen months," from 81 percent in the fall of 2001 to 59 percent in the spring of 2003. This rating is the "lowest in the poll's history" (*The National Catholic Reporter*, 23 May 2003, 8).

3. This would not, of course, rule out the papal veto in cases of genuine emergency or a papal intervention to guarantee the integrity of the process of selection. Of itself, "a decisive voice" does not rule out other decisive voices. What is at issue here, however, is the usual government of the churches. Such a papal intervention could be understood not as an habitual use of primatial authority, but as a substitutional one. For the substitutional use of papal authority in exceptional circumstances, see Buckley, *Papal Primacy*, 62–74.

4. *The Didache, or Teaching of the Twelve Apostles*, in *The Apostolic Fathers*, ed. with trans. Kirsopp Lake, Loeb Classical Library (London: William Heinemann, 1930), 15.1. Ferguson explains the term *cheirotonesate* in terms of its historical usage in Greece of the first and second century: "Magistrates in Greece were elected by the citizens. The vote was taken by a show of hands, which was the original meaning of cheirotonia."

Everett Ferguson, ed., *Encyclopedia of Early Christianity*, 2d ed. (New York: Garland Publishing, 1997), s.v. "Election to Church Office," by Everett Ferguson.

5. Buckley, *Papal Primacy*, 86.

6. Hippolytus of Rome, *The Treatise on the Apostolic Tradition*, ed. Gregory Dix and Henry Chadwick, 2d rev. ed. (London: Alba Press, 1992), 2:1–2, 2–3 (emphasis added).

7. See Hippolytus, *On the Apostolic Tradition*, an English version with introduction and commentary by Alistair Stewart-Sykes (Crestwood, N.Y.: St. Vladimir's Seminary Press, 2001), 56–57.

8. Thascius Caecilius Cyprianus, *Epistulae*, in vol. 3, pt. 2 of *Corpus Scriptorum Ecclesiasticorum Latinorum*, ed. W. Von Hartel (Vienna, 1871), Letter 55.8; the English translation used here is Saint Cyprian, *Letters (1–81)*, trans. Sister Rose Bernard Donna, in *The Fathers of the Church*, vol. 51 (Washington, D.C.: The Catholic University of America Press, 1964), 138. See W. H. C. Frend, *The Rise of Christianity* (Philadelphia: Fortress Press, 1984), 403.

9. Patrick Granfield, "Episcopal Elections in Cyprian: Clerical and Lay Participation," *Theological Studies* 37 (1996): 41 (emphasis added).

10. Frend, *The Rise of Christianity*, 428 n. 39. Frend is reporting the judgment of Origen as in Origen, *Homily on Leviticus*, ed. W. A. Baehrens, *Die griechischen christlichen Schriftsteller der ersten drei Jahrhunderten, Origen* (Leipzig: Hinrichs, 1920), III. 20.

11. Sozomen, *The Ecclesiastical History of Sozomen, Comprising a History of the Church from* A.D. *324 to* A.D. *440*, trans. Edward Walford (London: Henry G. Bohn, 1855), bk. 8, ch. 2, p. 364 (emphasis added).

12. Robert L. Benson, *The Bishop-Elect: A Study in Medieval Ecclesiastical Office* (Princeton: Princeton University Press, 1968), 33. One finds vestiges of this need for the consent of the people in the address of the bishop to the people during the Ordination of Priests in the previous *Pontificale Romanum*: "Not without cause did the Fathers direct that the people should also be consulted in the choice of those who are to minister at the altar. For sometimes what is unknown to the many of the life and conduct of a candidate may be known to the few, and a more ready obedience is given to a priest when assent has been given to his ordination. Now the conduct of these deacons, whom by God's help we are about to ordain priests, has been tried and found (as far as I can judge) pleasing to God, and deserving, in my opinion, of a higher ecclesiastical dignity. But as the judgment of one person, or even of several, may perhaps be mistaken or led astray by partiality, it is well to ascertain the general opinion." "The Ordination of Priests," in *The Rites of Ordination and Episcopal Consecration*, with English translation approved by the National Conference of

Catholic Bishops of the United States of America and confirmed by the Apostolic See (Washington, D.C.: National Conference of Catholic Bishops, 1967), 34. The revised "Rite of Ordination" omits this exhortation, the *ordinandi* being presented to the bishop with the assurance that the People of God have been consulted in the past.

13. Benson, *The Bishop-Elect*, 36.

14. See Henry Chadwick, *The Church in Ancient Society: From Galilee to Gregory the Great* (Oxford: Oxford University Press, 2001), 314.

15. Benson, *The Bishop-Elect*, 25. Benson is citing this dictum of Leo, which has remarkable similarities to a statement of Pliny the Younger, from *Ep.* 10, c.6, PL 54:634. See Benson for similar assertions of the election of the bishop by all concerned and the application in the early and Medieval church of the principle of Roman law: "*quod omnibus similiter tangit, ab omnibus comprobetur.*"

16. Benson, *The Bishop-Elect*, 25. Benson is citing this dictum of Celestine from *Ep.* 4, c.5, PL 50:434: "*Nullus invitis detur episcopus. Cleri, plebis et ordinis consensus ac desiderium requiratur.*"

17. Benson, *The Bishop-Elect*, 24–25.

18. See Jean Gaudemet, "The Choice of Bishops: A Tortuous History," in *From Law to Life*, ed. James Provost and Knut Walf, *Concilium* 1996/5 (London: SCM Press, 1996), 60–61.

19. William Henn, O.F.M. Cap., "Historical-Theological Synthesis of the Relation between Primacy and Episcopacy during the Second Millennium," in *Il primato del successore di Pietro: Atti del simposio teologico, Roma, dicembre 1996* (Vatican City: Libreria Editrice Vaticana, 1997), 225.

20. John R. Quinn, *The Reform of the Papacy: The Costly Call to Christian Unity* (New York: Crossroad Publishing Co., 1999), 133.

21. James O'Toole, "A Cardinal's Coverup," *The Boston Globe Online*, 12 January 2003, www.boston.com/dailyglobe2/012/focus/A_cardinals_coverup+.shtml (accessed 13 January 2003), 2.

22. Ibid., 3.

23. Ibid.

24. Quinn, *Reform of the Papacy*, 134–35. The archbishop continues: "[But] it should be possible to find candidates who are not only orthodox in the true sense, but who are also endowed with critical judgment, imagination, and who are open to new ideas. Fidelity to the mission of the Church requires candidates who can listen, listen to the world, listen to the people, and who have the spiritual discernment and critical judgment to endorse what is good, reject what is evil, and not stifle the Spirit" (135).

25. Augustine, *Contra epist. Parmen*, III. 24. PL 43, 101. For Newman's reception of this maxim, see John Henry Newman, *Apologia pro vita sua, Being a History of His Religious Opinions*, ed. Martin J. Svaglic (Oxford: Clarendon Press, 1967), 109–11.

26. Hamilton Hess, *The Canons of the Council of Sardica, A.D. 343* (Oxford: Clarendon Press, 1958), 71–75. See Buckley, *Papal Primacy*, 90–92.

27. Hess, *Canons of the Council of Sardica*, 73.

28. See Buckley, *Papal Primacy*, 93.

29. Hess, *Canons of the Council of Sardica*, 76–77.

30. The interviews with Cardinals Gantin and Ratzinger were reported in *Trenti giourni* and delivered to the press in the United States by ZENIT International Agency. See "Bishops Divided between Diocesan Fidelity and 'Careerism,' " *The Daily Catholic*, 21 July 1999, http://dailycatholic.org/issue/archives/1999Jul/135jul21,vol.10,no.135txt/jul21dc2.htm (accessed 15 January 2003) (emphasis added).

31. Brian Daley, "Structures of Charity: Bishops' Gatherings and the See of Rome in the Early Church," in *Episcopal Conferences: Historical, Canonical, and Theological Studies*, ed. Thomas J. Reese, S.J. (Washington, D.C.: Georgetown University Press, 1989), 28. See Christopher O'Donnell, *Ecclesia: A Theological Encyclopedia of the Church* (Collegeville, Minn.: The Liturgical Press, 1996), s.v. "Councils."

32. Daley, "Structures of Charity," 28–29.

33. Ibid., 41–42.

34. Ibid., 45.

35. One thinks, for example, of the treatment meted out to the National Conference's decision regarding the implementation of *Ex corde ecclesiae* and the decision on the age of confirmation. In 1982, the U.S. Conference of Catholic Bishops (USCCB) voted to permit a trial use of the Common Lectionary on a limited basis; the Congregation for Divine Worship and the Discipline of the Sacraments (CDWDS) denied the *confirmatio* of the bishops' decision the following year. Around 1993, the USCCB voted three separate acts of approval and submitted them to Rome for *confirmatio*: (1) the revised Lectionary based on the New American Bible (NAB), especially the revised NAB New Testament; (2) the liturgical use of the revised NAB psalter; and (3) the use of the New Revised Standard Version (NRSV) Lectionary. The CDWDS denied absolutely the decisions on the revised NAB psalter (largely for inclusive language reasons) and also denied the NRSV Lectionary (saying that each conference should have only one scripture translation for use in the liturgy). Rome also denied *confirmatio* of the NAB Lectionary and asked the USCCB to send representatives to Rome to discuss the matter. In September 1997, the CDWDS denied its approval or confirmation of the proposed International Commission for English in the Liturgy (ICEL) Ordination Rites approved by the USCCB. In March 2002, the same Congregation refused its approval or confirmation of the proposed ICEL translation of the second edition of the Roman Missal, despite the fact that it had been approved not only by the U.S. Conference of Catholic Bishops but by nine other conferences as well. The content or

justification of each of these various reversals is not in question here; what is at issue is that an episcopal conference can be so frequently overridden by Curial action, as if the bishops were incompetent to decide about the pastoral needs of their people, the translation of the scriptures into their own language, and the conduct of liturgy within their diocese or national conference.

36. See Vatican I, Fourth Session, *Pastor aeternus*, the First Dogmatic Constitution on the Church of Christ, 18 July 1870, DS 3061: "This power of the Supreme Pontiff is far from standing in the way of the power of ordinary and immediate episcopal jurisdiction by which the bishops who, under appointment of the Holy Spirit (see Acts 20:28), succeeded in the place of the apostles, feed and rule individually, as true shepherds, the particular flock assigned to them. Rather this latter power is *asserted, confirmed and vindicated by this same supreme and universal shepherd*, as in the words of St. Gregory the Great: 'My honor is the honor of the whole Church. My honor is the firm strength of my brothers. I am truly honored when due honor is paid to each and everyone.' " English translation from *The Christian Faith in the Doctrinal Documents of the Catholic Church*, ed. J. Neuner and J. Dupuis (New York: Alba, 1982) (emphasis added); see also ibid., DS 3050–51.

37. O'Donnell, *Ecclesia*, s.v. "Cardinals." Cardinals rank only after the pope in hierarchy: "Since the twelfth century, the cardinals have had precedence over archbishops and bishops, and since the fifteenth century, even over patriarchs (bull: *Non mediocri* of Pope Eugene IV, 1431–47." Salvador Miranda, "Cardinal," in *New Catholic Encyclopedia*, 2d ed. (Detroit, Mich.: Gale, 2002), 3:105. In the secret consistory of 10 June 1630, Urban VIII granted to the cardinals the title of "eminence."

38. John Paul II, *Ut Unum Sint* (25 May 1995), no. 55 (emphasis added).

39. Ibid., no. 56.

40. Ibid., no. 95. In this request to pastors and theologians of the church, the encyclical is citing from the homily of John Paul II in the presence of the Ecumenical Patriarch, Dimitrios I (6 December 1987), 3; *Acta Apostolicae Sedis* 80 (1988): 714.

# FIVE

## From Autonomy to Alienation: Lay Involvement in the Governance of the Local Church

### R. Scott Appleby

I n 1963, Daniel Callahan, associate editor of the lay Catholic weekly magazine *Commonweal*, lamented the sorry state of lay Catholic status, authority, and leadership within the U.S. church. Callahan's words, as his landmark book *The Mind of the Catholic Layman* demonstrated, could have been written about virtually any previous generation of American Catholic laity:

> Regrettably, a lack of freedom in some non-theological and non moral areas in the Church is recognized to be a major handicap to the development of the kind of layman the Church now needs in order to make its voice heard in the world. The layman is called upon to be vigorous, courageous and outspoken in secular society—but he is rarely encouraged (though he may be permitted) to be any of these things within the Church itself. He is told that the Church approves of the kind of give and take which prevails in American life—but he finds that it is hesitant to allow it within the Church. He is told that the Catholic school and college are as good a training ground for democracy as the public institution—yet he knows full well that the virtues often lauded within them are discipline, obedience and uniformity of opinion. He is asked, finally, to be a prophetic voice in society—but he may well be courting trouble if he tries to raise such a voice within the Church.[1]

In what follows, I sketch three patterns in the history of lay involvement, or lack thereof, in the governance and administration of the Catholic Church in the United States.

Notwithstanding the variations in the relative location, strength, and size of the laity vis-à-vis the clergy, certain themes ring true across the decades. They include a clerical suspicion of any form of independent lay activism; the bishops' claim to possess full temporal as well as spiritual authority over the church; and, legitimating this consolidation of power in the office of the bishop, an integralist ecclesiology that holds that power and authority within the church are indivisible and rooted in the sacrament of Holy Orders. This ecclesiology has relegated the laity to a secondary and subordinate status within the church. According to a dualistic view that sees the church as "in the world, but not of the world," the laity has been confined to "the world."

Against this formidable array of developments, the two major moments of lay initiative and relative autonomy—the trustee system of the early republican era, and the short-lived "liberation of the laity" during the years immediately following the Second Vatican Council—fell short of their promise to lift the laity to the permanent status and function of full-fledged members of the "People of God," coresponsible with the bishops, priests, and religious for the mission of the church in the world.

## The Crisis of Lay Trusteeism, 1785–1860

No episode demonstrates the dilemma of American lay involvement in ecclesial governance more clearly than the lay trustee controversies of the late-eighteenth and early-nineteenth centuries. Trusteeism was a lay movement that arose in the attempt to adapt European Catholicism to American republican laws and values by asserting exclusive lay control of Catholic properties, and the rights of lay governance over individual congregations. When Catholic bishops and pastors resisted the movement, claiming bitterly that congregational leaders had usurped apostolic (that is, episcopal) authority within the church, the laity fought back, refusing to yield control of local churches.[2] In some instances, the hostilities between laity and bishops dragged on for decades, with some priests caught in the middle and others taking one side or the other.

Though trustee conflicts were not a common event in antebellum parishes, neither were they isolated aberrations; a number of challenges to ecclesiastical authority occurred between 1785 and 1860. While the *casus belli* and the configuration of allies and enemies differed in each locale, a common tension underlay them all: How was the Catholic Church to govern itself in a democratic republic?

Lay trusteeism arose within the context of the early American republic, which was characterized by movements of democratization within the Protestant churches and a general cultural enthusiasm for self-governance and the dismantling of authoritarian structures.[3] According to American law during this period, every congregation that sought legal protection for its properties was required to elect a board of trustees who were corporately responsible for pastors' salaries, church debts, and for hiring and firing ecclesiastical personnel. From Louisiana to Maine, lay Catholics formed new congregations in this way and thereby received legal sanction for many of their powers and responsibilities within the congregation.[4]

The first major conflict unfolded in December 1785 when the lay trustees of St. Peter's, New York City's first Catholic congregation, voted to withdraw financial support from their duly appointed priest, Father Charles Whelan. According to the trustees, Father Whelan was unskilled as a preacher and demanded too much financial compensation. Though the trustees appealed to the superior of the American mission, Father John Carroll, to remove their rejected priest, they threatened to dismiss Whelan themselves through civil legal action if Carroll refused. It was both their right and their duty as trustees (specifically, *American* trustees) to oversee the temporal management of the parish, which in their minds included the selection of their priest.

While Carroll also sought to accommodate Catholicism to its new American environment, the trustees' claim of the right to appoint and dismiss clergy was simply out of the question; it smacked of Protestant congregationalism and threatened the very foundations of Catholic ecclesiology. Whelan would eventually leave on his own accord, but this simply delayed a direct challenge to the church hierarchy that would result from the trustees' and hierarchy's different conceptions of church administration and authority.[5]

Similar confrontations developed in Boston and in German parishes in Baltimore and Philadelphia. The most tumultuous conflicts occurred between 1815 and 1829 in Philadelphia, Norfolk, and Charleston. St. Mary's Catholic Church in Philadelphia, which boasted perhaps the wealthiest and most accomplished Catholic laity in the nation, was the site of a particularly prominent and protracted battle between a newly arrived Irish priest, William Hogan, and Bishop Henry Conwell. The laity backed Hogan, who returned the favor by demanding lay participation in the selection of pastors and bishops. Hogan and his lay colleagues of St. Mary's also argued that the laity, rather than the clergy, was best suited to manage the temporal affairs of the church and to control its physical assets. A virtual schism prevailed at St. Mary's throughout the 1820s. "The Hogan affair had national implications," writes the historian of lay trusteeism Patrick Carey. "It represented in dramatic and very public ways what was going on in many Catholic congregations across the country where laypeople, clergy and bishops struggled to define Catholic ecclesiology and ecclesiastical practices in the new environment of American democracy."[6]

In 1829, during a provincial council held in Baltimore, the U.S. bishops established national policies reasserting the bishop's control over all ecclesiastical temporalities and his exclusive authority to appoint and dismiss pastors. The policies were only partially effective, however, for lay trusteeism continued to flourish in certain cities, especially in New Orleans and Buffalo, where lay leaders sought redress in the civil courts.[7] Gradually, however, the bishops won the court battles—often arguing before the bench, successfully, that episcopal governance is a constitutive mark of a bona fide Catholic Church—and thereby gained civil legal control of parish properties, a victory that served further to validate their canonical legislation. After the Civil War, direct lay challenges to episcopal prerogatives were sporadic.

What was the enduring significance of the lay trustee crisis?

The newly formed republic of the United States posed a number of unprecedented challenges to the Roman Catholic Church. With the partial exception of Maryland, the British American colonies were dominated by Protestant cultures that were highly suspicious of their Catholic minorities. The republicanism that dominated the United States after the Revolutionary War defined itself in opposition to absolutism of all kinds, not least religious dogmatism. Only rule by law, governmental checks and balances, and the will of the governed (however that will was to be mediated) could prevent the return of the tyranny that had plagued the colonies and Europe itself. The lack of such "checks and balances" in Roman Catholicism led many American Protestants to the conviction that the Catholic Church was incompatible with republicanism.[8]

Voluntaryism and the rules of legal incorporation in the United States inspired the formation of Catholic lay trustee boards to hold and manage all church property. Though later boards would be headed by a priest or bishop or at least have clerical representation, many early boards consisted entirely of laymen. In many settlements, towns, and cities, lay ownership was unavoidable, given the dearth or absence of clergy. In addition, laymen and -women literally built and furnished the church building, so they came by their sense of ownership honestly.

Moreover, though these boards enjoyed significant authority, they also shouldered the responsibilities accompanying ownership; in addition to the actual management of the parish, trustees were legally responsible for the debts of the congregation.[9] In areas without an established ecclesiastical infrastructure, these same boards sought out a priest for the congregation and negotiated his salary. Such responsibility naturally led republican minds to conclude that they had a right to the cogovernance of their congregations.

American Catholic laymen who had accepted republican presuppositions used the lay trustee system as evidence that the two systems were compatible. Most lay trustees had no desire to democratize the church; but they did import republican ideas—especially regarding the separation of powers and the right of those invested in a community to participate in its governance—into their ecclesiology.[10]

It is important to recognize that few, if any, lay leaders harbored pretensions to authority in the religious or spiritual realms. They found fault with a priest's foreign accent and peculiar customs—that is, with his ethnicity—or with his personal behavior (e.g., alcoholism) more frequently than they objected to his preaching or teaching. If ecclesiastical authorities rightfully governed the spiritual matters of the church, however, this privilege and right did not endow bishops with the qualifications or authority to control the temporal affairs of the local church or even to appoint a pastor without consulting the parishioners he was assigned to serve. In the minds of these Americanizing lay leaders, any "interference" of the Catholic hierarchy in local church governance was an overextension of its authority, and the trustees would use civil courts if necessary to maintain a proper balance of power.

In the early stages of church planting and growth, lay trustees did not attempt to "displace traditional authorities, but insisted that the people must check their power."[11] In the trustees' minds, a sharing of power with the clergy and hierarchy not only resonated with their own ideas of judicious governance, but also served to ameliorate their Protestant neighbors' concerns over Catholicism's compatibility with republicanism.

John Carroll and later American bishops (many of whom were equally concerned with accommodating Catholicism to the American context) saw the situation quite differently from the trustees. Catholicism was compatible with the American system not because the church was itself a republican institution, but rather because of the constitutional doctrine of the separation of church and state. Lay trustee control—particularly over the selection of clergy—inhibited the freedom of the priest to carry out his duties. Even worse, the lay involvement of civil authorities, in many bishops' minds, was not only morally wrong, but also went against the separation of church and state.

*Every issue* related to the church, the bishops (and the popes) argued, is spiritual, not temporal, and thus should be under ecclesiastical jurisdiction. During the controversy at St. Peter's, the lay leaders of the congregation conveyed to Carroll their "opinion" that the congregation holds the right "not only to choose such parish priest as is agreeable to them, but discharging them at pleasure, and that after such election, the bishop or other ecclesiastical superior cannot hinder him from exercising the usual functions." In his role as Superior of the American mission, Carroll responded:

> If [such principles] should become predominant, the unity and catholicity of our Church would be at an end; and it would be formed into distinct and independent societies, nearly in the same manner as the congregational Presbyterians of our neighboring New England States. A zealous clergyman performing his duty courageously and without respect of persons would be always liable to be the victim of his earnest endeavors to stop the progress of vice and evil example, and others more complying with the passions of some principal persons of the congregation would be substituted in his room; and if the ecclesiastical superior has no control in these instances, I will refer to your own judgment what the consequences may be.[12]

In the subsequent controversies, four major groups of participants emerged. Trustees and their supporters constituted the first group. Trustees usually tended to be the wealthier members of the congregation; both the responsibility of congregational debt and the high cost of pew rents (which qualified one to vote in trustee elections) dictated this eventuality.[13] Because of this, poorer members of the congregation often constituted a second group in the controversies. In addition to differing socioeconomic situations, many of the second group were often recent immigrants—tied more to their European home country than to American political notions.[14] The third group consisted of those most often opposed to the trustees: the American bishops. American bishops were often caught in odd juxtapositions; in their struggles with Rome to create a national church, they often applied the same republican rhetoric that the lay trustees used to appeal to them (usually to no avail).[15] The final group consisted of those who were usually the immediate cause of the controversies: the local priests. Local clergy were also the most variable element: they could side with the trustees in republican solidarity against the "arbitrary" authority of the bishop; they could advocate full-blown democracy by pitting the laity against their trustees; or they could side with the bishops for the cause of ecclesiastical authority. Often the same priest would shift among these various roles.

For all the acknowledged rancor that the trusteeism controversies created, issues that were *not* contested are equally telling. As I have mentioned, there is no indication that trustees challenged the church's absolute authority in spiritual matters, only in what they considered to be temporal matters. Nor is there any indication that the Catholic hierarchy opposed accommodating what it deemed to be "reasonable" requests of a congregation (i.e., requests for clergy that spoke the predominant language of the laity and were sensitive to their culture) or even that it opposed muted forms of cogovernance (one might well find better things for a priest to do than oversee the mundane aspects of property management). Rather, conflicts resulted primarily from disagreement over what constituted a "temporal affair." This did not lessen the intensity of the conflict, but such intensity should not be misinterpreted as a crisis of authority. Trustees were simply attempting to appropriate for themselves (under the auspices of republican "popular sovereignty") concessions already given to European governments. Not surprisingly, the hierarchy attempted to use the same ideology to argue that these compromises were not necessary in the American context.

John England, bishop of the sprawling diocese of Charleston, South Carolina, from 1820 to 1842, effected a compromise of a different sort, and thereby left a distinctive and noteworthy legacy of lay incorporation into the governance of the church at the local and diocesan levels. Founder of *The United States Catholic Miscellany*, the first Catholic newspaper in the United States, England responded to the crisis of lay trusteeism by modeling his diocesan government after the U.S. Constitution and the convention system of the Protestant Episcopal Church. The written constitution of the diocese specified the proper procedures for founding a new church and for electing lay vestrymen, who served as consultants to (rather than employers of) the pastor. Bishop England's constitution also established a bicameral consultative body—the house of the clergy and the house of the laity—and an annual convention, to be attended by the bishop, the clergy of the diocese, and lay delegates from each district of the diocese.

The rules governing the annual convention illustrate the brilliance of England's compromise: laity would be duly consulted and thereby "empowered," but their role in "governance" would simultaneously be restricted to consultation.

The convention has no power or authority to interfere respecting any of the following subjects, viz.: 1. The doctrine of the church. 2. The discipline of the church. 3. The administration of sacraments. 4. The ceremonies of the church. 5. Spiritual jurisdiction. 6. Ecclesiastical appointments. 7. Ordinations. 8. The superintendence of the clergy.

The convention is not to be considered as a portion of the ecclesiastical government of the church; but the two houses are to be considered rather as a body of sage, prudent and religious counselors to aid the proper ecclesiastical governor of the church in the discharge of his duty, by their advice and exertions in obtaining and applying the necessary pecuniary means to those purposes which will be most beneficial, and in superintending the several persons who have charge thereof; to see that the money be honestly and beneficially expended; wherefore the convention has the following powers, viz.:

1. To dispose of the general fund of the church in the way that it may deem most advantageous. 2. To examine into, and to control the expenditures made by its own order or by that of a former convention. 3. To examine into, regulate and control, with the exception of their spiritual concerns, all establishments of its own creation; or which being otherwise created may be regularly subjected to its control. 4. To appoint the lay-officers and servants of such establishments. 5. The house of the clergy has power to examine into the ecclesiastical concerns of such establishments, and to make its private report thereon to the bishop or vicar, together with its opinion and advice, but such report of advice shall not be published in any other way, without the consent of the bishop or vicar first had and obtained in writing under his hand and seal. . . .

4. No act shall be considered a valid act of the convention except it shall have been passed by a majority of the clergy and by a majority of the house of the laity, and been assented to by the bishop or vicar.

5. In all elections to trust, or places or offices, the decision will be made by a majority of the clergy and laity voting conjointly, and

their choice assented to by the bishop, except when in any instance
a different mode of election shall have been provided for. . . . [16]

Bishop England's system was strikingly effective in adapting Roman
Catholic ecclesiology to American republicanism, but it did not survive
him. Further study of "England's compromise" seems appropriate in
the current situation when, alarmed by episcopal malfeasance and mis-
management of the sexual abuse crisis in the priesthood, increasing
numbers of American Catholic laity are demanding greater participation
in the administration of church affairs.

## Immigrant Church, Docile Laity

The U.S. Catholic episcopacy emerged from the lay trustee crisis as a
far stronger, more centralized institution. The bishops' victory virtually
eliminated any chance that lay Catholics would enjoy significant
decision-making authority in church affairs; indeed, the bitter memory
of lay recalcitrance only deepened the clergy's suspicions of lay involvement in the church.

The marginalization of potential lay leaders came at a moment in
the development of American Catholicism when the church needed all
the help it could get. A constant stream of Irish, German, and French
Catholics immigrating to the United States during the antebellum period
was followed by another wave of Italian, Polish, Lithuanian, and other
Eastern European Catholic immigrants after the Civil War. Yet the
overwhelming pastoral, institutional, educational, and administrative
needs of the immigrant church were met by religious, not laity. In the
strictest sense of the term, of course, the nonordained—the nuns and
religious brothers who themselves migrated from Europe to build and
staff the Catholic hospitals, orphanages, and schools during and after
the Civil War—fall into the category of "laity." But they lived as celibates
in a religious community, obedient to their religious superior, who in
turn negotiated the ecclesial terrain with the local bishop, who, according to canon law, was supreme in his diocese. Further empowered by
the steady rise in vocations to the priesthood, the immigrant church
was a strikingly effective provider of pastoral, educational, and other
services required to preserve the faith and practice of the majority of
immigrant Catholics. So dominant were the episcopacy and the clergy
during the century following the Civil War that historians still refer to
individual bishops and priests, not to laity, as the leading actors in
the drama that evolved around the challenges of Americanism and
Americanization.[17]

Immersed in a devotional religious culture that encouraged focus on things supernatural and consolidated the authority of the pope and the bishops in the Catholic religious imagination, the laity, with some notable exceptions, followed the Tridentine dictum to "pray, pay, and obey." The ordained were the custodians of the "sacred mysteries" necessary for salvation, and literally everything else having to do with the church was configured within and subordinated to this cultic function. The mundane business decisions taken by and for the church, no less than the administration of the sacraments, were legitimated by this sacred foundation. In this system the bishop, in whom the full powers of the priesthood alone resided, personified the church. Indeed, from the late nineteenth century even to this day, when laity refer to "the church," they often mean the pope, the bishops, and (perhaps) the clergy.

During these decades, the priesthood assumed an exalted status in U.S. Catholicism. "No office held by mortal man exceeds in dignity or sublimity that of the priesthood," wrote Rev. John A. O'Brien in a popular 1943 exposition of this theology. St. Thomas Aquinas declared that no act is greater than the consecration of the body of Christ, O'Brien reminded his readers. "In this essential phase of your ministry," he declared, "the power of the priest is not surpassed by that of the bishop, the archbishop, the cardinal or the Holy Father himself. Indeed it is equal to the power of Jesus Christ; for in this role the priest speaks with the voice and authority of Christ Himself." The priesthood is not, O'Brien concluded, a human usurpation of divine authority; nor is its authority "derived from the corporate will of the congregation."[18]

The priest was, in the theological terminology of the day, *alter Christus*. His competence in religious questions went unchallenged by a laity that perceived him as "a man set apart" from the crowd. His parishioners presumed him to be a man of holiness by virtue of his ordination. The church, itself an institution set apart from the sin of the world, guaranteed this. In both its form and its content, the priestly office was seen as objective and owing nothing essential to subjectivity. Suitable men could acquire and exercise its liturgical and extraliturgical responsibilities in a prescribed and uniform manner. "St. John's tried to prepare candidates so that they could absorb a sacramental character at ordination much as softened wax is impressed with a seal," wrote Robert E. Sullivan of the Boston Seminary.[19]

The theology that undergirded this image was ahistorical in that it posited unchanging, invisible essences as the principle of identity and reality (a person is a human being by virtue of a *soul*; a priest is a priest by virtue of an indelible mark on the soul); and this identity and reality remained substantially unaffected by the shifting tides of human history (a validly ordained priest remains a priest in spite of his external circumstances). The church, a perfect society, possessed its own objective body of canon law, precepts, and rubrics legitimated in and of themselves (*ex opere operato*) rather than by the personal, subjective qualities of its members. In short, the Catholic religious world of the period from the Civil War to World War II sustained a vertical rather than a horizontal faith.[20]

When the parish pastor interceded with the world on behalf of the immigrant, he did not relax the paternalistic stance by which he dealt with the laity from the sanctuary and the boardroom alike. The clergy of the immigrant church wielded influence with public officials because they represented a powerful constituency, namely, that closed society known as the Catholic Church. Yet the pastor was not "elected" by his constituency. Rather, the parishioners placed trust in the pastor because he represented to them something far greater than himself, namely, the triumphant church extending through time and space. The pastor's action was in behalf of this church. On many occasions, this action coincided with the needs and will of his parishioners.

On some occasions, it did not. In a 1930 article titled "Anticlericalism in the United States," Jerome D. Hannan pointed out that the priest's primary loyalty was not to the local church but to the Universal Church. Susceptible to the disedifying influences of American society, the laity could not always be counted upon, he complained, to defend the interests of Catholicism. Reporting on an interview he had conducted with a "deposed church committee," Hannan wrote:

> There are many reasons why a man should not be permitted to serve on a church committee, even though chosen by a majority ballot. He may be a bad Catholic. That type usually finds a way of squirming into the petty politics of church factions. The objection may arise to him because he has unjustly criticized the pastor's administration of the parish. Finally, he may by deed have interfered in parish administration to such an extent as to have hindered its development. . . . [When I made these points, the members of the committee] pretended exasperation. "Then all we can do is give, give, give," they exclaimed. I merely reminded them that they all had an obligation to contribute to the support of the church and that it was not a right, but a privilege, which permitted

some of the congregation to cooperate with the pastor in the administration of church affairs. . . . It was clear that they believed themselves to be of right the administrators of the congregation's property, and the priest was merely their hired servant, not the delegate of the Bishop. This is a view that is not so rare as one might believe. It springs from the democratic form of political government under which we live, and from the Protestant method of ecclesiastical government which is everywhere operative about us. Both types of government are essentially laical.[21]

Regarding the laity, the actions and attitudes of the priest were individualistic rather than corporate, independent rather than collaborative. As a rule, the priest did not empower the laity to act within the parish or in behalf of the parish out in the world. Instead, he took it upon himself to act. In the world, he alone represented the parish. And in the parish, he incorporated various ministries within his own. Better put: it did not occur to him that significant apostolic service might occur apart from his sacerdotal office. Intimations of a different way of priesthood did not disturb his serenity until the 1960s.

Given this complex of circumstances, and the demands placed upon priests in both rural and urban settings, it is not surprising that twentieth-century prelates such as William Henry O'Connell in Boston, Patrick Hayes and Francis Joseph Spellman in New York, Joseph Francis Rummel in New Orleans, and George William Mundelein in Chicago, among others, expected almost "universal competence" for a variety of ministries from each man receiving Holy Orders. Pastoral ministry was, in this context, "quite diversified, predominantly parochial, and isolated from other priests and laity."[22]

## A Lay Renaissance?

There were exceptions to this general pattern of lay docility. What Callahan calls, perhaps too charitably, "a lay renaissance" began in the late nineteenth century when some lay Catholics in Chicago, St. Louis, Detroit, and elsewhere, supported by progressive bishops such as John Ireland of St. Paul and John Lancaster Spalding of Peoria, began to consider ways in which their growing experience in U.S. civic and cultural life might be placed in the service of the church. In St. Paul, a group of laymen formed the Catholic Truth Society for the purpose of countering distortions in the press about Catholicism; some members of the society also established a network of Catholic benevolent and civic societies that worked in cooperation with the local bishop. During the 1880s and 1890s, the pages of *The Catholic World*, a journal published by the Paulists, featured candid discussions of the role of the laity, including calls for increased lay participation "in the public action of the Church" and criticism of "an exaggerated feeling of condescension toward the laity" displayed "among a large number of the priesthood."[23]

More significantly, a Catholic Lay Congress was held in Baltimore on November 11–12, 1889. Its leaders were William J. Onahan, a prominent Chicago politician, and Henry A. Brownson of Detroit, the son of Orestes A. Brownson, who expressed his hope that the congress would serve to "unite Catholics, giving them an opportunity to see and know one another, of proclaiming to the world that the laity are not priest-ridden, and of ratifying the declarations of the clergy."[24]

The major problem the organizers of the congress encountered, however, was to convince the bishops of the need, value, and safety of a lay congress. John Ireland, the sole initial episcopal supporter of the idea, was eventually able to sway James Cardinal Gibbons, Archbishop of Baltimore, to endorse the plan. Subsequently, an episcopal commission was appointed to "pass upon the character of the papers" to be delivered at the congress, in order to weed out any controversial subjects or treatments. The bishops' committee also prohibited any discussion of the papers on the floor of the meeting, so as to preclude any "surprises."

Nonetheless, more than 1,500 delegates attended the congress. The presenters struck several major themes, including the perfect compatibility of Roman Catholicism and the rights and liberties enshrined in the Constitution of the United States; a defense of the rights of workers against the evils of "untrammeled capitalism"; a call for greater Catholic solidarity in the face of hostility from anti-Catholicism in American society; and, not least, the need for Catholic laity to speak freely within the church and to think for themselves, apart from the dictates of the clergy.[25]

The success of the Baltimore congress led to another, the Columbian Catholic Congress, held in Chicago in 1893. Approximately 2,500 delegates attended and were treated to a series of thoughtful presentations on the social questions of the day, many of which engaged the themes of *Rerum Novarum* (The Condition of Labor), Pope Leo XIII's groundbreaking social encyclical of 1891. Episcopal resistance to lay congresses, however, was stronger than it had been in 1889, and after Chicago, there were no more lay congresses, and little coverage of lay Catholics in the religious or secular press.[26]

Among the primary causes of the eclipse of this brief "lay moment" were the papal condemnations of Americanism (1899) and Modernism (1907), which bred a climate of mistrust and suspicion within the American church. Any form of theological or ecclesiological innovation proved impossible in the first decades of the new century; seminary and other forms of Catholic education returned to a strict neo-Scholasticism; and lay Catholics were discouraged from departing in any significant regard from the Tridentine model of the church, which emphasized the centrality of the priesthood.

## Vatican II and a New Theology of the Laity

The path to Vatican II was paved in part by European theologians such as the Belgian theologian Gerard Philips and the great Dominican Yves Congar, whose writings on the laity informed the thinking of the Council Fathers. In 1955, Philips authored a short but influential book, *The Role of the Laity in the Church*, an examination of the nature and limits of lay apostolic activity. If the laity are seen "merely as an inferior part of a well-organized society," he wrote, then they are condemned to passivity, "and we would have no Christianity." On the contrary, baptism and confirmation bring laypersons "into the laos or people of God." In respect of this status, the layperson must cultivate "a spirit of initiative." Mere obedience and submission to the hierarchy, Philips insisted, "will not save . . . orthodoxy."[27]

Congar's *Lay People in the Church*, first published in French in 1953, called for the layperson to exercise a role in the eucharistic worship of the church, actively bringing the world and its concerns before God in Christ. In addition, the layperson may cooperate, through Catholic Action, in the work of the hierarchical apostolate. Finally, the layperson is called through baptism and confirmation to a direct evangelization of the world that is exercised independently of the hierarchical apostolate. These characteristics of lay apostolicity, Congar explains, are priestly roles. While the hierarchical ministry is a priesthood of a different order from that of the priesthood of the laity, lay priesthood is real in itself, and most certainly not derivative of ministerial priesthood. The laity who engage in apostolic actions are not mini-priests, but rather "lay priests."[28]

Congar, furthermore, challenged the clericalization of the church, and emphasized the fundamental parity of clergy and laity. Lay activity in the world is not something delegated to them by the clergy, but theirs by right and responsibility as laypeople. Significantly, Congar distinguishes Christ's spiritual authority in the church, where he reigns, from his temporal authority in the church, where he does not yet reign. If it is in the work of laity in the secular realm that Christ's temporal authority is forwarded, it is important to see that this temporal authority is not mediated through the spiritual authority within the church. Indeed, the laity's priesthood is a true priesthood, which has its place both in "the order of the holiness of life" and in "the order of sacramental worship." While the ordained priesthood has particular responsibilities not shared with the laity pertaining to the celebration of the sacraments other than baptism and Eucharist, all other aspects of priesthood are shared by clergy and laity.[29]

Congar's seminal works on the theology of the laity inspired Daniel Callahan's landmark work *The Mind of the Catholic Layman.* Writing his book in the early 1960s, Callahan noted the signs of hope and renewal all around him: the growth and dynamism of various lay movements inspired by Catholic Action; the fact that "a number of laymen were voicing complaints about their seemingly negligible role in the Church", the election of a lay Catholic as president of the United States; and the Second Vatican Council's attention to the special role of the laity in fulfilling the mission of the church.[30]

At the same time, Callahan remained skeptical about the prospects for the laity in the absence of a serious reform of clerical and hierarchical attitudes:

> Now the great difficulty here is not the divinely ordained authority of the Church in matters of faith and morals. Rarely does this pose a genuine problem of conscience of the layman. The real difficulty is authoritarianism: that cluster of inclinations, concepts and attitudes which is fearful of individual freedom, reliant upon the force of law and coercion to sustain belief, and convinced that the only discipline of any value is that imposed by others. It would be false to imply that the authoritarian spirit reigns supreme in the Church, especially in America. . . . The layman is urged to be a free man in society; but if he observes how reliant some bishops and priests are upon docile laymen, how alarmed they become when faced with even a respectful challenge to their wisdom, then it is difficult for the layman to believe that much store is set by freedom—within the Church or outside.

The laity, it seems to me, have a good basis for their complaints that clerical paternalism is a major obstacle to a more effective development of the layman. At the same time, there is considerable justice in the clerical retort that lay apathy is a reality of major proportions. . . .

A more plausible reason for this kind of apathy lies in the type of training the laity receives from the hands of a significant proportion of the clergy (and religious). If the layman is conditioned from his earliest days to be quiet and docile, to do what he is told, it is almost inevitable that he will be poorly prepared to act in a mature, vigorous way when he is an adult. The over-protective parent produces immature and dependent children; an over-protective clergy produces the same kind of layman.[31]

Even as Callahan was writing, however, the Council Fathers of Vatican II were incorporating into their description of the church some of Congar's seminal insights. The Decree on the Apostolate of Lay People declared that the laity, "carrying out this mission of the church, exercise their apostolate therefore in the world as well as in the church, in the temporal order as well as in the spiritual." These orders are distinct, the Council acknowledged, "yet they are nevertheless so closely linked that God's plan is, in Christ, to take the whole world up again and make of it a new creation, initially here on earth, totally at the end of time. The layperson, at one and the same time a believer and a citizen of the world, has only a single conscience, a christian conscience, by which to be guided continually in both domains."[32]

Vatican II did indeed trigger a renewal of the laity. The reforms instituted in the late sixties and seventies, designed to realize the concept of lay participation and collegiality on the local level, were significant. In many parishes, lay councils exercised significant consultative and advisory roles; laymen and -women took responsibility for financial planning and budgeting, as well as for religious education and liturgy. Lay ministries, beginning with eucharistic ministry, proliferated. Diocesan and international synods made an undeniable impact on the consciousness of laity and clergy alike. All of these initiatives raised expectations for a truly collaborative church.

The Council and the reforms it engendered nonetheless had their limits. In fact, Callahan's misgivings seem prescient, for it seems, forty years later, that Vatican II's Decree on the Apostolate of Lay People (*Apostolicam Actuositatem*, 18 November 1965), and the theology of the laity undergirding it, were not equal to the task of motivating the necessary reform in priestly attitudes.

The limits were embedded in the so-called "new theology" itself. Philips's basic conservatism was reflected in Vatican II's efforts to evaluate and promote the lay apostolate. Philips's book *The Role of the Laity in the Church* is both a call to the laity to recognize their spiritual adulthood and a resounding appeal to the clergy to relate to the laity as adults to adults, to expect and reward responsibility and initiative. It utilizes the language of the church as "people of God," anticipatory of Vatican II. As Paul Lakeland points out, however, nowhere does Philips envisage any real change in power relations in the church, nor does he investigate the nature of the priesthood and episcopacy in which that power is concentrated.

Congar's concerns, on the other hand, clearly address a theological evaluation of the laity as such. A number of the council documents, above all the chapter from *Lumen Gentium* on the laity, reflect much of his thought. Overall, however, Lakeland notes, the Council's words on the laity skirted the question of their theological status and concentrated on their apostolate. On the crucial question of lay involvement in governance and the exercise of authority within the church, Congar asserts that the real role of the laity resides in "the principle of consent" to decisions made by the episcopacy. Lakeland concludes:

> The huge role that Congar sees for lay consent in order to make the church not just a structure but a living community is greatly heartening. But perhaps not so the vigor with which Congar defends the notion that power in the church, the power of decision making, rests entirely with the hierarchy. The church is no democracy, he insists.[33]

## Conclusion: The Return of Alienation

Unfortunately, the early enthusiasms for the new independent layperson, and the reforms they generated and reflected, so much on display in the 1960s, now look distressingly like a period piece. In many parishes, parish councils, always dependent for their vitality on the discretion of the pastor, atrophied in the 1980s and 1990s. The long pontificate of John Paul II has not been kind to lay ministry in the United States; the pope's focus on revitalizing the priesthood has prevented a sophisticated theology of lay ministry from being incorporated into a working ecclesiology of the American church. As a result, lay ministry is a vocation in search of an official justification (beyond seeing the lay minister as a complement and subordinate to the ordained priest); not surprisingly, the career track for lay ministers in many dioceses is uncertain.

Moreover, the crisis of priestly sexual abuse has deepened an alienation of the laity from the hierarchy that may well have begun with the controversial reaffirmation of the church's ban on artificial contraception (in Pope Paul VI's encyclical *Humanae Vitae*) in 1968. The persistent failure of many members of the American hierarchy truly to consult with laity on personnel, financial, and other matters of church administration seem to echo previous generations of complaints of a two-tiered church, where decisions are made, often in secrecy, by a clerical/episcopal elite. The current crisis has demonstrated, moreover, that some members, at least, of that elite were concerned more with the preservation of their prerogatives and their sense of the church than with the needs, yearnings, and witness of the laity. Sadly, Callahan's protest against lay subordination within the church, written forty years ago, rings true today.[34]

The longer history of lay–clergy relations considered in this chapter, however briefly, suggests that the current experience of lay alienation from the hierarchy is the historical norm, rather than the exception. Lay trusteeism, in retrospect, was an epiphenomenon rather than a full-blown movement for church reform around the principle of lay–clergy cogovernance of the local church. The lay congresses of the turn of the twentieth century raised the intellectual profile of the laity in the church and generated enthusiasm for, and participation in, the Catholic response to the social question—the question of the plight of the worker— posed by rapid industrialization and urbanization. Whatever lay momentum was inspired by the congresses, however, failed to lead to any reform of the structures of the American church that concentrate all administrative as well as pastoral and theological decision-making in the hands of the clergy.

Finally, the "theology of the laity" proposed by Congar, Philips, and others had its moment in the spotlight during the preparations for the Second Vatican Council, and influenced the documents produced by the Council, not least in the retrieval of the biblical concept of the "people of God" as a description of the church. But the fragility of such innovations became unmistakably apparent during the pontificate of Pope John Paul II, when priests were told explicitly that "you are in the world, but not of the world." By contrast, the laity, in John Paul II's view, are presumably in *and of* the world; in any case, they were told implicitly (and, at times, explicitly) that their "apostolate" is exercised primarily in the world, not in the church. In addition to relegating the laity, once again, to second-class status within the church, this attitude reinforces, against the grain of Vatican II, the strongly dualistic church-world distinction that emerged in the Middle Ages and was formalized in the mid-sixteenth century by the Council of Trent.

In the absence of papal endorsement and "implementation" of a Vatican II–era ecclesiology that would insist on honoring the principle of collegiality at every level of church governance and ministry, any theology of the laity that attempts to erode the church-world, clergy-laity distinction will meet the same fate as Congar's, which serves today more as a historical period piece, now fading from memory as well as from practice, rather than as a rationale and justification for genuine reform. The problem is not a lack of profound, well-reasoned, theologically sophisticated, and perfectly orthodox theologies of the laity and of lay ministry, for such theologies, inspired by Vatican II, have been published and are being taught in Catholic university and college theology courses, and in lay ministry certification programs and seminars.

The problem, rather, is the unwillingness of the hierarchy, following the lead of the pope, to grant full consideration to such theologies, and to begin the process of restructuring the church in such a way as to promote genuine collaboration between clergy and laity in all aspects of Roman Catholic ministry. Instead, many laity feel, the emphasis over the past decades has been on putting the laity back "in their place" after the unfortunate enthusiasms of the 1960s and 1970s. Unfortunately for those who seek neither the alienation nor the autonomy of the laity from the clergy and hierarchy, and who prefer a model of the church based on collegiality and cooperation, the historical record of U.S. Catholicism on this question is not an unambiguous resource, to say the least. Rather, it tells the tale of a hierarchy that, in matters of religion, ministry, and administration of the church, has held the laity at arm's length, and of a consequent lay struggle for autonomy from the hierarchy, punctuated by periods of alienation and more benevolent, but fleeting moments of shared purpose and genuine collegiality.

## Notes

1. Daniel Callahan, *The Mind of the Catholic Layman* (New York: Charles Scribner's Sons, 1963), 175.
2. Patrick W. Carey, "Trusteeism," in Michael Glazier and Thomas J. Shelley, eds., *The Encyclopedia of American Catholic History* (Collegeville, Minn.: Liturgical Press, 1997), 1396.

3. Nathan O. Hatch, *The Democratization of American Christianity* (New Haven, Conn.: Yale University Press, 1989).

4. Carey, "Trusteeism," 1396.

5. Patrick W. Carey, *People, Priests, and Prelates: Ecclesiastical Democracy and the Tensions of Trusteeism* (Notre Dame, Ind.: University of Notre Dame Press, 1987), 1–13.

6. Carey, "Trusteeism," 1397.

7. David Gerber, "Modernity in Service of Tradition: Catholic Lay Trustees at Buffalo's St. Louis Church and the Transformation of European Communal Traditions, 1829–1855," *Journal of Social History* 15 (1983): 655–84.

8. John T. McGreevy, *Catholicism and American Freedom: A History* (New York: W.W. Norton & Co., 2003).

9. Carey, *People, Priests, and Prelates*, 59–72, 80.

10. Ibid., 156–73.

11. Dale B. Light, *Rome and the New Republic: Conflict and Community in Philadelphia Catholicism between the Revolution and the Civil War* (Notre Dame, Ind.: University of Notre Dame Press, 1996), 24.

12. Rev. John Carroll, "Letter to Trustees of St. Peter's Church," 25 January 1786, in John Tracy Ellis, ed., *Documents of American Catholic History, Vol. 1: 1493–1865* (Wilmington, Del.: Michael Glazier, 1987), 152.

13. Carey, *People, Priests, and Prelates*, 124–29.

14. Ibid., 136–46.

15. Light, *Rome and the New Republic*, 14.

16. "Constitution of the Roman Catholic Church of the Diocese of Charleston," in Patrick W. Carey, ed., *American Catholic Religious Thought: The Shaping of a Theological and Social Tradition* (New York: Paulist Press, 1987), 89–90.

17. See, for example, Thomas T. McAvoy, C.S.C., *The Great Crisis in American Catholic History, 1895–1900* (Chicago: Henry Regnery Co., 1957); Robert D. Cross, *The Emergence of Liberal Catholicism in America* (Cambridge, Mass.: Harvard University Press, 1958); and Christopher J. Kauffman, *Tradition and Transformation: The Priests of Saint Sulpice in the United States from 1791 to the Present* (New York: Macmillan, 1988).

18. Rev. John A. O'Brien, *The Priesthood in a Changing World* (Paterson, N.J.: St. Anthony Guild Press, 1943), 3.

19. Robert E. Sullivan, "Beneficial Relations: Toward a Social History of the Diocesan Priests of Boston, 1875–1944," in Robert E. Sullivan and James O'Toole, eds., *Catholic Boston: Studies in Religion and Community, 1870–1970* (Boston: Archdiocese of Boston), 219.

20. R. Scott Appleby, "Present to the People of God: The Transformation of the Roman Catholic Parish Priesthood," in Jay Dolan, R. Scott Appleby, Patricia Byrne, and Debra Campbell, *Transforming Parish Ministry: The*

*Changing Roles of Catholic Clergy, Laity, and Women Religious* (New York: Crossroad Publishing Co., 1989), 11.

21. Jerome D. Hannan, "Anticlericalism in the United States," *America* 62 (8 April 1930): 8.

22. Philip Murnion, *The Catholic Priest and the Changing Structure of Pastoral Ministry, New York 1920–1970* (New York: Arno Press, 1978), 151.

23. "The Laity," *The Catholic World* 67 (April 1888): 12.

24. Henry A. Brownson, "The Catholic Congress," *Michigan Catholic* (12 December 1889).

25. Callahan, *The Mind of the Catholic Layman*, 66–69.

26. Ibid., 72.

27. Gerard Philips, *The Role of the Laity in the Church*, quoted in Paul Lakeland, *The Liberation of the Laity: In Search of an Accountable Church* (New York: Continuum, 2003), 45–46.

28. Lakeland, *The Liberation of the Laity*, 53.

29. Yves Congar, *Lay People in the Church: A Study of the Theology of the Laity* (Westminster, Md.: Newman, 1955); Lakeland, *The Liberation of the Laity*, 54–61.

30. Callahan, *The Mind of the Catholic Layman*, ix.

31. Ibid., 177–78.

32. "Decree on the Apostolate of Lay People (*Apostolicam Actuositatem*)," in Austin Flannery, O.P., general editor, *Vatican Council II: Constitutions, Decrees, Declarations* (Northport, N.Y.: Costello Publishing Co., 1996), 410.

33. Lakeland, *The Liberation of the Laity*, 56–57.

34. "In the past . . . [the layman] was not welcome on the secular campus, in secular welfare work or in non-Catholic organizations in general. If he was tolerated, his opportunities were limited because of his Catholicism. Thus it was natural for him to stay closer to Church organizations; if there were frustrations there, they were at least more tolerable than those he met in the outside world. Today all that has changed; the situation is reversed. It is the direct service of the Church which entails the greater number of frustrations. The result of this shift is apparent: a great many of the better-educated, more assimilated laymen are coming to choose the secular world as the more congenial place to exercise their lay vocation. . . . That is not all. In our society, the Catholic as a citizen is able to exercise his constitutional freedoms to the fullest degree; the contrast between the kind of role he plays within the Church and the kind he plays within society is unmistakable. . . . [S]hould the layman wish to use his human talents to the utmost, he has a far better chance of doing so in the service of society than in the service of the Church. In society, imagination, initiative, and leadership are rewarded and respected; in the Church they may be the cause of suspicion and suppression." Callahan, *The Mind of the Catholic Layman*, 178–80.

# Part II

# Contemporary Perspectives

# SIX

# Participatory Hierarchy

## TERENCE L. NICHOLS

In this chapter, I will propose that the Catholic Church is meant to be a participatory hierarchy, sourced in the Holy Spirit, in which the will and mind of the Spirit is expressed both through the magisterium and through the laity, priests, and religious. The contemporary crisis in the church has come about because over the centuries participatory hierarchy has been supplanted by a one-sided command or monarchial hierarchy.

As is well known, the Second Vatican Council favored the image of the church as the People of God. This has led to widespread calls for a democratic church. Yet Vatican II also emphasized that the church is hierarchical. Chapter III of the Dogmatic Constitution on the Church (*Lumen Gentium*) is titled "The Hierarchical Structure of the Church." The church, it says, is a "hierarchically structured society" (*LG* no. 20). The bishops have, by divine institution, succeeded the apostles as shepherds of the church (*LG* no. 20). Yet the bishops can only exercise their offices of teaching and governing in "hierarchical communion with the head and members of the college" (*LG* no. 21). The Roman Pontiff has "full, supreme and universal power over the Church," and he can always exercise this power freely (*LG* no. 22). The Dogmatic Constitution on Divine Revelation (*Dei Verbum*) states: "The task of authentically interpreting the word of God, whether living or handed on, has been entrusted exclusively to the living teaching office of the Church" (*DV* no. 10). So the church is the People of God, yet it is also hierarchically structured. Can the church be both democratic and hierarchical?

This is problematic because the notion of hierarchy is increasingly thought to mean domination, oppression, authoritarianism, and patriarchy. Joann Wolski Conn writes: "Ideas and projects in the relational feminist tradition feature a non-hierarchical, egalitarian vision of social organization."[1] For authors such as Elisabeth Schussler Fiorenza, Rosemary Radford Ruether, Leonardo Boff, Sallie McFague, and others, hierarchy means domination *tout court*. The alternative to hierarchy, for these authors, is an egalitarian church. It seems, then, that the church must be either hierarchical and authoritarian, or democratic and egalitarian.

Many authors argue for an egalitarian church. One of the leitmotifs of John Dominic Crossan's *The Historical Jesus* is that the original Jesus movement was egalitarian. Jesus was not even a mediator, according to Crossan. He was a radical egalitarian who ate with prostitutes and tax collectors. "[F]or Jesus, the Kingdom of God is a community of radical or unbroken equality in which individuals are in direct contact with one another and with God, unmediated by any established brokers or fixed locations."[2] It was Jesus' followers who set up a hierarchical church, and so betrayed Jesus' own mission. Other authors, such as Elisabeth Schussler Fiorenza, also argue that the pristine Jesus movement was egalitarian.

Yet it is hard to imagine how a worldwide institution such as the Catholic Church could survive as an egalitarian society. Even simple social structures, like families, school classes, sports teams, and so on, need some kind of hierarchy to function. A family in which the children have an equal vote on every issue would disintegrate. A class in which the opinions of the students were equivalent to those of the teacher would accomplish nothing. In a family, a class, an orchestra, a sports team, a university, a corporation, or a church, the alternative to some kind of hierarchy would seem to be fragmentation and paralysis. Some social hierarchy seems necessary for even a minimal level of unity and operation. One purpose of hierarchy in the Catholic Church is to preserve the unity of the church.

It is also difficult to see how the worldwide church could function as a democracy. Would each parish elect its priest and decide what the priest should teach? This is a congregational ecclesiology, in which ultimate authority is vested in the congregation itself. Free churches and Baptist churches follow this model. But a striking feature of these churches has been disunity and fragmentation. They have been unable to preserve unity in teaching and doctrine, or unity among their congregations. The Roman Catholic Church, on the other hand, has never followed a purely congregational or democratic ecclesiology. Rather, it has relied on bishops to preserve unity in teaching and communion at least from the time of Ignatius of Antioch.

Yet it is also true that many hierarchical structures are dominating, patriarchal, oppressive, and authoritarian. Such a hierarchy, based on a top-down exercise of power, might be called a *command hierarchy*. The question is: Is this the only model of hierarchy? Interestingly enough, both those who want an authoritarian hierarchy, and those who reject it in favor of an egalitarian society, have the same image of hierarchy: a command hierarchy.

I will propose here an alternative model of hierarchy, namely *participatory hierarchy*. In this model, the aim of those in authority is not to suppress but to foster participation and inclusion, and to lead those in their charge into a sharing of the goods that the leaders themselves possess. It is this kind of hierarchy that ought to characterize the church.

An example of participatory hierarchy is teaching. The wise teacher wishes to bring her students to a sharing of the same knowledge or skills that she herself possesses. (Knowledge, like love, is not diminished by being shared; rather, it is enriched.) Another example of participatory hierarchy might be a parent–child relationship. Certainly there are abusive parents who dominate their children, but good parents wish for their children to grow into the maturity that the parents themselves possess. A third example is the religious master–disciple relationship. In some cases, such as Zen Buddhism, the authority of the master over the student is almost absolute. But the enlightened master seeks not to dominate, but to pass on the very enlightenment that he possesses.

In a command hierarchy, the source of authority is power: the hierarch has the power to compel obedience. In a participatory hierarchy, however, the source of authority is what might be called competence or *virtue*, which may take the form of knowledge, wisdom, love, or holiness. The learner seeks to participate in the knowledge, wisdom, love, or holiness that the master already possesses. This kind of hierarchy, based on competence and virtue, is recognized in all human societies.

The idea of participatory hierarchy is analogous to hierarchy in biology. All complex entities in nature are systems, which are made up of subsystems, which are made up of subsystems, etc. Thus, an animal is made up of organs, which are made up of cells, which are made up of macromolecules (e.g., proteins), which are made up of simpler molecules and atoms, which are made up of subatomic particles. In such systems, the more comprehensive levels do not "suppress" or "dominate" the lower. Rather, they build on them and organize the simpler systems into a larger whole. The lower systems have a degree of autonomy, which is regulated and organized but not otherwise interfered with by the higher system. A cell of a human body, for example, can be kept alive and even reproduce *in vitro*, but once incorporated into an organ, its activity is regulated by that organ (except in the case of cancer cells, which grow in unregulated fashion). Similarly, the heart can be kept alive and will even beat erratically *in vitro*, but within the body its beating is regulated by the body.

Such a hierarchy is based on the principle of inclusion and subsidiarity. Simpler systems are integrated into more comprehensive systems without losing their nature. This kind of hierarchy is also found in societies. National systems are federations of regional or state systems, which are themselves made up of local systems, which are made up of families. The Catholic teaching on subsidiarity therefore states that it is wrong for the higher levels of government to interfere with lower, more local levels, unless those levels are dysfunctional. A society that is entirely controlled from the top, a command hierarchy, lacks subsidiarity and is despotic.

As institutionalized, however, there is usually a tension between command hierarchy and participatory hierarchy. In situations requiring quick, decisive action, a command hierarchy is more appropriate. Such is the situation in emergencies, wars, and periods of crisis, and therefore command hierarchies are the rule in fire and police departments and military units. Even these require some degree of participation, however. If the members do not feel as if they are engaged in a pursuit in which they all share, they will perform poorly. An army defending its homeland is typically more formidable than an army of mercenaries or an army of slaves. But as a long-term strategy for governance, command hierarchies do not work well. They typically result in despotic regimes, which are detested by their members, provoke revolt, and are vitiated by apathy and resentment.

At the other end of the spectrum, the pure form of participatory hierarchy, found for example among master and disciples, is difficult to embody in an institutional structure. Most religious bodies and social institutions inevitably contain some elements of a command hierarchy. In a college classroom, for instance, we hope that the students are there to gain knowledge, but we do have to depend also on forms of coercion (grading). Even pacifist groups, like the Amish, have developed their own forms of coercion (shunning). In almost all social groups, both forms of hierarchy are found.

Nonetheless, I will defend here the thesis that the church ought to emulate participatory hierarchy as far as possible. There are several reasons for this. First, it is the kind of hierarchy Jesus practiced (I will have more to say about this below). Second, hierarchy means "sacred source" (*hiera arche*). The sacred source of the church is the Holy Spirit, whose mission is to draw all humanity into participation in the divine life of God. And this is also the mission of the church—to bring its members into mutual participation in God's divine life (*LG* no. 2) and into a community that freely embodies God's love. Such love cannot be coerced; it is given through participation in the Spirit: "God's love has been poured into our hearts through the Holy Spirit that has been given to us" (Romans 5:5, NRSV). Third, the church is meant to be "a kind of sacrament of intimate union with God, and of the unity of all mankind, that is, she is a sign and instrument of that unity" (*LG* no. 1). But the church can only be such a sign if it embodies a participatory hierarchy. If it embodies a command hierarchy, on the other hand, it becomes a countersign, a stumbling block to the faithful, a sign not of participation but of domination, authoritarianism, and oppression. And if this is the case, it cannot be a sacrament of union with God and unity with humankind. It will fail in its mission.

In the remainder of this chapter, I will consider participatory hierarchy in the history of the church and in the contemporary church. I will end by arguing that the crisis in the church today has been brought on by the displacement of participatory hierarchy by command hierarchy.

## Participatory Hierarchy in Church History
Hierarchy emerges in the Hebrew scriptures with the Book of Genesis.[3] God is totally sovereign in the act of creating, but creation itself is an expression of the goodness of God and participates in God's own goodness. Only humans are made in the image of God. "Image" here can mean many things, but modern commentators note that ancient kings were in the habit of installing "images" of themselves in all corners of their kingdoms, since they could not be present everywhere at once. These images might be statues or deputies, whose charge was to govern the kingdom as the king would if he were present. Humans, then, are charged with the responsibility of governing the earth as God's stewards or regents. Thus, in Genesis 2, God places Adam in the garden "to till and to keep it." In this state, the first humans participate in God's blessings and presence: God walks in the garden and talks to his creatures. There is no indication of dominance either between the man and the woman, or between humans and the animals. To be sure, God gives the man and his wife a command (not to eat the fruit of the tree of the knowledge of good and evil), but this is more tutelary than despotic.

It is a warning. Command hierarchy sets in for real only after the first sin. The woman becomes subject to the man (Gn 3:16), the animals subject to humans (it is only after the fall that humans are told to eat meat—Gn 9:3), and the humans subject to God. The "fall," then, is a fall from full participation in the life of God. Domination is a condition of a sinful world and is a distortion of the participatory hierarchy found in paradise.

The several covenants initiated by God—that of Noah, Abraham, Moses, David, Jesus—are attempts by God to bring human beings back into the state of full participation in the divine life, symbolized by the paradise account in Genesis. These covenants are mediated by prophets, priests, and kings. Note that there were many mediators through which the Spirit taught Israel, not just one. Now priests, prophets, and kings are hierarchical figures. But their aim was to bring the people into the blessings of God. (The good king brought unity, justice, and blessings to Israel, whereas domination was characteristic of an evil king: cf. 1 Sam 8:1–18). Further, the people themselves were called upon to ratify the work of the prophets and kings. The whole people ratified the covenant presented through Moses: "Everything that the Lord has spoken, we will do" (Exod 19:8). Though anointed by Yahweh, both Saul and David were acclaimed by the people (1 Sam 11:15, 2 Sam 2:4, 2 Sam 5:3). Rehoboam was rejected as king because he failed to receive the consent of the people (1 Kings 12). Hierarchy in the Hebrew scriptures is not, then, just a matter of God imposing rules on people. It is fundamentally participatory.

The same is true in the New Testament. I am not persuaded by the arguments of Crossan and others that the Jesus movement was egalitarian. After all, the disciples address Jesus as Rabbi (teacher) and Lord—he has the kind of authority in his movement that other religious teachers (Moses, Buddha, Muhammad) had in theirs. His followers are not called "equals," but "disciples" (learners), and there is never any indication that they thought of themselves as his equals. He promises the twelve that they will sit on thrones and judge the twelve tribes of Israel (Luke 22:30). He himself prays to God as "Abba" (Father, Daddy). Scholars as various as Rudolf Bultmann, Joachim Jeremias, Norman Perrin, Ben Meyer, E. P. Sanders, and John Meier agree that the core of Jesus' message was the coming kingdom or reign of God over a renewed Israel. But the kingdom is a hierarchical symbol. It is also eschatological, and Jesus' eschatological sayings typically involve judgment, and so hierarchy (e.g., Matthew 25:31–42, the parable of the sheep and the goats).

However, if there is hierarchy in the Jesus movement, it is not dominance or command hierarchy. Jesus denounces those in positions of
hierarchy and flouts social convention by eating with tax collectors and
sinners. He declares that authority is service (Mark 9:35), and he so
represents it (the washing of the feet in the Gospel of John). When Jesus
sends out disciples, he gives them the same powers to preach, heal, and
exorcise that he has (Matthew 10; Luke 9). His aim seems to be to
bring the disciples into the kind of loving relationship with God that
he himself experiences. He thus exercises the kind of hierarchy characteristic of teachers, parents, and religious masters.

Much the same is true of St. Paul. Paul can sound authoritarian
when he is defending his apostolic authority (cf. Galatians 1). His whole
aim, however, is to bring the Christian disciples into the life in the Spirit
that he himself enjoys. This is clear in Galatians, Corinthians, Romans,
and other letters. Paul's insistence on apostolic authority is not for
purposes of domination, but to open the way to participation. He prays:
"that your love may overflow more and more with knowledge and full
insight . . . so that in the day of Christ, you may be pure and blameless"
(Philippians 1: 9–10). His metaphor of the church as the Body of Christ
(1 Cor 12) emphasizes the participation of all in the gifts of the
Spirit.

Personal, charismatic authority, such as Paul's, begins to yield to
institutional authority in the early church. We see this in Acts 15. There,
the apostles and disciples must decide whether to demand circumcision
(and observance of the Jewish law) of Gentile converts, or to admit them
uncircumcised. The decision is shown as involving extensive discussion
among apostles and elders. Peter speaks authoritatively, as he does also
in Acts 1 and 6, as a spokesperson for the apostles. The final decision
is rendered by James (the head of the Jerusalem church), and is represented as a consensus decision of the whole church (Acts 15:22). This
consensus is taken as a sign that the decision expresses the will of the
Spirit: "It has seemed good to the Holy Spirit and to us . . ." (Acts 15:28).

The account of this "council of Jerusalem" is idealized in Acts.
We know from Paul's letter to the Galatians that there remained a
circumcision faction (Gal 2:12). But I would argue that Acts 15, as
inspired scripture, represents a "narrative charter" of how decisions
ideally ought to be reached in the church. Here we see the early church
wrestling with its most momentous decision—in opening its doors to
uncircumcised Gentiles, it became a truly universal church. The process
involves hierarchical leadership (the apostles), but also broad participation. The Spirit is mediated through many (as it was in Israel), not just

through one. And the achievement of consensus is a sign that the decision expresses the will of the Holy Spirit, not merely human will.

The ideal of consensus also inspired early ecumenical councils. At the Council of Nicaea, the aim of the bishops was not to impose the will of a majority on the minority, but through discussion to reach consensus. Though the emperor Constantine summoned the council, and recommended the use of the term "*homoousios*," he did not impose a decision. According to Socrates' *Ecclesiastical History*, "whatever could be fittingly advanced in support of any opinion was fully stated."[4] The decision was a near consensus (two bishops of some 300 present refused to sign). This was taken by Constantine and by the bishops as evidence that their decision represented the will of the Holy Spirit. Nonetheless, the creed of the Council of Nicaea was not fully accepted by the wider church for many years. Subsequent councils (Constantinople, 381; Chalcedon, 451) declared the Council of Nicaea to be ecumenical and hence binding on the whole church. Thus, the creed of Nicaea became uncontested orthodoxy only when it had been accepted by the universal church.

It might be argued that Nicaea was not really participatory hierarchy; after all, it was a council of bishops, not of laymen (except Constantine), much less laywomen. But these early bishops were usually elected by their local churches (e.g., Ambrose, Augustine), and so represented their people. Hippolytus, writing about 215, describes an ordination thus: "Let the bishop be ordained being in all things without fault chosen by all the people."[5] Thus, one might say that the Holy Spirit operated at several levels: that of the people, the presbyters, and the ordaining bishops. The people, then, though not present at Nicaea, were in effect represented by their bishops. Furthermore, the fact that Nicaea was not accepted until after a long period of reception, involving the whole church, also indicates that participation was involved. But hierarchical leadership was also necessary: without the leadership of Constantine, the council would not have occurred.

In this way, through discussion and reception, the creed of Nicaea became established as normative. This principle of common discussion was later affirmed by the Second Council of Constantinople (553):

> The holy fathers, who have gathered at intervals in the four holy councils, have followed the examples of antiquity [i.e., the apostles at the Council at Jerusalem]. They dealt with heresies and current problems by debate in common, since it was established as certain

that when the disputed question is set out by each side in communal discussions, the light of truth drives out the shadow of lying. *The truth cannot be made clear in any other way when there are debates about questions of faith, since everyone requires the assistance of his neighbor.*[6]

Thus, it is *only* through participatory discussion (and not by the imposition of a command hierarchy) that the truth can be made clear.

The conciliar model, which remained strong in the church in the east, was gradually challenged by the emerging model of a monarchial papacy in the west. Peter certainly acts as the spokesperson for the apostles in the gospels and in Acts. But he seems to act as the facilitator and proclaimer of consensus, not from a command hierarchy. However, by the time of Pope Siricius (384–389), a different style has emerged. According to Klaus Schatz, in Siricius's decretals, "we find . . . the commanding style of the imperial court. . . . Before this, only synods could create new law in the Church. Now papal writings were placed *de facto* on the same level as synodal law."[7] Pope Leo the Great (440–461) saw himself as the head of the whole church, because he was the vicar of Peter. As he wrote: "When, therefore, we utter our exhortations in your ears, holy brethren, believe that he is speaking, whose representative we are (*cuius vice fungimur*)."[8] Yet Leo also wrote (in a letter): "Let whoever is to be set over all be elected by all."[9] Pope Gelasius (492–496) argued that the Roman See judges the whole church, but can itself be judged by no one.[10] Gelasius thus prepared the way for the papal monarchy of the Middle Ages.

The factors that led up to the medieval papal monarchy are complex. The bishops had fallen under the control of local lay lords, who claimed the right to install the bishops. The reform of Pope Gregory VII (1073–1085), with its extraordinary claims of papal hegemony, originated in a (successful) attempt to wrest control of the church from lay lords. But the result was, according to Yves Congar, "the greatest turning which Catholic ecclesiology has known."[11] Ecclesiology changed from a conciliar mode to an imperial mode, in which the authority of the church derives from the pope, its head, who alone represents Christ on earth, and who has not only primacy, but jurisdiction over all other churches.[12] The ancient idea that the unity of the Body of Christ was to be found in the principle of consensus was replaced with the idea that its unity is based on monarchial papal authority and obedience. The Spirit is mediated only through one, not through many. By the reign of Innocent III (1198–1215), the title "Vicar of Christ" was reserved for the pope alone, whereas in earlier times it had been used for both kings and bishops. It was Innocent who declared: "The Pope is the meeting point between God and man . . . who can judge all things and be judged by no one."[13]

The papal monarchy was a major factor in the schism with the east, which began in 1054, but which culminated in the crusade of 1204 (which sacked Constantinople) and with Innocent III's appointment of a Latin patriarch of Constantinople. Byzantine historian Aristeides Papadakis gives this diagnosis of the schism:

> [T]he decisive change in the Roman church was the unprecedented transformation of its legitimate primacy into monarchy. The theoreticians of the Gregorian movement were to devise a new ecclesiological model in which Rome was conceived legalistically and juridically as the head and mother of the Churches. . . . Indeed, the autocratic basis of the new ecclesiology, in contrast with Eastern Christendom's traditional collegial and synodal structure, left little room for accommodation or compromise. The shrill demand of the Roman Church for submission was to become an invariable feature governing its relations with Byzantium. . . . Historically, the mounting hostility which gives the period 1071–1453 a certain recognizable unity . . . has its origins in the eleventh century, in the highly centralized papacy and its novel claims.[14]

The British historian Sir Stephen Runciman agrees: "The East had no wish to submit to the West and the West would accept nothing less than submission."[15]

Although we think of the Middle Ages as the period of papal monarchy, it is well to remember that there was a strong conciliar movement that flourished all through that period. And the authority of the pope was de facto limited by the authority of kings and local lords. What the medieval period did bequeath to the later church was the *ideology* of papal monarchy, in which ecclesial unity was understood as due to obedience to one's superiors, that is, to the acceptance of a command hierarchy, rather than to a conciliar principle.

The papal monarchy continued into the Renaissance and was a major factor in the Protestant Reformation. Pope Boniface VIII, in his bull *Unam Sanctam* (1302), had claimed: "We declare, state, define, and pronounce that it is altogether necessary to human salvation for every human creature to be subject to the Roman pontiff" (*DS* 875).[16] This statement was repeated at the fifth Lateran Council (1517), and was part of the reason for Martin Luther's reaction against the papacy. Again and again in his writings, Luther accuses the pope (and the Curia) of "tyranny." What Luther (and other Reformers) rejected was a command hierarchy of the pope *over* the church. Unfortunately, they did not seriously consider more participatory models of the papacy. Philip Melancthon, however, in the interests of unity, was prepared to accept the pope as the first among equals (as the Orthodox understand it).[17]

The emergence of a command hierarchy within the papal office was partially responsible for both the schism with the Orthodox and the Reformation separation. Indeed this is still the case. Insofar as the papacy is conceived monarchially, it is unacceptable to the Orthodox or to the Protestants. However, a more participatory form of papal authority, such as that adumbrated by John Paul II in *Ut Unum Sint*, may be acceptable. The doctrines that stand in the way, however, are the doctrines of papal infallibility and universal jurisdiction, laid down at the First Vatican Council (1869–1870).

Vatican I was largely controlled by Pope Pius IX, the Curia, and the Ultramontanist party. Its Dogmatic Constitution on the Church of Christ (*Pastor Aeternus*) enunciates the doctrines of infallibility and the universal jurisdiction of the pope. The pope's infallible definitions, it says, are irreformable *ex sese, non ex consensus ecclesiae* (by themselves, and not from the consent of the church—*DS* 3074). However, these statements can be interpreted in different ways. *Pastor Aeternus*, says that the infallibility exercised by the pope is the infallibility "which the divine Redeemer willed His church to enjoy in defining doctrines" (*DS* 3074). Papal infallibility, then, is rooted in the infallibility of the whole church. When speaking infallibly, the pope speaks the mind of the church; he cannot invoke an infallible definition *against* the mind of the church. Thus, it is possible to interpret Vatican I more moderately than in the usual Orthodox and Protestant interpretations.[18]

## The Second Vatican Council and Beyond

*Lumen Gentium* repeats many of the assertions of Vatican I, such as that the pope has "full, supreme and universal power over the Church" (*LG* no. 22). But the Vatican II document also modifies this, saying that each bishop (and not just the pope) is a Vicar of Christ (*LG* no. 27). The church is the whole People of God, not just the magisterium. And *Lumen Gentium* asserts that the bishops and the pope govern the church together: "Together with its head, the Roman Pontiff, and never without its head, the episcopal order is the subject of supreme and full power over the universal Church" (*LG* no. 22).

Vatican II was unusual in another way. The bishops were able to set their own agendas and, for the most part, craft their own documents. Furthermore, the bishops learned from the many *periti* (expert advisors) who attended the council, and from the Protestant and Orthodox observers. The council, then, was not controlled from the top (as Vatican I had been). It is a good, though not perfect, example of participatory hierarchy in action. As in the Council of Nicaea, the bishops proceeded by careful discussion, until they reached a near consensus (most documents were approved by about 98 percent of the bishops). This discussion aided the bishops in discerning the will of the Spirit. Two crucial issues, however, were not discussed by the council, but were reserved by the pope for his own decision. These were the decisions concerning artificial birth control and clerical celibacy. As is well known, the pope, Paul VI, resisted the advice of the majority (over 90 percent) of his own Commission on the Family to modify the teaching on birth control, and issued the encyclical *Humanae Vitae* on his own authority. Had Vatican Council II been allowed to participate in the process, it is likely that the decision would have been different. This is one more example of the failure of a command hierarchy.

The movement to restore participation in the contemporary Catholic Church has been uneven. Participatory hierarchy is probably best exhibited in local parishes, where priests often cooperate with lay parish councils and lay administrators. In my own diocese (Minneapolis/St. Paul), Archbishop Harry Flynn inaugurated a pastoral advisory council, staffed by laypersons, whose task is to listen to and consult with parishes and carry their advice back to the archbishop. A lay advisory board has been in place since the early 1990s to cooperate with the bishop in dealing with cases of clerical abuse. Archbishop Flynn met with the theological faculties of the University of St. Thomas and the College of St. Catherine several times to discuss the implementation of the mandatum (an acknowledgment by a bishop that a Catholic theologian is teaching within the full communion of the Catholic Church). Because of his pastoral and participatory style of leadership, the church in Minneapolis and St. Paul is healthy and vigorous. There is not a great deal of alienation among Catholics, and donations are strong. In fact, the diocese recently completed a record-breaking fund drive.

By contrast, in Boston, Cardinal Bernard Law resisted the advice of his brother bishops in 1992 to install a lay review board to help handle

cases of priestly abuse. Cardinal Law insisted on handling these cases
on his own, and would not let anyone else tell him what to do in his
own diocese. The unfortunate results are well known, another failure
of command hierarchy.

Participatory styles of leadership are not faring well in the universal
Catholic Church. Power and decisions remain centered in the Vatican.
Two examples illustrate this. In 1992, the Celam IV conference of Latin
American bishops was controlled by Rome, so that a discussion of the
issue of clerical celibacy was not on the agenda and was not allowed.
(This at a time when the church in Latin America is desperately short
of priests and is losing thousands to evangelical Protestant groups, who
are flourishing because of their participatory structure.) John Paul II's
encyclical *Ordinatio Sacerdotalis*, which prohibited even the discussion
of the ordination of women by Catholics, is another example of a
document issued by command, with little participatory discussion.

However, the encyclical *Ut Unum Sint* has aroused hopes that the
papacy may be open to a more participatory style of leadership. There,
John Paul II affirms that the leadership of the papacy must always be
done in communion with the whole body of bishops (no. 95), and that
the exercise of the primacy is "open to a new situation" (no. 95). Let
us hope so. The problem is that this theology is far ahead of actual
practice. It will take decades to move the whole church in the direction
of participatory hierarchy. A good start would be to recover the ancient
practice of the election of bishops. Walter Kasper has proposed that
bishops be appointed by a "joint act of the relevant local church, the
fellow bishops in the district . . . and the universal church, i.e., the Pope
as the head of the College of Bishops."[19] The Curia would certainly
have to be reformed. Right now it outranks the bishops themselves, so
that a Curial member can overturn the request by bishops to revise
their own national lectionaries. National and international bishops'
synods need to have more than merely advisory authority. Other such
structural changes also need to be considered, including more effective
lay participation in decisions at the diocesan level.

Participatory hierarchy, however, is not just a matter of structure.
It is also a matter of style. Even within present structures, a bishop or
priest who is willing to listen, consult, and accept advice can be a very
effective pastor.

The move toward participatory structures and styles of leadership
is crucial for any progress in the ecumenical movement. Our interlocutors in ecumenical discussion, from Orthodox to mainline Protestants
to Evangelicals and Pentecostals, will respond more to what the Catholic

Church does than to what it says. *Ut Unum Sint* has elicited an encouraging response. But if the old monarchial structures and styles of leadership remain unchanged, its vision of ecumenical reunion will remain barren.

What might a participatory hierarchy in Rome look like? The pope's real mission of unity, I believe, is to facilitate (near) consensus among the bishops and to proclaim it, just as Peter does in Acts 1 and Acts 6. To be able to facilitate consensus, he must have real (and not merely honorific) authority, which should however be exercised in communion with the bishops. The loss of such papal authority by Orthodox and Protestants has resulted in the fragmentation of their churches. But this loss was occasioned by the perversion of the papacy into a command hierarchy. The recovery of the papacy as a vital force for unity in the church will depend on its recovery of a participatory mode of operation, in which the laity have real authority in the selection of bishops, and the laity, religious, and bishops have real authority in governing the church. The best expression of this is an ecumenical council. The exact balance of authority and power in such a participatory hierarchy, however, will have to be worked out through discussion, not only among Catholics, but also in concert with our ecumenical dialogue partners.

Participatory hierarchy, as described here, is not the same as a democratic church. In a democracy, authority is vested with the people. Democratic ecclesiologies typically result in congregational or representative churches with no bishops (e.g., the Presbyterian). The Catholic principle of the Spirit operating through the bishops, as the successors of the apostles, is not present in such churches. Thus, in a Catholic participatory hierarchy, authority is vested in the bishops and the pope, but also in the priests, the theological community, the religious, and the people. The Spirit acts simultaneously at many levels.

The current crisis in the church has been precipitated by its long drift into command modes of hierarchy. This has affected popes, bishops, and priests. Yet if the Spirit is given to the whole church (1 Cor 12), then we must believe that the Spirit speaks to the church through many members, not just through the pope or even the pope and the bishops. The parallel here is ancient Israel, to whom the Spirit spoke through many mediators, not just one. This is why the church needs a participatory form of hierarchy, subsidiarity, and conciliar models of discernment (like the ancient councils), in which all voices, including dissenting voices, are heard. There needs to be leadership and hierarchy, but also participation. For conciliarity requires the leadership of primacy if it is to be effective. But equally, primacy requires conciliarity.

# Notes

1. Joann Wolski Conn, "New Vitality: The Challenge from Feminist Theology," *America* (5 October 1991): 217.

2. John Dominic Crossan, *The Historical Jesus* (San Francisco: Harper, 1991), 101.

3. In this section, I can only offer a sketch of my views on this matter. For more detail, see Terence Nichols, *That All May Be One: Hierarchy and Participation in the Church* (Collegeville, Minn.: Liturgical Press, 1997).

4. Socrates Scholasticus, *The Ecclesiastical History*, in Nicene and Post-Nicene Fathers, Second Series, ed. Philip Schaff and Henry Wace (Grand Rapids, Mich.: Wm. B. Eerdmans, 1989), I:9, p. 14.

5. Hippolytus, *The Treatise on the Apostolic Tradition of St. Hippolytus of Rome*, ed. Gregory Dix, reissued with corrections, preface, and bibliography by Henry Chadwick (London: The Alban Press, 1992), 2–3.

6. Emphasis added. Latin text and English translation in Norman Tanner, ed., *Decrees of the Ecumenical Councils* (Washington, D.C.: Georgetown University Press, 1990), vol. 1, 108.

7. Klaus Schatz, *Papal Primacy: From Its Origins to the Present* (Collegeville, Minn.: Liturgical Press, 1996), 29–30.

8. Leo, *Sermo* 3, 4, in J. P. Migne, ed., *Patrologiae Latinae cursus completus* (Paris, 1881), vol. 54, p. 147A.

9. *Qui praefecturus est omnibus ab omnibus eligatur.* Leo, Epist. X, 4, in Migne, ed., *Patrologiae Latinae*, vol. 54, 628.

10. Gelasius, *Ep.* 10, c.5: *illam [sedem] de tota ecclesia iudicare, ipsam ad nullius commeare iudicium.* Cited in Walter Ullmann's *The Growth of Papal Government in the Middle Ages* (London: Methuen, 1955), 27, note 7.

11. Yves Congar, *L'Église de Saint Augustin à l'époque moderne* (Paris: Cerf, 1970), 103.

12. Ibid., 96.

13. Innocent III, *Sermo* 2, PL, 217:658, cited in Patrick Granfield, *The Limits of the Papacy* (New York: Crossroad Publishing Co., 1987), 32.

14. Aristeides Papadakis, *The Christian East and the Rise of the Papacy* (Crestwood, N.Y.: St. Vladimir's Seminary Press, 1994), 14–15.

15. Stephen Runciman, *The Eastern Schism* (Oxford: Clarendon, 1955), 168.

16. H. Denzinger and A. Schönmetzer, eds., *Enchiridion Symbolorum*, 36th ed. (Barcinone: Herder, 1965); hereafter *DS*; English translation in S. Ehler and J. B. Morrall, eds., *Church and State through the Centuries* (Westminster, Md.: Newman Press, 1954), 91–92.

17. See Philip Melancthon, *Treatise on the Power and Primacy of the Pope*, in *The Book of Concord* (Philadelphia: Fortress Press, 1959), 320–34.

18. See Hermann Pottmeyer, *Towards a Papacy in Communion* (New York: Crossroad Publishing Co., 1998); see also Nichols, *That All May Be One*, 226–36.

19. Walter Kasper, "The Church as Communio," *New Blackfriars* (May 1993): 242.

# SEVEN

## Feminist Theology and a Participatory Church

LISA SOWLE CAHILL

Although women are the mainstay of Catholic parish life, Catholic education, religious education in the home, and Catholic health care, women's channels of official authority in the church are now, as ever, few and far between.[1] If the current sex abuse crisis in the Catholic Church urges a call for greater lay participation, it is the participation of women in decision-making roles that, above all, must be enhanced. The exclusion of women from ecclesial authority was in the past based on theories of women's innate inferiority and necessary subordination to men, theories that validated long-standing and culturally pervasive sexist practices. Although today's teaching church recognizes such practices for what they are,[2] it still interprets men's and women's natures as "complementary." This can all too easily reinforce the expectation that women's sole sphere of decision making is domestic and even there comes under the authority of the male head of the household. To the contrary, if women do possess, as John Paul II believes or hopes, a special "genius" by which they "see persons with their hearts,"[3] and that "can ensure sensitivity for human beings in every circumstance,"[4] women's judgment is all the more necessary to guide the internal affairs of an organization ostensibly devoted to faith, compassion, harmony, and service—especially to the most vulnerable, including children.

The sex abuse crisis was not directly caused by the absence of women's voices in church governance; the resolution of the crisis will require that church members address many more immediate and glaring errors than the omission of women's viewpoints. First and foremost, the crisis reached mammoth proportions and caused irreversible scandal due to the dereliction of duty by "shepherds" who can be, should be, and are being called to account well within the structures of responsibility that already exist, focused even as they are around male leadership. Nonetheless, many observers have noted that the isolation of this leadership from women's influence—and, to an extent, from the influence of men who are married to women, and who together with women are parents—has contributed to an ecclesial decision-making environment likely to conceal abuse and even to create it.

A veteran pastor and seminary educator who embarked upon his own priestly training in 1965 (at the age of fourteen) laments: "Before I was 19, I learned that when it came to sexual matters, the clerical culture winked." As the explanation for this, he cites a "connecting tissue" of "affective bonds" among priests and priests-to-be, who "lived, worked, prayed and played together," developing a mutual need for loyalty, understanding, compassion, and protection. Even today, he admits: "Many of us do not have the self-awareness, understanding, articulation and sometimes the courage to face straightforwardly the complex questions that surround male sexuality, adult human growth and development, or even the spiritual disciplines required for deepening growth in chastity."[5] Moreover, "a very few among those who repress their sexuality are positively dangerous to themselves, others and the church." Among other things, this spokesman recommends that Catholics "include more women and men in church governance."[6]

Following this line of thought further, Notre Dame theology department chair John Cavadini notes that church structures have managed to "distance and muffle even the pleas of parents who are concerned about grave danger to their children. No one can hear—that is the essence of the scandal." Cavadini suggests the following:

> Employ the gifts of the laity in all situations not essentially pertinent to the functions of the presbyterate or episcopacy. Why couldn't the president of a pontifical council, say of justice and peace, be a layman or laywoman? What about the staff of these councils. . . . Even only a few such highly visible appointments of laypeople can be immensely symbolic, something not to be underestimated in a sacramental church. Note that the issue is not simply lay involvement in the church, but upward visibility and access.[7]

This is even more true of women's involvement than of men's. Peter Steinfels has proposed that "lay Catholics, especially women" be appointed by the bishops as members of a panel to address the crisis, help provide leadership, and demand collective action for change.[8]

## Contributions of Christian Feminist Theology

What can feminist theology bring to the current crisis? How does it discern the need for, legitimate symbolically, and effect practically, greater levels of participation by women in church leadership roles? Feminist theology arises out of the experience of women's suffering, critically evaluated in light of Christian faith. Feminist theology reappropriates and reinterprets biblical narratives, and the theologies of Christ, Trinity, church, and sacraments. It thus brings the equality of men and women under the aegis of Jesus' preaching of unity in the inclusive reign of God, and St. Paul's call to Christians to become a new family as brothers and sisters in Christ. Feminist theology identifies forgotten images and roles of women in scripture and tradition, roots out patriarchal distortions, and proposes renewed forms of community and new roles for women within the church.

## Defining Feminist Theology

The narratives recorded in scripture, the doctrines of the church, and the ecclesial structures have all been constructed almost exclusively by men, with a primarily male audience in view. In this, the church reflects the assumptions and practices of age-old and worldwide cultures and of all the major religions. According to today's foremost Catholic feminist theologian, Elizabeth Johnson:

> In our day we are witnessing the phenomenon that all over the world the "other half" of the human race, women, are waking up to their own dignity and finding their own voice. One result has been that within the community of disciples, faith is now being reflected upon explicitly from the perspective and experience of women. This type of theology is commonly called feminist theology, or theology based upon the conviction that women share equally with men in the dignity of being human.[9]

Johnson's guiding vision for feminist theology is "a new human community based on the values of mutuality and reciprocity," a community structured neither by domination and subordination nor by sameness, but by the participation of all "according to their gifts, without preconceived stereotyping."[10] At the heart of the feminist Christian vision is neither complaint nor criticism, but hope—hope that change is possible and that justice and love can be realized more completely in society and in the church.[11]

## Feminist Theology and Ecclesiology

Feminist theology follows both the New Testament and the Second Vatican Council in seeing the church as the People of God, living under God's "kingdom" or "reign," but still in pilgrimage toward the fulfillment of its identity.[12] Biblical scholar Raymond Brown points out that the diversity of models of church in the New Testament itself underwrites the multiplicity and complementarity of a number of models for the church today. To accentuate or reinforce different aspects of the church may be appropriate for different eras or situations and their distinctive needs. Brown notes that the early churches too confronted various historical circumstances that influenced their ecclesiologies. For example, the epistles written by Paul and those attributed to him by later followers (the so-called "pastoral epistles," 1 and 2 Timothy and Titus) had to respond to very different views current among Christians about their future relation to the Jews. While Paul himself envisioned that Jews and Gentiles would ultimately be united in one community, the heir of Israel (Rom 11:11–26), later leaders and their communities were troubled by sharpening differences between traditional Jews and Jewish and Gentile followers of Christ. The pastoral epistles thus exhibit a stress on united, authoritative teaching in order to stave off those who wanted to universalize for all Christians Jewish practices like circumcision.[13]

In the pastorals, presbyter-bishops have strong authority over sound doctrine and practice (Titus 1:2–2:1; 1 Tim 4:1–11, 5:17).[14] The author of the pastorals wants to preserve a heritage against "radical ideas and teachers," by enforcing "safe institutional virtues" and a "sharp distinction between those who teach and those who are taught."[15] There is a danger, however, in institutional control that becomes the way of life for the church,[16] for then "those who ask probing questions about the standard doctrine will be presented as the opponents of God's truth." Such a situation would hardly be true to the realities of "ordinary church life."[17] Brown himself concludes that "at one time or other every Christian is or should be part of the teaching church and everyone should be part of the learning church."[18]

Brown finds a corrective model in the Gospel of John, which, interestingly, was written around the same time as the pastoral epistles, but for a different community. In John's community, there had been a definitive split between the Jews who worship in the temple, and converts to Christianity who have been driven out because of their unorthodox views compared to traditional Jewish norms.[19] John emphasizes unity, reciprocity, mutual support, and equality within the beloved community of Jesus' disciples. While the pastorals view women as likely to be misled and unable to teach (2 Tim 3:6–7), John's Gospel's attitude is "remarkably different," portraying "major male and female believers" with "no difference of intelligence, vividness, or response." Taking over the role given to Peter in Matthew's Gospel (Mt 16:16–17), Martha's confession of faith is exemplary: "You are the Christ, the Son of God" (Jn 11:27). An entire village comes to believe in Jesus through the word of the Samaritan woman (Jn 4:39), and in John's Gospel, not Peter but Mary Magdalene is the first to see the risen Jesus, and the first to give the Easter proclamation, "I have seen the Lord" (Jn 20:14).[20]

In the Johannine community, real status comes from the love of Jesus; no special offices are distinguished as more authoritative.[21] Although Brown regards Johannine ecclesiology as "the most attractive and exciting in the New Testament," he acknowledges that it is "also one of the least stable."[22] Just as the Johannine community eventually had to confront the fact that some of those claiming to follow Jesus were distorting his message (the gnostics), so the church must incorporate some lines of structure and control over what can be regarded as genuinely Christian. As Brown displays, however, the challenge now as then is rightly to balance both structured authority and the charismatic, critical impulse that identifies even some parts of "tradition" as distortions of genuine Christianity.

As Christianity spread and became more global in its reach, and especially after the reign of the emperor Constantine (fourth century), when Christianity became an officially accepted religion within the Roman empire, the institution of the church became increasingly organized according to a formal structure. The hierarchical structure even came to be seen as that dimension of the church that above all participates in and communicates to believers the presence of the divine on earth. Leadership became more centralized in Rome, and understood on an imperial model.[23] The local churches, especially the laity (and among the laity, women), were viewed as the passive recipients of church teaching.

With Vatican II, the concept of church as communion, structured according to the principle of collegiality, comes into the foreground.[24] The practical meaning of collegiality continues to be contested. According to Avery Dulles, the model of the church as a "community of disciples" has "the advantages of being closer to our experience and of suggesting directions for appropriate renewal."[25] Dulles mentions the potential of this concept to constitute the church as a "contrast society." A feminist theologian, following Brown, might more readily find a model of inclusive participation and equality in the church.

A major topic of debate in contemporary ecclesiology (and in essays in this volume) is the priority among and the relationship between the local churches and the universal church. Michael Fahey points out that even for St. Paul, the earliest author in the New Testament, and the one who writes most explicitly and consistently to and about particular Christian communities, there is still an assumption that the church (in the singular) enjoys a reality that transcends local embodiments.[26] Most theologians see the local church and the universal church as both necessary and complementary.[27]

Even though a "certain priority" is given to the local church in thinking after the Second Vatican Council, the universal aspect of the Catholic Church is kept in balance. "As a mystery it is realized in every local community; as institutionally organized it becomes a communion of communities, presided over in charity by the local Church of Rome and its bishop, the servant of the servants of God."[28] If charity and servanthood, not rigidity and imperial authority, should characterize the church even in its institutional, universal, and formal aspects, then this opens the door to inclusive participation of laypeople, including women, all up and down the spectrum of even those structures and offices that are arranged in appropriate hierarchies of responsibility.

The Council's ecclesiology includes the laity as sharing in the *sensus fidei*, the "sense of the faith" that is "found in Christians that allows them to recognize what is authentic or unauthentic as well as what is central or what peripheral to the Christian faith (*Lumen Gentium* [*LG* 12])."[29] As Michael Fahey infers, the roles of the faithful thus include "co-responsibility" or "shared decision-making." Fahey's caveat—"This may ring hollow in some parts of the church where the faithful, if called upon at all to speak, are not always heard, or where the lay faithful are never asked to participate in crucial decisions, such as the naming of a local bishop"—has the tragic ring of truth after the year 2002.[30]

From the standpoint of feminist theology and ecclesiology, the patriarchal and one-sidedly hierarchical structures of the church are still indeed a glaring problem, especially for women and their meaningful participation and authority. Feminist ecclesiology, like other liberationist critiques of the church, tends to begin its constructive project with reflection upon Christian community as experienced in small grassroots or "base" communities where women's voices are strong and valued.

Women in small, intentional communities ponder their experience in the light of scripture and imagine a transformation of the church.[31] Mary Hines declares: "A massive transformation of the church's structures is needed to free them from the patriarchal, hierarchical, and clerical assumptions that prevent the church from becoming a prophetic community of equal disciples committed to the task of liberation for all people."[32] According to Hines, the main issue is not adherence to the form of traditional structures, but which structures will best serve the mission of the church today. Hines builds on three models of the church proposed by feminist theologians: discipleship of equals, democracy, and "world-church."[33] Briefly, these models indicate a church that follows Jesus' example of inclusive community, and that of the early church; that grounds authority in consent and respect, and that takes participatory decision making for granted; and that sees in the globalization of the church a sign that its unity must respect and build upon many local cultures.

Even for feminist ecclesiology, community and hierarchy are counterparts. For example, feminists appreciate the Catholic "voice" on social issues that is possible because of the popes and national bishops' conferences. The tradition of Catholic social encyclicals can be mentioned, along with specific issues like economic development, unrestrained global capitalism, human rights, violence against women, and the war in Iraq. In fact, critics of church handling of recent abuse cases typically think that the bishops and other institutional representatives should have acted more energetically and authoritatively to restrain miscreant priests. However, for feminist theology, hierarchical teaching needs to remain in a dialectical relation to communion and participation, much as different New Testament models of church interact dialectically within the New Testament canon. The need at the present time is to redress the balance in favor of reciprocity and participation. Also, the norm of participation does not apply only to local communities, but to representation of the laity (women and men) within and along the structures that enable the church's universality.

It would be naïve to assume, however, that all Catholic women, or even all feminist theologians, intend the same thing by an inclusive ecclesial communion, or want women's participation to look the same. Two issues on which women disagree are women's ordination to the priesthood, and whether women's nature is properly to be described as "complementary" to that of men. (Both of these issues will be discussed further below.) Catholic women may see the church as relating to the changing roles of women in society (at least U.S. society) in different ideal ways. A symposium designed to bring together more traditional and more reformist Catholic women to discuss "the church women want" in the twenty-first century exposed some of these differences.[34] Not all women had an equal interest in changing the more or less standard forms of authority in the Catholic Church as we know it (ranking pope, bishops, [male] clergy, and laity in that order). But all seemed to advocate and to exemplify by their very presence a greater voice for women.

Miriam Therese Winter describes most women as staying within the church in order to change it, and celebrates, for instance, nontraditional liturgical rituals crafted by women to express their distinctive experience and its spirituality.[35] On the other hand, Susan Muto looks to historical figures like Teresa of Avila and Catherine of Siena to illustrate the riches of the traditions handed down, and urges more respect for Catholic women making their contributions, and sometimes challenging authority, through the accustomed (and too often neglected) roles of religious vocation and the single life.[36] Of these two speakers, the symposium organizers wrote that their "embodiment of dialogue, mutual respect, humor, and willingness to speak their truth and to listen to one another across significant differences images what most participants wanted."[37] The participatory church that most Catholic women want would expand the role and authority of women, while allowing nondivisively for some differences in theological and liturgical standpoints among all members of the laity.

## Feminist Theology and Trinity

Although the shape of the church is integrally related to all the dimensions of faith and theology, there has been a recent turn in feminist theology to the doctrine of the Trinity to ground and enable more reciprocal and equal relationships in an ecclesial *communio*. Historically, Trinitarian doctrine emerged as an attempt to answer questions about the identity of Jesus Christ, specifically an array of fourth-century proposals that assigned him a lesser status (as "begotten") than the unoriginate God and Creator of all.[38] The solution of the Council of Nicaea (351) was to insist that the Father and Son are equal and "the same" in substance or essence, in a formulation (*homoousion*) explicitly extended to include the Holy Spirit by the Council of Constantinople (381). The Trinity is seen by some feminist theologians as a doctrine that affirms equality over subordination as a model for human relations and community as well.

Catherine LaCugna has done groundbreaking work in Trinitarian theology,[39] arguing that theories about God's interior self-relations (the "immanent" Trinity) should never be detached from the experience and theology of salvation (the work of the "economic" Trinity) and of the Christian life.[40] The Christian life shares in the life of the Trinity. "Christians believe that God bestows the fullness of divine life in the person of Jesus Christ, and that through the person of Christ and the action of the Holy Spirit, we are made intimate partners of the living God (*theosis*, divinization)."[41] Salvation is possible precisely because God is self-communicating love, a relationship that God chooses to express externally, to us, as well as internally, in God's own eternal relationality.[42] The Greek Cappadocian fathers (Basil, Gregory of Nyssa, and Gregory of Nazianzus) brilliantly drew out the insight that the unity and life of God are located in the communion among equal persons, not in the superiority or hierarchy of one person over another.[43]

This is the crucial point for feminist Trinitarian theology; it becomes the basis of a Trinitarian approach to human relations in the church as a faith community called to be the Body of Christ united in the Spirit. "Humanity is created in the image of God, and God exists as the communion of love, as a reciprocal exchange of love and persons in which humanity has graciously been included as a partner."[44] In the divine image, human and ecclesial community is a communion of persons-in-relation whose genuine diversity or difference is essential and not inimical to their equality.[45] The point of Nicaea (in reply to the subordinationist Arian heresy) was that, though different, the Son is not subordinate to the Father *in any sense*.[46] Whether this point can be better respected today by expanding metaphors for the divine persons beyond the "Father–Son" terminology will be addressed in the next section, on feminist theology, gender, and Christology. In any event, Trinitarian theology helps ground the doctrine of the church in a model of divine life that is highly encouraging to the full participation of women.

## Feminist Theology and Christology

The person and teaching of Jesus Christ, especially in their biblical presentation, have been perhaps the major focus of feminist reforming theology. One of Christian feminism's key inspirations is the recovery of biblical texts that portray Jesus interacting with women, calling women to be his disciples, appearing as risen first to women, and sending a woman (Mary Magdalene) to announce the gospel to the other disciples (John 20:11–18).[47] On the other hand, the maleness of Jesus, and the postresurrection proclamation of Jesus Christ as the Son of God, have been used historically, doctrinally, and theologically to make women second-class citizens in the Catholic Church and to exclude them from many roles reserved, either by official norms or by widespread practice, for men.

Elizabeth Johnson puts the problem very directly:

> I do not think one can overestimate the seriousness of the charge brought against Christology, that of all the doctrines of the church it is the one most used to oppress women. . . . The fundamental problem lies in androcentric interpretations of the maleness of the human Jesus, which lift his sex to the level of ontological necessity, and the incorporation of Jesus as a male so interpreted into a divine Father-Son relationship, which totally excludes women from the most intimate of divine exchanges.[48]

The problem of Christology thus brings us to the heart of the problem of exclusion of women from full participation in the Catholic Church, and the reason why women suffer this exclusion more radically than do lay men. Although the biblical depictions of Jesus in the Gospels in no way require the minimization or subordination of women's role in the church—far from it—the historical interpretations of Jesus that have formed official Catholic views of women participate in the sexism of centuries of cultural patriarchy. The doctrine of the Trinity has from ages past validated a view of the divine nature in whose image humans are made as a communion in which subordination is impossible; New Testament models of church affirm equal participation to be at least as crucial to Christian community as hierarchical authority; and neither Nicaea's Trinitarian affirmation of the relational life of God nor New Testament ecclesiology offers definitive arguments for excluding women from full communion and participation as disciples. Nevertheless, the figure of a male Jesus as the savior and model for discipleship has *functioned* or been *used* to put women in a subordinate position in the church.

Johnson sees the maleness of Christ as having an "effective history" (not an intrinsic meaning) that perpetrates three distortions. First, when the man Jesus is confessed as the Christ and the revelation of God, his maleness is mistakenly assumed to be an essential characteristic of divine being itself, a distortion that is exacerbated by the exclusive use of male metaphors for God (Father and Son). Second, male human beings are then assumed to resemble God and Christ more than women do, with the result that men alone are seen as able fully to represent Christ. Women cannot be public representatives, on behalf of the church, of Christ's role in and for the church. Third, the maleness of Christ jeopardizes women's salvation, since, as the early church taught, whatever of humanity that is not assumed in the incarnation cannot be redeemed.

What are the essentials of the church's proclamation of Jesus as savior and Christ, and how are these represented in Christological doctrines? As early as the New Testament, there are different answers to the questions "Who is Jesus?" and "What does it mean to confess Jesus as the Christ?" Perhaps most primitively, Jesus is represented as the awaited eschatological prophet, like Moses, promised to Israel by God. Jesus is also represented as Son of man and coming Lord who will judge the world. He is represented as a "divine man," in whom God works, e.g., by miracles and exorcisms. And he is presented as the emissary of divine wisdom or of wisdom incarnate,[49] a portrayal that has been especially important in feminist theology. Common to all of these is the faith that God's salvation is decisively present in Jesus.

The historical Jesus, to whom this faith is inextricably linked, is available to us through the interpretive lens of post-Easter portrayals. Nevertheless, it is possible to describe some key aspects of Jesus' life, as attested by all four Gospel authors. The center of Jesus' preaching is the kingdom or reign of God (Mark 1:15), which is expected to arrive in the near future, but is already present among those who believe the words of Jesus and put them into action. In Jesus, his first followers experienced the inbreaking of God's reign. The preaching of the kingdom during Jesus' life is confirmed in its relevance for salvation by Jesus' death on a cross and his resurrection. The meaning of the crucifixion, its relation to Jesus' life, its inevitability, and Jesus' own expectation of it, are complicated biblical and theological issues. Likewise, the nature and meaning of the raising of Jesus from the dead is presented in a variety of ways biblically (e.g., in appearance accounts such as 1 Cor 15, and in the empty tomb stories with which the Gospels conclude) and theologically.

While the best characterization and explanation of the saving effect of the death and resurrection of Jesus have always been matters of dispute, Christians in the main agree that the crucifixion and resurrection are crucial to salvation in Christ, and that these events are in continuity with the historical life of Jesus. Feminist and other liberation theologies represent a developing strand of thought in which God, through the self-sacrificial death of Jesus, is experienced to be in solidarity with human suffering, and to be present to us in the midst of suffering, even while decisively redeeming humans from suffering and death. The resurrection is both the vindication of Jesus and the inauguration of a decisively new mode of existence in which believers begin already to share. The cross and resurrection, therefore, are for feminist theologians the basis on which meaning is attributed to human life despite even radical human suffering, and the basis on which hope for a change in the human condition is established.[50]

From the historical memory of Jesus filtered through the early post-resurrection churches, it is obviously easier to see that Jesus is human than that he is God. Therefore, the first challenge for Christian theology and doctrine in the first few centuries of Christianity was to hold the line against identifications of Christ that saw him as a creature or as in any way less than fully divine. Nicaea affirmed the definitive Christian experience that, in encountering Jesus, one encounters "the reality of the one true God."[51] Controversies continued, however, and the tendency, after Nicaea, to deny that Jesus is fully human, or human only in appearance, was refuted, after much politicking, at the Council of Chalcedon (451). Like Nicaea, Chalcedon captured Christian experience with the help of Greek philosophical terminology. Chalcedon's formulation is that Jesus is one person with two natures; he is both completely human and completely divine (the hypostatic union).

It is not through his maleness that Jesus saves, but through his humanity, which is united fully with his divinity. This is the legacy of Nicaea and Chalcedon. Of necessity, then, Jesus shares in the humanity of women as fully as he shares in the humanity of men; in Jesus, God stands with the suffering of women as fully as with that of men; and Jesus inaugurates the kingdom and resurrection life as completely in the faith and life of women as he does in those of men. Likewise, women are included in the newness of Christian community as richly as are men. It is not Jesus' maleness that is represented most essentially by the presider of the central ritual of that community, the eucharist, but Jesus' humanity, shared as deeply by women as by men.

One creative angle of feminist reinterpretation of Jesus as the Christ turns on the image of divine wisdom found especially in the biblical books of Proverbs (1, 8, 9) and the Wisdom of Solomon, and associated with Jesus in one strand of developing New Testament Christology.[52] The appeal of this image for feminists is that, in the Old Testament or Hebrew Bible, it functions as a female personification of God, of an emissary of God, or of the immanent activity of God in human life. Wisdom

> is an aura of the might of God
>
> and a pure effusion of the glory of the Almighty;
>
> . . . she is the refulgence of eternal light,
>
> the spotless mirror of the power of God,
>
> the image of his goodness.
>
> And she, who is one, can do all things, and renews everything
>     while herself perduring. . . . (Wisdom 7:25–27)

So at a first level, the importance of the figure of Wisdom is that it offers a biblical example of a female metaphor for God. This encourages the consideration of female imagery for the Holy Spirit and for Jesus Christ also. Feminist theologians have reminded us that although in the Hebrew Bible the spirit of God appears more as an impersonal force or power, there are some connections between the divine spirit and female imagery, especially the symbolism of a bird caring for its young (Ex 19:4, Dt 32:11–12). In Jewish tradition after the close of the biblical canon, the Spirit of God was imaged with the female symbol of the *shekkinah*. In the New Testament, Spirit designates the power of God present in Jesus' ministry (Lk 4:18), and is likened to a woman giving birth (Jn 3:5–6). The Spirit is also the Spirit of Christ, present in the church, enabling disciples to share in the love of God (Rom 5:5; Acts 1:8).[53]

Perhaps most importantly for the concrete prospect of women's participation in the Catholic Church, the female image of Wisdom is associated with Jesus in the New Testament. Even though Jesus is a man, his significance for salvation can be represented by a female figure. The most explicit identification between Jesus and Wisdom is made early on by Paul: "we preach Christ crucified, a stumbling block to the Jews and folly to the Gentiles, but to those who are called, both Jews and Greeks, Christ the power of God and the wisdom of God" (1 Cor 1:22–24).[54] Connections between Jesus and the roles of and imagery for Wisdom—as found, for instance, in the Gospels of Matthew (11:28–30, 23:37–39) and John (1; cf. 11:25–27)—can correct an unbalanced view of Jesus' maleness. Wisdom can also be named as "Sophia," the Greek word for wisdom, and is so called by feminist theologians.

Viewing Jesus Christ as "the human being Sophia became," Elizabeth Johnson believes that biblical proclamations of the significance of Christ exhibit a fluidity in use of male and female images that "breaks the stranglehold of androcentric thinking that circles around the maleness of Christ."[55] Jesus' humanity (not his maleness as such) is united with his divinity, and offered in sacrifice on the cross. The truth that women and men are equally close to the figure of Christ is brought home when the Bible identifies Christ with a feminine figure. Wisdom Christology reflects the fact that the mystery of God, the incarnation, and the redemption of humans by Jesus Christ can be conveyed by the use of female as well as male symbols, for women and men participate equally in these realities.

At a fundamental level, of course, such insights recommend the full participation of women in the church. They also lead naturally to the question whether women should and must be defined without exception as members of the "laity," or whether women's participation could also take place through ordained ministry, even priesthood.[56] A collection of essays on *lay* participation is not the most appropriate place to engage in a lengthy discussion of priesthood. While it is fair to say that most Catholic feminist theologians do not view gender as an irreversible barrier to ordination, it is also true that there are many Catholic women who are either not in favor of women's ordination,[57] do not see ordination as a central agenda item in the advancement of women,[58] or would even view women's ordination to the priesthood as we know it as a betrayal of the Christian feminist goal of a truly participatory church for everyone.[59] The expansion of roles for lay women in the church will be addressed in the next section.

## Feminist Theology, Gender, and Women's Roles

The idea that biological sex differences imply different and complementary psychological characteristics and separate social and ecclesial roles for men and women is fundamental in defining the avenues of participation that are open to women in the church today. In a work on sacramental theology, Susan Ross observes that the way Catholics define and celebrate all seven sacraments is affected by assumptions about gender difference and its meaning. Although the eucharist is meant to be a sacrament of unity, only men can represent the self-offering of Christ; although baptism is supposed to unite all in one community, despite differences of sex, class, and ethnicity (Gal 3:28), gender still separates us as Christians into different categories. The sacrament of holy orders is most evidently affected by the fact that "half the human race is deemed incapable of representing God incarnate," and this applies as well to the sacraments of reconciliation and anointing, which only priests can mediate. Marriage too is understood according to a natural sexual complementarity that results in different roles in marriage and family for men and women.[60]

In his Apostolic Letter *On the Dignity and Vocation of Women*,[61] Pope John Paul II recognizes the striking interactions of Jesus with women in the Gospels, including his resurrection appearance first of all to women, and his sending of Mary Magdalene to announce the gospel, for which she has been called rightly "apostle to the apostles." Intending to praise women, the pope attributes to the women disciples "a special *sensitivity which is characteristic* of their *femininity*."[62] Although the pope believes that men and women are equal in "dignity,"[63] he also holds that their personalities are intrinsically different. There is an innate maternal aspect of women's make-up that can be expressed either in marriage and biological motherhood, or in virginity as spouse of Christ. Even for those who are not literally mothers, the special vocation of women is to love and care for others; love and sensitivity constitute a special "genius" that is the mark and fulfillment of women's feminine identity.[64]

The pope does not believe that women should be excluded from any specific social vocations, even though he believes motherhood is our highest calling. He has also condemned sexism and violence and discrimination against women, and praised women's liberation.[65] However, he still believes that the creation of humans in two sexes, as described in Genesis, means that women and men have natures that are not only different but complementary. "Womanhood and manhood are complementary not only from the physical and psychological points of view, but also from the ontological. It is only through the duality of the 'masculine' and the 'feminine' that the 'human' finds full realization."[66] Because maternal and domestic roles are seen as most important for women, there is a pervasive bias in official Catholic teaching and practice against the leadership and authority of women in other roles, both inside and outside the church.

Some Catholic women do accept gender complementarity as not necessarily incompatible with equality. Psychosexual difference is seen to be both intrinsic and basic to personal identity, and a characteristic that enables the relationship and communion that make human beings the image of the Trinity.[67] Other women, reacting no doubt to the exclusionary way gender difference has been used to allot women roles that in fact are not equal, insist that humanity is first, and sexual differentiation second, in creating identity. Many so-called innate gender differences have really arisen in response to social conditions in which certain things were required of women, and in which women needed to adapt and survive.[68] Still others hold that while there may be some innate differences between women and men, they are not polar and complementary, nor can they be used to assign men and women clearly different personalities and roles. The church's teaching that men and women are fully created in the image of God and fully redeemed in Christ should be reinvigorated to preclude any idea either that women more than men can imitate Christ's loving service, or that men and not women can be "christomorphic" in ecclesial and sacramental functions.[69]

Leaving aside the question of women's priestly ordination, then, how about women's equal treatment in other areas of church life? Do the ramifications of the complementarity theory result in a sexist organization of church life, of liturgy, of the Catholic symbol system, and of women's experience of being Catholic? No one would deny that women are excluded from priesthood, and that priesthood is at least a tacit precondition for most roles of higher leadership in the church. One only has to envision the Roman curia, the Congregation for the Doctrine of the Faith, a meeting of the national bishops' conference, or a conclave gathered to elect a new pope, to get the picture—in which all the actors are male. While Catholic women who grew up before the Second Vatican Council may have accepted more or less without question the rarity or at least invisibility of women's ecclesial leadership, younger women take for granted the goals of equal education and equal vocational opportunity. They often notice a gap between the roles open to women in their society and those in the church, as well as between the images of women that are or are not presented in either sphere.

A young theologian who has worked for the National Conference of Catholic Bishops, is active in the pro-life movement, and received her doctoral degree from Boston College in 2001 remarks that she questioned as a child "why I referred to myself as a man when professing my faith," even though she had the opportunity "to present the gifts at the altar, to serve at the altar and to proclaim the Word to the community." After entering theological studies, she became "increasingly aware of the way in which the institutional church can be an alienating force in a woman's relationship with God and in a woman's service of God's people." She recalls a conversation with a young man who had confronted a presider after Mass, arguing that the Nicene creed should not be used without the words "men" or "man." The questioner simply assumed on the basis of the English usage to which he was accustomed that the original Latin was *vir* ("man"), instead of *homo* ("human"). The phrase in question, *homo factus est*, when used of Christ, raises, as the young woman put it, "soteriological questions," if translated in a way that focuses on Christ's maleness.[70]

Similarly, an undergraduate biology major tells a poignant story:

When I think about the main messages of the bible, particularly the New Testament, what comes into my mind are the ideas of compassion, forgiveness, and love exemplified by Jesus. As a young girl attending church with my family I loved listening to the readings each week. I wanted to help the poor and the sick and do all of the things that were part of being a compassionate person. Perhaps this is why by the time I was in seventh grade I became a lector at my parish's youth mass, an activity I continued throughout high school, concluding with my final reading the Sunday I left home to attend Boston College.

Each year however there was always something that bothered me about Paul's letter to the Ephesians. "Wives should be subordinate to their husbands as to the Lord" (Eph 5:22). "Husbands, love your wives, even as Christ loved the church . . ." (Eph 5:25). Every time I heard these words read or read them myself they bothered me. After all it seemed rather unfair that as a woman I should subordinate myself to my husband when all he would have to do was love me in return. Before I knew anything at all about feminist theology and interpretation of the canonized bible I felt strangled by these words and others like them that can be found throughout the New Testament. For me as a woman of faith it is hard to disbelieve the bible, but it is harder to accept the words condemning me to a quiet and subordinate existence cleaning the home and caring for children. My solution until now was to ignore these passages. Most Sundays I would go to church and enjoy the readings and homilies and when these passages were read I would refuse to think about them.[71]

Both of these young Catholic women have taken advantage of opportunities for women in the church that were nonexistent before Vatican II. Nonetheless, they are aware of current attitudes toward women that are, consciously or unconsciously, sexist. Moreover, they experience these attitudes as having an impact on the way they themselves will be treated as Catholics, and even on their relationship to God and on their vocation to follow the message and example of Jesus. The view of women that the Catholic Church presents is out of alignment with their hopes for their own futures and for their contributions to the faith community to which they are strongly committed.

Having decided that their attempts to write a pastoral letter "on women" were doomed to failure and perhaps misguided in the first place, and after the pope had published *Ordinatio Sacerdotalis* (barring women from the priesthood), the United States bishops in 1994 wrote a "pastoral reflection" on issues related to women's church participation.[72] In this document, they express the aim of welcoming and respecting "the gifts and competencies of all persons," and assert that "[w]omen are essential in ministry both within the church and to the world."[73] They recognize and enumerate many ways in which women are already involved in parishes, in education, in social justice programs, and in advocacy for women's issues. They even cite a study estimating that 85 percent of nonordained ministerial positions in parishes are now held by women.[74]

Nonetheless, the bishops admit that an unresolved "important issue for women is how to have a voice in the governance of the church to which they belong and which they serve with love and generosity." Consultation is one way the bishops name, but the obvious shortcoming here is that the means, degree, and use of consultation are still in the hands of the bishops. Another, more innovative and challenging way is "through cooperation in the exercise of authority."[75] The bishops cite in favor of this route Canon 129 of the 1983 Code of Canon Law. This canon provides that "those who have received sacred orders are capable of the power of governance, which exists in the church by divine institution." It continues: "[L]ay members of the Christian faithful can cooperate in the exercise of this power in accord with the norm of law."[76] The bishops suggest that not all forms of church governance that are now restricted to priests need to be assigned exclusively to priests in the future. There may be no real reason, as far as even present church law is concerned, that women cannot be involved in the higher administration of local dioceses, or even of the Vatican and its offices. Some argue that changes in church law, for example, to permit the ordination of women as deacons, would more accurately reflect the practices of an earlier church.[77] An entrenched bias against such developments is another matter. Rightly the bishops cite the continuing use of exclusive language in catechetical, pastoral, and liturgical materials as a source of women's pain and as a contributing factor to the persistence of sexism.[78]

The recent sex abuse crisis that has devastated the U.S. Catholic Church offers an unhappy occasion to realize that few if any of the bishops' recommendations have been put into practice or even seriously explored by the church hierarchy ten years later. Indeed, analysts such as Peter Steinfels and John Cavadini are in the position of repeating the very same themes and exhortations. Although this state of affairs may inspire cynicism or even despair in some, feminist theology clings to the hope that Wisdom's Spirit, the Spirit of God, can still enliven the Catholic Church. Elizabeth Johnson's reclaiming of the theology of the Holy Spirit, who makes Christ present in the church, provides a keynote for the challenges ahead: "Brokenness and sin are everywhere. . . . Spirit-Sophia is the source of transforming energy among all creatures. She initiates novelty, instigates change, transforms what is dead into new stretches of life."[79]

## Notes

1. See John J. Fialka, *Sisters: Catholic Nuns and the Making of America* (New York: St. Martin's Press, 2003); Paul Hoffman, *The Vatican's Women: Female Influence at the Holy See* (New York: St. Martin's Press, 2003); and the review of the latter by Margaret O'Brien Steinfels, "The Purple Ceiling," *New York Times Book Review*, 16 February 2002, 16.

2. See especially John Paul II, "Letter to Women," prepared in anticipation of the United Nations World Conference on Women in Beijing, 1995 (*Origins* 25, no. 9 [1995]: nos. 3–6, pp. 139–41).

3. Ibid., no. 12, p. 143.

4. John Paul II, *On the Dignity and Vocation of Women* (*Mulieris Dignitatem*) (Washington, D.C.: United States Catholic Conference, 1988), no. 30, p. 112.

5. Michael L. Papesh, "Farewell to 'the Club': On the Demise of Clerical Culture," *America*, 13 May 2002, 8–9.

6. Ibid., 11.

7. John C. Cavadini, "After the Sex-Abuse Scandal: What Lies Ahead?" *Commonweal*, 13 September 2002, 22.

8. Peter Steinfels, "The Church's Sex-Abuse Crisis: What's Old, What's New, What's Needed—and Why," *Commonweal*, 19 April 2002, 19.

9. Elizabeth A. Johnson, *Consider Jesus: Waves of Renewal in Christology* (New York: Crossroad, 1990), 97.

10. Ibid., 99.

11. Margaret A. Farley, "Feminist Theology and Ethics: The Contributions of Elizabeth A. Johnson," in Phyllis Zagano and Terrence W. Tilley, eds., *Things New and Old: Essays on the Theology of Elizabeth A. Johnson* (New York: Crossroad, 1999), 18.

12. For much more extensive and nuanced general discussions of ecclesiology than will be possible here, see Michael A. Fahey, "Church," in Francis Schüssler Fiorenza and John P. Galvin, eds., *Systematic Theology: Roman Catholic Perspectives, Volume II* (Minneapolis: Augsburg Fortress, 1991), 3–74; and Edmund Hill, O.P., "Church," in *The New Dictionary of Theology*, ed. Joseph A. Komonchak, Mary Collins, and Dermot A. Lane (Wilmington, Del.: Michael Glazier, 1987), 185–201.

13. Raymond E. Brown, S.S., *The Churches the Apostles Left Behind* (New York: Paulist Press, 1984), 21.

14. Ibid., 34.

15. Ibid., 37.

16. Ibid., 39.

17. Ibid., 43.

18. Ibid., 45.

19. Ibid., 22.

20. Ibid., 94–95.

21. Ibid., 99.

22. Ibid., 123.

23. Hill, "Church," 199.

24. See *Lumen Gentium* 22, 26, for instance.

25. Avery Dulles, S.J., *Models of the Church*, expanded edition (New York and London: Doubleday, 1987), 222.

26. Fahey, "Church," 21. Fahey here draws on Raymond Brown.

27. See, for example, Dulles, *Models of the Church*, 206, 226.

28. Hill, "Church," 200.

29. Fahey, "Church," 44.

30. Ibid., 45.

31. Mary E. Hines, "Community for Liberation: Church," in Catherine Mowry LaCugna, ed., *Freeing Theology: The Essentials of Theology in Feminist Perspective* (New York: HarperCollins, 1993), 162, 178.

32. Ibid., 163–64.

33. For these three she draws on Elisabeth Schüssler Fiorenza, Edward Schillebeeckx, and Karl Rahner.

34. Elizabeth A. Johnson, ed., *The Church Women Want: Catholic Women in Dialogue* (New York: Crossroad, 2002).

35. Miriam Therese Winter, "Feminist Women's Spirituality: Breaking New Ground in the Church," in Johnson, ed., *The Church Women Want*, 23–31.

36. Susan Muto, "Called to Holiness as Women of the Church," in Johnson, ed., *The Church Women Want*, 11–22.

37. Elizabeth Johnson and Catherine M. Patten, "Introduction," in Johnson, ed., *The Church Women Want*, 5.

38. For an overview, see Edmund J. Dobbin, O.S.A., "Trinity," in *New Dictionary of Theology*, 1046–61.

39. See especially Catherine Mowry LaCugna, *God for Us: The Trinity and the Christian Life* (New York: HarperCollins Publishers, 1991).

40. Catherine Mowry LaCugna, "The Trinitarian Mystery of God," in Francis Schüssler Fiorenza and John P. Galvin, eds., *Systematic Theology: Roman Catholic Perspectives, Volume I* (Minneapolis: Augsburg Fortress, 1991), 177.

41. LaCugna, *God for Us*, 3.

42. LaCugna, "The Trinitarian Mystery of God," 178.

43. Catherine Mowry LaCugna, "God in Communion with Us," in LaCugna, ed., *Freeing Theology*, 87–88. Sarah Coakley stresses the importance of not developing a "social" doctrine of the Trinity that seems to construe the three persons as three separate consciousnesses that are in "community" rather than "communion." Sarah Coakley, *Powers and Submissions: Spirituality, Philosophy and Gender* (Oxford, U.K., and Malden, Mass.: Blackwell, 2002), 119–20.

44. Ibid., 188.

45. LaCugna, "God in Communion with Us," 92.

46. Ibid., 98.

47. A landmark of feminist biblical scholarship is Elisabeth Schüssler Fiorenza's *In Memory of Her: Toward a Feminist Reconstruction of Christian Origins* (New York: Crossroad, 1983).

48. Elizabeth A. Johnson, "Forging a Conversation with Colleagues," in Zagano and Tilley, eds., *Things New and Old*, 108.

49. See John P. Galvin, "Jesus Christ," in *Systematic Theology, Volume I*, 249–324, for an overview of these approaches (258–59) and of the development of Christology in general.

50. Elizabeth Johnson, *She Who Is: The Mystery of God in Feminist Theological Discourse* (New York: Crossroad, 1994), 246–72.

51. William Loewe, "Jesus Christ," in *New Dictionary of Theology*, 536.

52. See Johnson, *She Who Is*, and Elisabeth Schüssler Fiorenza, *Miriam's Child, Sophia's Prophet* (New York: Continuum, 1994).

53. Johnson, *She Who Is*, 82–86, 124–49.

54. Among those titles for Jesus that New Testament authors borrowed from their Jewish heritage to capture his radical significance, Wisdom is the one that most clearly alludes to his divinity (Son of God, Messiah, and Lord

all having been used traditionally to refer to human beings, and Son of Man to refer to an apocalyptic figure who will judge on the last day).

55. Johnson, *She Who Is*, 99.

56. The two main arguments of the Catholic Church against the ordination of women are that women cannot represent the male Christ on the altar and that there is an unbroken Catholic Christian tradition of the priestly ordination of men only. See the Congregation for the Doctrine of the Faith, *Inter Insigniores*, 1976 (*Declaration on the Question of the Admission of Women to the Ministerial Priesthood*); John Paul II, *Ordinatio Sacerdotalis*, 1994 (*Apostolic Letter on Ordination and Women*), and Congregation for the Doctrine of the Faith, *Responsum ad Dubium*, 1995 (*Response Concerning Ordinatio Sacerdotalis*).

57. Sara Butler, M.S.B.T., "Questio Disputata: 'In Persona Christi'," *Theological Studies* 56 (1995): 61–80.

58. This is probably especially true of "Third World" women, for whom the basic necessities of life and violence against women are much more urgent issues.

59. Mary Hines states that "most Catholic feminists no longer view being ordained into such a system as ideal. The struggle for ordination has been decentered in favor of working for systemic change" (Hines, "Community for Liberation," 170). For alternative forms of women's ministry and liturgy, see Rosemary Radford Ruether, *Women-Church: Theology and Practice* (San Francisco: Harper and Row, 1985).

60. Susan A. Ross, *Extravagant Affections: A Feminist Sacramental Theology* (New York: Continuum, 1998), 204.

61. John Paul II, *On the Dignity and Vocation of Women* (*Mulieris Dignitatem*) (Washington, D.C.: United States Catholic Conference, 1988).

62. Ibid., no. 16 (italics in original).

63. Ibid., no. 25.

64. Ibid., nos. 18 and 30.

65. See especially John Paul II, "Letter to Women," *Origins* 25, no. 9 (1995): 137, 139–143.

66. Ibid., no. 7.

67. Sara Butler, M.S.B.T., "Embodiment: Women and Men, Equal and Complementary," in Johnson, ed., *The Church Women Want*, 35–44.

68. Colleen Griffith, "Human Bodiliness: Sameness as Starting Point," in Johnson, ed., *The Church Women Want*, 60–67.

69. Elizabeth A. Johnson, "Imaging God, Embodying Christ: Women as a Sign of the Times," in Johnson, ed., *The Church Women Want*, 45–59.

70. Angela Senander, "Theological Synthesis: Interim Report," unpublished paper, January 2003.

71. Meredith Halpin, "Feminist Theology and Ethics: The Household Codes," unpublished paper, January 2003.

72. United States Conference of Catholic Bishops (USCCB), "Strengthening the Bonds of Peace: Pastoral Reflection on Women in the Church and in Society," *Origins* 24, no. 25 (1994): 417, 419–22.

73. Ibid., 419, 421.

74. Ibid., 419.

75. Ibid.

76. *Code of Canon Law*, English translation by the Canon Law Society of America (Washington, D.C.: Canon Law Society of America, 1983).

77. Phyllis Zagano, "Catholic Women Deacons: An Update on the Discussion," *America* 188, no. 5 (17 February 2003): 9–11.

78. USCCB, "Strengthening the Bonds of Peace," 421.

79. Johnson, *She Who Is*, 135.

# EIGHT

## Belonging to the Laity: A Baptist Perspective

### S. MARK HEIM

The recent turmoil over sexual abuse in the American Catholic Church is felt far beyond the boundaries of that communion. When one part of the body of Christ sorrows, all sorrow. As a Baptist Christian, my own experience over the past several months bears this out. In my circle of Protestants there has been anguish and prayer over what the Catholic community has undergone. In the recent past, this would not necessarily have been the case. Even in such sadness, we may note the transformation reflected in using the word "ours" to name this pain. We feel solidarity because we know that sexual misconduct and abuse of power and trust are present in our churches as well, but above all because we recognize each other as part of the same household of faith. It is in that light that I welcome the opportunity to participate in this ecumenical conversation.

The current crisis has led many within the Roman Catholic communion to ask whether there are ways of reforming and refiguring the place of the laity within the church—ways that will help the church deal with the current crisis more faithfully and effectively and address some of the structures that, if they did not foster the abuses directly, still allowed them to occur on such a scale in the first place. There is no lack of diagnoses of problematic areas in need of reform: clericalism, unaccountable forms of hierarchy, a theology of "scandal" in the church that places high priority on discretion or secrecy. Depending on whom you listen to, the problem is either an isolated and unrealistic priestly formation, or a permissive and lax one. The crime of sexual abuse may be the catalyst, but the discussion it has prompted runs into virtually all areas of ecclesiology. And the role of the laity is a thread that connects virtually all of the issues raised. The resulting reflection looks back at least as far as the Second Vatican Council, with its treatment of the church as the People of God, and spreads across the whole sweep of the church's present life. What the outcome of this reflection will be, it is too early to say. But surely we can expect that lay Roman Catholics will increasingly be exploring and exercising new roles of leadership within the church.

Given that prospect, I would like to offer a perspective on the laity from within the Baptist tradition,[1] a tradition that could hardly be more different than the Roman Catholic tradition on this subject. The Baptist way has its own ills in full measure, but I offer these thoughts in the hope that this experience may be of some value for those developing new approaches to lay participation. If nothing else, it may offer the relief of contrast, a change from contemplating the defects of Catholic ecclesiology to contemplating the defects of another—like exchanging the distress of a stomach virus for a brief spot of extreme toothache! We can gain a helpful understanding of our own situation in grasping the pros and cons of other traditions. Despite the current crisis, there is no danger that Roman Catholics will collectively by acclamation adopt Baptist ecclesiology. But a view from the other side of the fence may be useful as Catholics consider empowerment of the laity. It may help Catholics recognize benefits in their approach that are, from my perspective at least, obvious, and it may alert them to new problems that come with new solutions.

I will offer a rather comprehensive look at the way Baptist churches have framed the position of the laity, because I think this foundational approach is the most helpful. It is too easy to treat questions of the laity as purely functional and practical questions (alongside deeply theological treatments of sacramental ministries, for instance), like a "patch" for a computer program. Such a perspective is unlikely to yield long-term change.

## No Visible Means of Support: Laity in the Baptist Tradition
It is common to find in Baptist churches little pamphlets that outline "Baptist principles" or "Baptist distinctives." That list would be some variation on these points: the authority of Scripture, believer's baptism, regenerate church membership, the priesthood of all believers, soul competency (or soul liberty), congregational autonomy, and religious freedom. This sounds like a string of separate convictions, but in fact they are linked by an emphasis on the laity and by a fundamental shared root, a distinctive Baptist view of the church itself. The best way to

grasp this is to consider the basic question of how to be the church. That is, how are the church's continuity and identity and life to be maintained across time, from generation to generation?

Historically, the church east and west agreed that the basis for this continuity was provided in Scripture and tradition. There is a given, written, normative Scripture. There are also normative elements of tradition: creeds, liturgical forms, writings of authoritative teachers. Though tradition interprets Scripture, the meaning of both is open to question. So the church further accepted a living authority to give decisive interpretation of Scripture and tradition. This is the magisterial teaching office of the church, preeminently present in the bishops individually and collectively and (in the west) in the papacy.

The church is built around Christ and Scripture. How do we know about Christ accurately and how do we interpret Scripture? Tradition is the source used to answer this question. How is tradition to be understood? A particular set of interpreters—and these interpreters are ordained clergy—guide the answer to that question. For most of Christian history, a unity was also presumed between the church and the state, so that the process just described can be backed up with political power at crucial points, even though the church's authority remains distinct from the state. This complex in its entirety is the means by which the church seeks to be consistent and faithful from one age to the next and from one locality to another.

With the Reformation, Protestants challenged this view of the church with a different one. They wanted two fundamental changes in the picture. They challenged the accumulated authority of tradition, saying it should not be equal or superior to that of Scripture, and they challenged the idea of a magisterial teaching office that could, by cumulative decisions, define what Scripture was to be understood as saying. In arguing for "Scripture alone," it was these two things that Protestant reformers were primarily attacking. Protestants claimed that it was possible to return again and again "for the first time" to Scripture, as it were. Scripture should be the authority in the church's life, and one should look to it directly for guidance. And in principle, each person, lay or ordained, secular or religious, could do this himself or herself. The Protestant definition of the church—where the word is rightly preached and the sacraments rightly administered—assumed that you could tell each of these things by reference to Scripture alone, and it left aside specification of a structure of human authorities in the church that would be part of the church's essential nature.

Now already during the Reformation, the classic argument against this approach was raised. "Scripture alone?" If that is your standard, surely it is obvious that people will not agree about what scripture says or means. And when they disagree, how will you resolve the disagreement? Reformers clearly saw the problem, and they had answers to it. The answers tended to revolve around three elements: creeds, liturgy, and a learned ministry. The three main branches of the magisterial ("teaching") reformation (Lutheran, Reformed, Anglican) all have confessional formulas. That is, they accept creeds like the Nicene and Apostolic creeds, and they also have their own confessions. In principle, these Protestants say that these confessions are summaries or "short forms" of scriptural truth. They are derived from scripture and are subordinate to scripture. Protestants routinely say that if anything in these confessions were to be contrary to scripture, the contrary elements would not be authoritative. So they try to make it clear that these confessions are not over and above scripture, but are nevertheless taken as authoritative guides to knowing when someone is reading and understanding scripture correctly.

The second guide is normative liturgy. Here perhaps the best example is the Anglican Church and the Book of Common Prayer. A fixed form of scriptural worship is developed, again on the principle that its authority is derived from scripture itself. By maintaining uniform use of and adherence to this liturgy, one can ensure that scripture is interpreted correctly and one can resolve the most important disagreements that arise—those that bear on worship and sacramental life. So in the Anglican Church, as in the Eastern Orthodox Church, the liturgy is a source of theology. The rule of prayer is the rule of faith, and the continuity in worship life is an absolute foundation for the church's continuity and identity.

The third element is a learned ministry. Protestants said that each person is capable of understanding scripture: there could be no other absolute human intermediary between people and the word of God than Christ. But this did not mean for them that every individual could give interpretive and normative guidance to the church. Not everyone is equally prepared both intellectually and spiritually to give the best and most consistent interpretation. Here there is a special role for the ordained minister, not primarily as a sacramental figure but, in Presbyterian language, as a "teaching elder."

And in these Protestant churches a dimension of magisterial structure remained also. A connected and authoritative church structure was seen as necessary to govern with authority on the basis of scripture and these three "guides." The focus for Anglicans and Lutherans remained bishops, whereas for Reformed it became synods and presbyteries, representative councils of the church that could decide authoritatively whether the guides to right scriptural interpretation were being rightly followed.

Baptists, along with a few others, advanced a quite different way of being the church. Or we might say that they pushed the Protestant way several dramatic steps further. Baptists agreed with the Reformation critique of the magisterial teaching authority and of tradition. And they did not disagree with the vast majority of what was contained in the Protestant confessions. But whereas the Reformers had attacked the magisterium and an extensive formulated tradition, Baptists extended that attack to include the three elements I have just noted, the elements on which Protestants depended to make up for the normative authorities they had rejected. Baptists proposed to do without creeds, fixed liturgy, and learned ministry. Our cousins, the congregationalists, took a similar track, but in a fundamental way kept the learned ministry.

All Christians hold to the authority of scripture. And all recognize that this authority itself gives rise to disagreement. How are we to deal with that disagreement and preserve the church's identity? Baptists faced the same criticism from Protestants that Protestants had faced from Catholics: they were accused of having removed the very organs by which faithfulness could be preserved. Baptists themselves were keenly aware of the problem. To appeal to "scripture alone" does not resolve differences.

Baptists made the distinctive proposal that the local, congregational community should be the primary and determinative instrument in interpreting scripture. If we want to know what the Bible means or teaches, the best way to proceed is for a small community of committed Christians ("regenerate believers" in the language of our tradition), who know each other face to face and are covenanted together, to pray and counsel together and seek God's will. This, Baptists believed, provided the situation in which the Holy Spirit could speak and be heard most freely. The church aimed to be a "theocracy of the Holy Spirit." All the intermediary authorities of church magisterium, accumulated tradition, great theologians, ancient creeds, fixed liturgies, and learned ministers were strongly devalued. Baptists themselves were divided over whether these things were simply limited and imperfect or positively distorting. For instance, some held that a learned minister is a good to be desired, but not a necessity, while others considered an uneducated pastor to be in principle better than one corrupted with human learning. Similarities to early Quakers are striking, though Quakers went a step further and severely limited any instrumental "helps," such as any sort of ordained ministry at all. In the place of all these authorities, Baptists placed the congregation of the laity. A glimpse at this history helps us to see the thread that connects the list of Baptist distinctives I mentioned earlier. They are all unified by this conception of the church.

Baptists were not naïve. They were well aware of the criticism that their program depended too exclusively and unrealistically on the work of the Holy Spirit. They were acutely aware that if this way of being the church was going to work, it would require a very special and unusual kind of community. If neither bishop nor creed nor fixed liturgy nor learned ministry was to have definitive authority, but rather the gathered community of believers, they knew they needed a disciplined and committed body. Only a community of people voluntarily, personally committed and covenanted—with each devotedly seeking God's will through scripture—could hope to reach enough agreement to maintain their continuity in the gospel and to live effectively together. Church discipline, the power to control membership, was virtually the sole tool left for preserving identity.

Believer's baptism points to the importance of personal faith for a Christian. But it is also the only possible form of baptism for a community such as I have described. Baptism is initiation into the Christian life, and it is also the gateway to responsible membership in the church. If the church is to be as Baptists have imagined it—a congregation freely constituting its life not only from generation to generation but from year to year—then it must be composed only of those who can make personal and free confession of their faith as part of their act of baptism. Of course, Baptists believed that it was just this pattern that they found illustrated in the New Testament, confirming their conviction that the church could be so maintained.

Baptists affirm regenerate church membership. "Regenerate" does not mean "perfect," but it means "converted"—people who can give good testimony and evidence that they have direct knowledge of God in their own lives, that they have tasted God's grace and are serious in their intentions about the Christian life. This is why the path to membership in a Baptist church has always been through testimony, testimony judged by deacons or elders and then affirmed by the membership. Ultimately it is a vote of the entire congregation that admits new members to a Baptist church. It is unusual for a Catholic priest or Lutheran pastor to consult the congregation about the decision to admit someone to the church. Baptists focus on this point, because when someone is admitted to membership in the congregation, they are given an equal portion of responsibility for *every aspect* of the church's life and teaching. They have standing to take part in the magisterial decisions of the church's life.

Because of their name, many people believe that Baptists must place baptismal practice above every other concern. But the understanding of Baptist principles that I have just summarized is confirmed by the fact that from their very beginnings, there has been variation in the practice of baptism among Baptists. Some early Baptist congregations insisted that all members must have been baptized as believers. Others accepted people who had been baptized as infants and did not require them to undergo believer's baptism. Occasionally there have even been Baptist congregations that accepted certain individuals into membership who had never had any rite of baptism at all. Baptists have all agreed that believer's baptism is the normative form of Christian baptism, but this variety in practice reflects the fact that it is regenerate church membership that is the primary issue. In all the cases I have just noted, the crucial common point that is required is the personal testimony or confession of faith given by the candidate. Those Baptist churches that do not require believer's baptism of all their members nevertheless require testimony of all members. A person who is received into membership apart from baptism is received "by Christian experience" or "by profession of faith."

Baptists affirm and, in fact, pioneered religious liberty. For them, this follows from the same vision of the church. If the congregation must be a voluntarily covenanted body of regenerate believers, then there must be social space to create such a congregation. And there cannot be such space without religious liberty. When people are coerced to be at least nominal members of a church without personal confession or when they are prevented from forming congregations voluntarily on such a basis, the church as Baptists understand it is impossible. This is why Baptists have defended the liberty to belong or not to belong to religious bodies. Only on such a basis could they maintain the character of Christian initiation that they understand as essential to the church.

Congregational autonomy is another of the principles I listed. In the Baptist view of the church, the local congregation is the primary instrument for "reading" scripture, and is its authoritative interpreter.

The process by which that community seeks the Spirit and the truth cannot be foreclosed by any outside authority, any council, creed, or form that is not subject to the congregation's revision or decision. The associational impulse in Baptist life has always been strong. It is based on the view that though congregations are the optimal instruments for interpreting scripture, there is tremendous value in consultation and cooperation with those outside one's local community. But these connections are always voluntary covenants: the congregation can form and dissolve these relations as it chooses.

If the Baptist vision of the church is to work, then the priesthood of all believers, the idea of "each member a minister," is crucial. Those in this tradition believe that God gives to every church, every local Christian community, all the gifts necessary for its life. This means that every function of the church, including every function ordinarily performed by the ordained, *can* in some circumstances be performed by any lay member. Preaching, sacramental ministry, and governance are all responsibilities that can fall on any member, according to the community's need and the calling from God.

The principle of soul liberty completes this list. If a congregation is to find a sound interpretation of scripture through the leading of the Holy Spirit, then the Baptist conviction was that each regenerate member in the community should sincerely, independently, and prayerfully be engaged in seeking the divine will. When the congregation came together, each person would share his or her insight and belief. The community would then seek consensus. This system cannot function unless each individual is free to make an independent inquiry and to share the results with the community. Baptists had no illusion or conviction that everyone's opinion was equally valid, or that God would always speak through a majority vote. They exhorted each other to listen and pray, since in some cases it might be only the few or even the one who had rightly heard the Spirit's calling for the community. This was one virtue Baptists perceived in their ecclesiology. From their perspective, the still, small voice of the Spirit was too often drowned out in traditional church structures. In the local congregation, it would have a chance to break through.

Baptists were not partisans of democracy in the abstract. Their primary concern was in knowing and doing the will of God, in being faithful communities. They certainly would never have viewed their ecclesiology in the terms that "everyone has a right to their own opinion." Soul liberty does not exist by itself: it was defended as a means for the community to discern the truth more effectively. Full liberty of conscience was something Baptists affirmed for the sake of the church, not as a private entitlement. Religious liberty is the social form of soul liberty—a freedom that relates to entering into membership in the church from the surrounding social order, while soul liberty relates to ongoing life in the church.

## Implications

Most Christian bodies have reservoirs in which they maintain the sources of identity. The special organs and authorities that I have reviewed—special teaching offices, creeds, governing bodies, fixed liturgies—guide the entire community to become a faithful church in continuity with the apostolic witness. These reservoirs are insulated and preserved from alteration. They stand beyond the community, so to speak, and are not open to revision by local or even collective authority. In the Baptist tradition, these reservoirs are almost entirely lacking. It is only the community itself that exercises the oversight and interpretation of the content of the faith. The guardrails are largely absent.

Baptist congregations are an ongoing experiment as to whether one can have church on this basis, whether it is possible to maintain strong identity, faithful continuity, effective witness, and mission through a "structure" that leans heavily—some would say simplistically—on the Holy Spirit. Since in the Baptist model of the church there is no overarching structure of governance, disagreement that cannot be reconciled usually follows a path of separation. There is no Baptist doctrine or authority or governing body that can set limits to how diverse people can be within the Baptist model of church, within any single local congregation. That limit is set only by whether the community can sustain itself as a living and faithful community. Baptist congregations historically exercised discipline in admitting and expelling members. Minorities within congregations who were convinced that the community had ceased to function faithfully in some essential way frequently withdrew. Sometimes they withdrew into new congregations that remained in close relation to the one from which they parted, sometimes into quite opposing ones. Connected associational life beyond the local congregation is based on covenant. Baptists have not been certain that such association was essential to the church's nature as such, but they have been certain that it was essential to the church's *mission*, and hence their connectional life has always had a strong mission orientation, and relatively little sacramental or organic emphasis.

Why have I taken this brief tour through a Baptist view of the church? Because in it we see one vision of a church centered on the laity. Some observers have suggested that the Baptist approach actually represents the abolition of the laity, in that no member of a Baptist church can be regarded "only" as a layperson. In principle, the members of a Baptist church stand in line for a portion of every aspect of the church's ministry, including its teaching and governing ministries. Any church that would elevate or extend the role of the laity will have to consider how extensively and how comprehensively it wants to pursue that goal. The Baptist example represents an option close to one end of the spectrum, and it may be illustrative of the drawbacks as well as the benefits of such movement.

Given current circumstances, the democratic aspects of Baptist life may have obvious appeal to some Roman Catholics. These would include the congregation's right to call, supervise, and discipline its own ministers, the selection of regional and national church leaders who serve at the pleasure of the elected representatives of the churches, and a structure in which all the members in a local community take part in its governance, a governance that includes every aspect not only of the church's program and ministry but of its faith and worship. In a local Baptist congregation, there are actually two prime leaders: the ordained minister whom the congregation has called to that position, and the moderator, a layperson elected by the community as its chief governing officer. As the title indicates, the executive power of this second office is largely instrumental. The person who holds the office is responsible for chairing and overseeing the congregational meeting process by which people seek agreement and make decisions about church life. Every question can ultimately be referred to a full congregational meeting, in which the minister and the moderator each have one vote, as do each of the members.

This model has many strengths. Decisions are made at the immediate level, and no one is far removed from that process. Issues are addressed in a community where people know each other on a direct and firsthand basis. There is extensive freedom for different communities to explore variations in their approach and their common life. Since scripture is the sole major "reservoir" of Christian identity that is universally affirmed among Baptists, it is a center of lively study and devotional concern. But there are clear weaknesses in this ecclesiology also. The sense of the universal church is often weak. The sacramentality and worship life of a congregation can become thin and narrow, constrained to the knowledge of the current members and the memories that extend only to recent generations in this single congregation. The same can be true of theology, since there is no necessary formation in a wider tradition. The local congregation can become sectarian, focused on its own composition and absorbed by the extensive work involved in complete local governance. And not least of all, it is always a struggle to maintain equilibrium in the community: without external authorities, internal conflict can spin out of control, or an entire community can veer in a highly idiosyncratic direction.

The challenge faced by clergy and laity in the Roman Catholic Church who wish to renew the role of the laity is how they may do so in ways that preserve what I, as a Protestant, respect as the genius of the Catholic tradition. I have tried to indicate that what some may view as attractive democratic mechanisms in Baptist churches are deeply grounded in a complete ecclesiology. They make sense only as part of a coordinated vision of the church, where other features of the congregation's life are consistent with them. They are fragile enough in their own setting: they could hardly be transplanted in a piecemeal way. Analogous developments in a communion like that of the Roman Catholic Church will have to be adapted to that ecclesial soil. An increase in the role and power of the laity does address certain problems directly: problems of participation, accountability, and clericalism. But hand in hand with such changes there also come new responsibilities and expectations for the laity. I do not mean this only in an individual sense, in that more is asked of specific individuals. I mean it in an institutional sense. The church gives over parts of its essential life to the leadership of laity, and this requires a new kind of accountability, formation, and organization for the laity themselves.

I admire and (sometimes) envy the Catholic Church's clear and substantial reservoirs of the faith in its liturgical, doctrinal, and structural norms. The very firmness of these sources allows the church an extraordinary openness in many ways. I have a friend who is a minister in one of the more liturgically ordered Protestant churches. She once noted that in her parish, on any given Sunday, she would not presume that a majority of the attending communicant members at that service could themselves affirm most or even any of what was affirmed in the service. To her mind, this was one of the positive features of her denomination. The worshipping community—and indeed the membership itself—could have a highly open character. People were free to come and to participate at whatever level they wished. At the same time, the content of the church's faith and life was preserved through the set liturgy, through the standards of ordination for the clergy who taught and preached, through the oversight of bishops and church councils that set the clear standards within which the local community must live. The gospel was present, so that people could come, explore it, and be nourished and converted by it.

I see a similar benefit in the Catholic tradition, where the strength of the reservoirs and the clarity of identity allow for a certain openness and inclusivity. There is no need to draw a bright boundary between those who are members and those who are not. There can be extraordinary openness in Catholic educational institutions, toward various disciplines and views, since there need not be great fear that such interaction will obscure the Catholic identity. This is seen also in the fact that the Catholic tradition as a whole has been at the forefront of dialogue with other religions and of enculturation and indigenization of Christian worship and life in various cultures. It has done this in part, I believe, precisely because of its strong mechanisms for preserving identity and continuity in its own tradition.

As I acknowledged to my friend, in a local Baptist church, one would have to recognize that all the *content* of the church's worship and witness could, in principle, be changed from one week to the next by a decision of the members who fill the pews. In that context, the "laity" becomes a magisterial office, and the qualifications and standards for people to enter that office become much more important. That is why Baptists have placed such focus and emphasis there.

As Catholics consider the role of the laity and seek to give the laity greater authority, they will find a question that will become less and less avoidable: Who are the members of the laity? Are they all who have been baptized as Roman Catholics? Are they all who have been received by confirmation or initiation or who are regular communicants? Are they those who have a recognizable relation with a Roman Catholic parish or diocese? As it becomes more common, as I believe it will, for members of the laity to have a voice in the major counsels of the church, these questions will be sharpened. If there are organizations that seek to speak for the laity, what is their appropriate constitution and who are the members of their legitimate constituency? There is a need for a spirituality of the baptized, in which baptism is recognized as every Christian's ordination to ministry. Such a spirituality stresses the need for an education and formation that would prepare the baptized to see this as a part of their Christian life and to carry out responsibilities within the church. In the Rite of Christian Initiation for Adults, the church already has a pattern and example for this kind of formation. As the role of the laity grows, the need for such identifiable paths of entry into the community of responsible laity will also grow.

Another question has to do with the appropriate organization of lay participation. It is natural for me as a Baptist to think of the means for lay participation on a congregational model, with an organized lay body in a local parish as the most basic unit for all other lay representation in the church. It may well be, however, that another model would fit the Catholic context. Voluntary societies, in which laypeople organize around certain apostolates within the church's mission, might be another avenue where such voices could be given official place. Laypeople have for centuries been members of religious orders, and perhaps there are models from that direction also for the way in which the laity may exercise its calling.

Another key question is whether there are limits to *what* the laity's voice and responsibility cover. Is some dimension of the church's teaching and deposit of faith to be reserved from the process of lay determination? In principle, there is a deposit of faith that is beyond alteration by the bishops and clergy collectively. Are there areas to be left primarily to the interpretation of the magisterial authorities, and others to be shared by the laity, and still others to be left to the laity without normative guidance from the ordained? These are questions for which I do not propose answers, but they are questions that call for reflection. Insofar as the authority of laity is extended, the church needs to ask what the structures are that assure this authority will maintain continuity and identity with the sources of faith.

This is but a sampling of the relevant questions. There are many others, and only Catholics are competent to answer them. But I hope that this brief excursion into another ecclesial perspective has underlined one important fact: significant changes in the role of the laity in the church will need to go hand in hand with a full vision of the kind of church that prepares, incorporates, and depends upon those lay ministries. Beginnings may come from specific changes driven by specific needs, but the new place of the laity will be sustained when there is a shared vision of the church that itself naturally calls forth and expects lay leadership. This new place will be assured when Roman Catholics, lay and ordained alike, presuppose an ecclesiology that is incoherent, theoretically and practically, without lay leadership.

# Note

1. For background, see Curtis W. Freeman, James Wm. McClendon, Jr., and C. Rosalee Velloso da Silva, *Baptist Roots: A Reader in the Theology of a Christian People* (Valley Forge, Pa.: Judson Press, 1999); Winthrop S. Hudson, ed., *Baptist Concepts of the Church* (Philadelphia, Pa.: Judson Press, 1959); and Michael Novak, "The Free Churches and the Roman Church: The Conception of the Church in Anabaptism and Roman Catholicism," *Journal of Ecumenical Studies* 2 (1965): 425–39.

# NINE

## Weathering "The Perfect Storm": The Contribution of Canon Law

JOHN BEAL

### The Genesis of the "Perfect Storm"

In late October of 1991, a classic nor'easter began to rage in the North Atlantic off the coast of Nova Scotia. This would have been a nasty storm under the best of circumstances, but these were not to be the best of circumstances. A once-in-a-lifetime meteorological convergence caused the nor'easter to merge first with a weak hurricane coming from the south and then with a massive Arctic cold front racing in from the west. The result was "the perfect storm."[1]

We may be witnessing a similar but rare convergence of powerful currents to form another perfect storm, not in the North Atlantic but throughout North America. This gathering storm is not a meteorological phenomenon, but an ecclesiological cataclysm. The original gale in this scenario is, of course, the storm of outrage occasioned by the revelation that hundreds of priests had sexually abused young people and that diocesan bishops had not acted decisively to remove these priests from ministry.[2] These revelations would have been sufficient to spawn a howling gale all by themselves. However, this nasty storm is in the process of being joined, from different directions, by two even more powerful storms, two historical gravamina that have been swirling undercurrents of American church history since the nineteenth century.

The first of these is the long-standing resentment of the lay faithful (but also, and more quietly, the lower clergy) at the lack of accountability, transparency, and opportunities for participation in church governance. This resentment surfaced most visibly in the long and often bitter conflict over what church historians, usually writing from the point of view of the victorious bishops, have called "lay trusteeism." Essentially, the lay trustees and their supporters demanded a significant role in the governance of their parishes and accountability and transparency in their administration from bishops and pastors. Often, this demand included the trustees' claim to authority to engage and dismiss the parish priest—and here is where conflicts between the trustees and their pastors and bishops often erupted into violent storms. Beginning with the First Plenary Council of Baltimore, the bishops eventually vanquished the lay trustees and wrenched from them control over church property.[3] Nevertheless, the bishops' victory did not make the demand of the laity for accountability, transparency, and participation in church governance disappear. It only pushed this swirling hurricane of resentment out to sea to drift harmlessly until the occasion presented itself for it to latch on to another storm and regenerate its fury.[4]

This occasion presented itself in January 2002 as reports multiplied of abusive priests being knowingly transferred to new parishes where they abused again, of parishioners being left uninformed about the dark side of their priests' pasts and about the reasons for their sudden removals or disappearances, of confidential settlements with victims and large sums expended with no disclosure or public accounting, and, more generally, of the appearance of the abuse of discretion and the arrogance of power. As a result, the once meandering hurricane has gathered strength and, as it has converged with the sex abuse storm, has achieved new ferocity.

The other turbulent current whose leading edge has only recently appeared on our ecclesial radar is the historic resentment of the lower clergy (and, to a lesser extent, their lay supporters) at allegedly arbitrary and capricious treatment of them by diocesan bishops. The demands of presbyters for "due process" when accused of wrongdoing, for tenure in office for parish priests, for a voice in diocesan governance and in the selection of bishops, and for the imposition of canon law in the United States to protect them from episcopal arbitrariness raised a gale that howled throughout the nineteenth and early-twentieth centuries.[5] As they had in the lay trustee conflict, the bishops squelched their presbyters' challenges to their unfettered authority, but it was a triumph that left a high pressure system of resentment and suspicion lurking just beyond the horizon. The United States Conference of Catholic Bishops' enactment in June 2002 of a Charter and Essential Norms for dealing with complaints of sexual abuse,[6] and its reenactment, after the intervention of the Holy See, of a revised Charter and Norms in November 2002,[7] as well as subsequent attempts to implement them, have created the conditions for this massive high to come roaring into the already hurricane-fortified nor'easter.[8] In short, if these gales continue on their present courses, their convergence will place the Catholic Church in the United States at the eye of the perfect storm.

## The Role of Canon Law

The church's future will depend on how it weathers this perfect storm. Especially precarious and perilous is the situation of the church in the United States, which was "a people adrift" even before the current storm began to break.[9] Storms as intense and dangerous as those now battering the church can shake faith and induce panicked reactions. In the eye of the storm, the temptation can grow strong to grasp whatever strategy seems expedient. Weathering the current storm, however, depends on the ability of the church as a community of faith to stay the course by holding fast to its fundamental canons: the canon of holy scripture, the canon of baptismal faith, and the canon of eucharistic prayer.[10] Those who lose their grips on these canons will surely drown in the dark sea of troubles now crashing over the church.

Nevertheless, holding fast to the canons of seamanship in the midst of howling gales and towering seas can be difficult without the assistance of canonical laws that translate the other three canons into concrete principles for action in the present. At their best, these canonical laws "regulate the daily living and due processes of assemblies of Christians in conformity with the . . . canons of scripture, creed, and prayer."[11] In fact, when these canonical laws are ignored or flouted, the church is soon set adrift at the mercy of the roaring sea. As Aidan Kavanagh has pointed out:

> Canonical laws, which are often denigrated as unimportant, attempt to render the other three canons specific in the small details of faithful daily life. When canonical laws are overlooked for too long, the other three canons are likely to drift away from the church's consciousness and to be honored only in the breach. When this happens, such a church will invariably discover its apostolate to be compromised, its faith dubious, its worship more concerned with current events than with the presence of the living God, and its efforts bent more to maintaining its own coherence than to restoring the world to God in Christ.[12]

As a result, canon law has only a modest contribution to make to keeping our fragile ecclesial boat afloat in the perfect storm, but it is a contribution that may make the difference between weathering the perfect storm and being swallowed by "the hungry ocean."[13] As a canonical contribution to the church's weathering the perfect storm, I would like to recall two sets of canons of ecclesial seamanship that have long been ignored in the church in the United States. The first deals with the ownership and administration of church property and the second with the administration of justice in criminal cases. Observance of these canons will not cause the current crisis suddenly to blow over, but it may help the church to ride out the storm without being shipwrecked.

## The Emergence of an Ecclesial "Corporate Culture"

Commentators, both secular and religious, of the left and of the right, have complained that the leadership of the Catholic Church has responded to the clergy sexual abuse crisis since January 2002 much as a large corporation would.[14] Indeed, the handling of the clergy sexual abuse crisis by church leaders has been subject to invidious comparisons to the ultimately futile attempts by corporate spokespersons to give a positive "spin" to the implosion of the Enron Corporation and the almost daily revelation of new forms of "creative accounting" and financial skullduggery in the business world. Nevertheless, it should not be surprising that church leaders responded to their crisis with tactics reminiscent of those of large corporations. The truth is that the Catholic Church in the United States *is* a "large corporation" or, more precisely, 186 more or less large corporations.

In canon law, dioceses are "juridic persons,"[15] that is, artificial persons that are

> distinct from all natural persons or material goods, constituted by competent ecclesiastical authority for an apostolic purpose, with a capacity for continuous existence and with canonical rights and duties like those of a natural person (e.g., to own property, enter into contracts, sue or be sued) conferred upon [them] by law or by the authority which constitutes [them].[16]

Juridic persons are the canon law equivalents of secular law corporations. However, not only dioceses but also parishes, religious institutes, and their provinces and houses are juridic persons—and the same is true, at least potentially, of a large range of church-related institutional apostolates.[17] Each of these juridic persons, and not the diocese in which it is located, owns and administers the property it legitimately acquires.[18]

The fact that the church has conferred corporate status on these forms of ecclesial organization has always been of no consequence to American law. As a result, church leaders have always had to secure civil recognition of their ownership of property by availing themselves of the vehicles available under the laws of their respective states. Thus, dioceses and parishes have become simultaneously public juridic persons in the church and corporations or quasicorporations (or components thereof) in the state, subject to both canon law and American law. Diocesan bishops have historically opted for the available forms of civil organization that maximize their own control of church property within their jurisdictions.[19] A favorite civil law vehicle for maximizing episcopal control of church property has been the "corporation sole" of which the diocesan bishop and his successors are the sole members and which holds title to all church property (save that held by religious institutes) within the diocese.[20] Although the corporation sole method of incorporation of a diocese and its parishes maximizes episcopal control, it also blurs, if it does not entirely obliterate, parishes' canonical distinctness from the diocese and their independent ownership and administration of their own property.

This incongruity between canon law and civil law models such as corporation sole prompted the intervention of the Sacred Congregation of the Council in 1911 to promote use of the parish corporation model for holding property as the one that most closely mirrored canon law[21] and to give merely provisional approval of the corporation sole model until such time as the parish corporation model was available and on condition that the bishop observe the requirements of canon law for consulting and receiving consent from advisors prior to engaging in certain transactions.[22] Nevertheless, there is no evidence that bishops responded to the Congregation's directive by lobbying their state legislatures to make the parish corporation model available or by changing to this model where it was available.

Even where corporation sole was not available or the organizational model of choice, diocesan bishops have found other ways to centralize control over church property in their dioceses in their own hands. For example, throughout the nineteenth and early-twentieth centuries, bishops in the United States doggedly resisted pressure from their own priests and people and from the Holy See to establish canonical parishes.[23] In the absence of canonical parishes, the property of these missions remained, at canon law, under the control of the diocesan bishops regardless of the civil law method chosen for their civil incorporation, and their rectors were subject to removal *ad nutum Episcopi* (at the will of the bishop). At the diocesan level, the bishops thwarted Vatican efforts to impose cathedral chapters, which would have provided for genuine coresponsibility in diocesan administration. When they finally had to succumb to Vatican pressure to appoint priests as diocesan consultors, they succeeded "in restricting the rights of consultors as much as possible" and retaining almost total control over their appointment.[24]

Despite the imposition of the requirement to appoint diocesan consultors to advise bishops on financial matters at the Third Plenary Council of Baltimore in 1884 and the somewhat accidental recognition of the separate juridic identity of parishes in 1922, old and deeply ingrained patterns of strongly centralized episcopal control of church property neither died nor faded away during the twentieth century. Indeed, centralized episcopal control over more and more aspects of local church life expanded throughout the last century as dioceses increasingly became and came to see themselves as "central service bureaucracies."[25]

The centralization that has characterized the evolution of diocesan organization since the nineteenth century has been paralleled in the business world. Despite the prevalence of republican rhetoric from the Jacksonian era on, nineteenth-century America witnessed an inexorable trend toward centralization of authority in the political, economic, and religious spheres.[26] In the business world, this centralization took the form of vesting the control of enterprises in fewer and fewer hands and minimizing the role of stockholders in the management of the corporation. This development in the business corporation was mirrored in the church. Indeed, A. A. Berle and G. C. Means's classic description of the evolution of the business corporation could, with a few minor modifications, also be applied to the evolution of church administration:

> The concentration of economic power separate from ownership has, in fact, created economic empires, and has delivered these empires into a new form of absolutism, relegating "owners" [i.e., the faithful] to the position of those who supply the means whereby the new princes may exercise their power.[27]

Once it embarked on the course of adopting made-for-business models for ecclesiastical organization, the church was caught in the strong undertow generated by these models' own internal dynamics.

The undertow of the corporate models it has chosen for ecclesiastical organization helps explain why the Catholic Church in the United States has historically had a strong business orientation whose emphasis is on diocesan "administration," in contrast to canon law's governmental orientation whose emphasis is on diocesan "governance."[28] As this business orientation has permeated the ecclesial organization, bishops and their associates in diocesan administration have been shaped by institutional cultures and ethos remarkably similar to those of their counterparts in corporate boardrooms.[29] Shielded by the First Amendment from most of the governmental interventions of the twentieth century designed to bring some measure of public accountability and transparency to business corporations, and used to ignoring canon law with impunity when doing so serves institutional interests, bishops remain largely unfettered by internal institutional constraints on their exercise of power. Their Achilles' heel, however, is their continued reliance on the voluntary offerings of the faithful to support their activities and programs.[30]

The option for business models for diocesan organization also helps to explain why official responses to church blunders bear the hallmarks of corporate damage-control operations. When disastrous mistakes by diocesan administration come to light as they have in the current clergy sex abuse crisis, they may eventually prompt apologies and promises not to repeat the mistakes. However, apologies and promises, no matter how sincere, do not alter the structural arrangements that have bred the corporate climate in which these mistakes could occur and fester until they reached disastrous proportions. Structural dysfunctions require structural solutions. Therefore, the current crisis calls for something more than apologies for what happened and promises of stricter vigilance over the lower clergy in the future.

Canon law suggests that the church might begin by abandoning the wholly uncanonical corporation sole model for diocesan organization, and the corporation sole mentality that it has spawned among church leaders even when other models of diocesan organization have been chosen. Instead, organizational models should be chosen that more faithfully mirror canon law's recognition of parishes as juridic persons distinct from but dependent on the diocese. Although canon law's attribution of distinct juridic identity to parishes has been criticized as a relic of the feudal era,[31] it is, in fact, a recognition that the church is most fully realized where a community assembles under the presidency of a priest to celebrate the eucharist. In most places, this occurs on a regular basis in parish Sunday liturgies, not in diocesan events.

The decentralization of responsibility for carrying out the church's mission that alternate forms of incorporation would entail would be consistent with the principle of subsidiarity, but it would also have implications beyond the area of the administration of temporal goods. It would involve the shift of primary responsibility for liturgy, religious education, Catholic schools, social outreach, and numerous other functions to the parish level from the diocesan central services bureaucracy with its "ingrained tendency . . . to create permanent dependence among parish leaders."[32] Such a transfer of the locus of responsibility for core elements of the church's mission to parishes will not occur without pain and struggle. In the end, however, the vitality of a diocese depends on the vitality of its constituent parishes, and central service bureaucracies can only hide, as they often do now, but not remedy fundamental weaknesses in the local units.[33] This transition to local responsibility will result in the thinning, not the disappearance, of diocesan offices. Some functions intimately connected to the bishop's own role (e.g., supervision and administration of justice) will still need to be supported at the diocesan level.

A transition to parish-centered local churches will not threaten or even diminish the legitimate authority of the diocesan bishop over the portion of the People of God entrusted to his care. If anything, it will make his personal involvement in the life of the local church even more critical than it is now. A focus on parish ministry will demand that the bishop be actively engaged in offering vision and leadership, in supervision and oversight, in coordination of apostolic initiatives and selection of local leaders, in allocating resources and challenging the temptation to parochialism, and in forming and re-forming ministers— in short, all of the ministerial activities historically associated with *episcope*. The thinning of diocesan bureaucracy may also create the space where the presbyteral council can actually be "like a senate of the bishop . . . which assists the bishop in the governance of the diocese," where the pastoral council can be an effective vehicle for pastoral planning, and where the finance council and college of consultors actually play prominent roles in financial affairs.[34] Such a restructuring of the local church would not result in a "democratic church," but it could lead to one in which the voice of the faithful calling for accountability, transparency, and participation is heard.

## Accountability and Transparency in Financial Matters

Canon law already contains provisions which, if creatively and effectively implemented, could bring a large measure of accountability and transparency to the church's finances. A promising, hitherto overlooked, step in the direction of accountability and transparency in financial matters was the U.S. Conference of Catholic Bishops' enactment in November 2002 of binding norms to govern fundraising drives. Modeled on guidelines enacted in 1977, these norms, if granted the *recognitio* of the Holy See, will require timely reports on funds raised in drives and on their disbursement:

10) Fund-raising reports should be prepared in scope and design to meet the particular concerns of those to whom reports are due:
    a) the governing body and membership of the fund-raising organization;
    b) competent authorities who approved and monitor the fund-raising effort;
    c) donors to the organization;
    d) the beneficiaries of the funds raised.
11) Annual fund-raising reports should provide both financial information and a review of the apostolic work for which the funds were raised. They should set forth, at least, the amount of money collected, the cost of conducting the fund-raising effort, and the amount and use of the funds disbursed.[35]

Canon 1277 authorizes the episcopal conference to designate those financial transactions by diocesan bishops that are to be considered acts of extraordinary administration: that is, those for whose valid performance the bishop must receive the consent of the diocesan finance council and the college of consultors. To date, the efforts of the U.S. Conference of Catholic Bishops (USCCB) to implement this mandate have been unimaginative at best and have placed few restraints on the authority of diocesan bishops beyond those already contained in universal law.[36] In light of the actions of other episcopal conferences and in light of economic conditions in the United States, the USCCB could revisit this issue and designate as extraordinary such episcopal acts of administration as the following: any expenditure outside the approved diocesan budget; undertaking a capital campaign; foreign or long-term domestic investments; purchasing real estate; erecting a cemetery or school; mortgaging real estate; making loans or acting as surety for third parties; settling lawsuits; borrowing from endowment funds; and selecting health-care plans, insurance plans, or pension funds.

Accountability and transparency in diocesan finances would be enhanced by a realistic catalogue of acts of extraordinary administration for diocesan bishops and the consequent involvement of the diocesan finance council and college of consultors, "who are to be thoroughly informed about the economic state of the juridic person" before the bishop undertakes these transactions.[37] The diocesan bishop already has authority to designate what constitutes extraordinary administration for pastors and administrators of other juridic persons subject to his jurisdictions when their statutes are silent on the subject.[38] By requiring consultation with or consent of the parish finance council as a condition for his own consent to acts of extraordinary administration by pastors,[39] the diocesan bishop could bring an enhanced level of accountability and transparency to parish financial management.

Although the 1983 Code of Canon Law encourages bishops and pastors to prepare detailed budgets of projected income and expenditures for each year,[40] it leaves to particular law the determination whether such budgets should be required and how and to whom they are to be presented. In the interest of accountability and transparency in financial management, the diocesan bishop could require all administrators, including himself, to prepare annual budgets and specify the form they are to take, those who are to be involved in their preparation, and the publicity they are to be given. The code itself assigns responsibility, under the direction of the diocesan bishop, for preparation of the annual diocesan budget to the diocesan finance council.[41] Particular law could designate the parish finance council under the leadership of the pastor as the body responsible for the preparation of the annual parish budget and the publicity to be given to this budget.

The code requires all pastors to submit financial reports to the diocesan bishop at the end of each fiscal year, and these reports are to be submitted for examination by the diocesan finance council.[42] The diocesan finance council, and not the diocesan bishop alone, is to receive a detailed accounting of diocesan receipts and expenditures prepared by the diocesan finance officer at the end of each fiscal year.[43] The code's requirement of annual financial reports and their examination by the diocesan finance council assures a measure of accountability and transparency in church finance. This accountability and transparency could be enhanced by particular law requiring financial reporting to the faithful, a requirement that is foreseen but not mandated by the code.[44]

Accountability and transparency in church finance is a value in itself. In fact, the lack of these qualities in Catholic Church finance is an important reason why Catholics lag behind members of other religious bodies in the amount of their charitable giving.[45] However, accountability and transparency in financial matters leads inevitably to accountability, transparency, and, ultimately, participation in other areas of church life. The watchword of the Watergate scandal is also applicable in the church: "Follow the money."

## Penal Law Revisited

In response to the storm of outrage prompted by revelations of sexual abuse of young people by priests and inadequacies of episcopal oversight, the bishops of the United States have pledged themselves to a regime of "zero tolerance" for sexual abusers among the clergy and have enacted procedural norms to make that pledge a reality. In doing so, the bishops may have, perhaps unwittingly, reopened a chapter of American church history that is neither hopeful nor edifying. A perennial undercurrent of church life during the nineteenth century was the battle between bishops and the lower clergy over, depending on one's position, the need to impose ecclesiastical discipline on recalcitrant clerics or the arbitrary and capricious abuse of authority by bishops. In a scenario ominously similar to present events, priests appealed to canon law and sought protection from the Vatican, while bishops bridled at Roman meddling and asserted their episcopal responsibility to protect the church from scandal.[46] This chapter from nineteenth-century history would be colorful but of interest mostly to antiquarians if the protagonists did not seem intent on repeating it in the twenty-first century.

There is perhaps no better example than the current sex abuse crisis of the disastrous consequences for the church of ignoring canon law—and no better example of the pervasiveness of the corporate mentality in both the popular and the episcopal mind. On the one hand, ignorance of canon law (and the theology that underlies it) has made it extremely difficult for the faithful and sometimes even bishops to understand why delinquent clerics cannot simply be cashiered like sticky-fingered employees of a business enterprise. One bishop even testified that priests are "independent contractors" whose services to a diocese can be terminated at will. On the other hand, by eschewing canonical penal discipline in favor of a more "pastoral" approach to dealing with priest-abusers, bishops unintentionally perpetuated the cycle of abuse with distinctly unpastoral consequences.

When the USCCB norms, revised at the insistence of the Holy See, called for trials to dismiss abusive priests, the media seemed nonplussed at the suggestion there might actually be such things as canonical trials. In fact, sexual abuse of minors by clerics has been an ecclesiastical crime since at least the fourth century,[47] and criminal procedure has been a staple of canon law since at least the Middle Ages and has actually influenced the development of Anglo-American criminal procedure.[48] Unfortunately, in their recent effort to show that they have both a will and a way to "get tough" with abusive clerics, the bishops have devised a penal regime that, particularly as it is being applied in practice, falls considerably short of guaranteeing the "due process" that both our American and our canonical traditions demand of a criminal justice system.

While it is still too early to know how the revised procedural norms approved by the USCCB in November 2002 will play out in practice, early signs are not promising. Many dioceses are not conducting thorough investigations of complaints of sexual abuse. As a result, when a complaint that seems at least plausible is received, the burden of proof is shifted to the accused priests, who must then prove their innocence. Proving innocence is difficult under the best circumstances, but accused priests often find several additional hurdles to surmount: the apparent absence of recognized rules of evidence; the unwillingness of dioceses to allow serious questioning of accusers lest such "hard ball legal tactics" be construed as "re-victimizing the victim"; the refusal of dioceses to lend their resources and assistance to priests in mounting their defenses; and the unauthorized admission of psychological and other confidential communications into the record. The steep nature of these evidentiary hurdles is exacerbated by an apparent unwillingness to recognize any statute of limitation for these offenses, despite the obvious difficulty in proving that what is alleged to have happened thirty years ago did not actually occur. The extent to which this procedural deck is stacked against the accused priest is evidenced by the procedural norms' rather liberal allowance for "administrative leave,"[49] which allows the bishop to impose all the disabilities, except loss of the clerical state and forfeiture of support, that could be imposed as penalties as a result of a penal trial before the trial even begins. In some cases, these disabilities are continued indefinitely when no trial is even contemplated.[50]

Revisions of these norms required as a condition for the Holy See's *recognitio* mitigate but do not eliminate these problems. One does not have to be a clairvoyant to predict that, as these procedures continue to be applied in practice, complaints of arbitrary and capricious action by bishops will increase. This perceived unfairness, as well as what appears to some to be a willingness of bishops to jettison priests in order to salvage their own reputations and authority,[51] will further strain priest–bishop relations and depress clergy morale. If this occurs, the perfect storm will no longer be merely looming just beyond the horizon.

## Conclusion

Weather forecasting is an inexact science in the physical world; it is even more inexact in the ecclesial world. Although meteorologists had recognized that conditions were right for the emergence of a perfect storm in 1991, they were not able to forecast this storm until it was already breaking. The suggestion that the ecclesial conditions are right for the emergence of a new perfect storm in the Catholic Church in the United States may prove alarmist. If this once-in-a-lifetime gale actually does form in the church in the United States, however, ecclesial seamanship hewing to canon law may make the difference between sharing the fate of the *Andrea Gail* and weathering the perfect storm.

## Notes

1. Sebastian Junger, *The Perfect Storm: A True Story of Men against the Sea* (New York: W. W. Norton, 1997), 95–106, 147–51.
2. See Jason Berry, *Lead Us Not into Temptation: Catholic Priests and the Sexual Abuse of Children* (New York: Doubleday, 1992); Philip Jenkins, *Pedophiles and Priests: Anatomy of a Current Crisis* (New York: Oxford University Press, 1997); and The Investigative Staff of *The Boston Globe*, *Betrayal: The Crisis in the Catholic Church* (Boston: Little, Brown, 2002).
3. See Jay P. Dolan, *The American Catholic Experience* (New York: Doubleday, 1985), 158–94; James Hennessey, *American Catholics* (New York: Oxford University Press), 96–100; Eugenio Corecco, *La formazione della Chiesa Cattolica negli Stati Uniti d'America attraverso l'attività sinodale con particolaree riguardo al problema dell'aminnistrazione dei beni ecclesiastici* (Brescia: Edizioni Morcelliana, 1970); Patrick Carey, *People, Priests, and Prelates: Ecclesiastical Democracy and the Tensions of Trusteeism* (Notre Dame, Ind.: University of Notre Dame Press, 1987).
4. Carey, *People, Priests, and Prelates*, 284–92.
5. Robert F. Trisco, "Bishops and Their Priests in the United States," in *The Catholic Priest in the United States: Historical Investigations*, ed. John Tracy Ellis (Collegeville, Minn.: Liturgical Press, 1971), 111–292.
6. United States Conference of Catholic Bishops (USCCB), "Charter for the Protection of Children and Young People" and "Essential Norms for Diocesan/Eparchial Policies Dealing with Allegations of Sexual Abuse of Minors by Priests, Deacons, or Other Church Personnel," *Origins* 32 (27 June 2002): 102–8.

7. United States Conference of Catholic Bishops (USCCB), "Charter for the Protection of Children and Young People, Revised" and "Essential Norms for Diocesan/Eparchial Policies Dealing with Allegations of Sexual Abuse of Minors by Priests or Deacons, Revised," *Origins* 32 (28 November 2002): 409, 411–18.

8. See John P. Beal, " 'Hiding in the Thickets of the Law': Canonical Reflections on Some Disturbing Aspects of the Dallas Charter," *America* 187 (7 October 2002): 15–19.

9. See Peter Steinfels, *A People Adrift: The Crisis of the Roman Catholic Church in America* (New York: Simon and Schuster, 2003).

10. Aidan Kavanagh, *On Liturgical Theology* (Collegeville, Minn.: Liturgical Press, 1992), 140–41.

11. Ibid., 141–42.

12. Ibid., 142.

13. See Linda Greenlaw, *The Hungry Ocean: A Swordboat Captain's Journey* (New York: Hyperion, 1999).

14. See, for example, George Weigel, *The Courage to Be Catholic* (New York: Basic Books, 2002), 87–100; and William Bausch, *Breaking Trust* (Mystic, Conn.: Twenty-Third, 2002), 13–15, 82–87.

15. Code of Canon Law *(CIC)*, c. 373.

16. Robert T. Kennedy, "Juridic Persons," in *A New Commentary on the Code of Canon Law*, ed. John P. Beal et al. (Mahwah, N.J.: Paulist Press, 2000), 155.

17. *CIC*, cc. 515, §3; 634, §1; 114. Whether these institutional apostolates founded and sponsored by other public juridic persons are themselves public juridic persons in the church and, if not, what their canonical status may be is a much controverted question in canon law. See Robert T. Kennedy, "McGrath, Maida, Michiels: Introduction to a Study of the Canonical and Civil-Law Status of Church-Related Institutions in the United States," *The Jurist* 50 (1990): 351–401; and Robert T. Kennedy, "Note on the Canonical Status of Church-Related Institutions in the United States," in Beal et al., eds., *A New Commentary*, 172–76.

18. *CIC*, c. 1256.

19. See Chester Bartlett, *The Tenure of Church Property in the United States of America*, Canon Law Studies #31 (Washington, D.C.: Catholic University, 1926); and Brendan Brown, *The Canonical Juristic Personality with Special Reference to Its Status in the United States of America*, Canon Law Studies #39 (Washington, D.C.: Catholic University, 1927).

20. Although authorized by statute in many jurisdictions, the "corporation sole" originated in common law. See *Black's Law Dictionary*, s.v. "corporation, aggregate and sole": "A corporation sole is one consisting of one person only, and his successors in some particular station, who are incor-

porated by law to give them some legal capacities and advantages, particularly that of perpetuity, which in their natural persons they could not have had."

21. The "parish corporation model" referred to by the Congregation was first enacted in the state of New York. This model allowed for the separate civil incorporations of each parish in a diocese with five trustees: the diocesan bishop, the vicar general, the pastor, and two laymen.

22. Sacred Congregation of the Council, letter, 29 July 1911: *Canon Law Digest* (Milwaukee, Wisc.: Bruce, 1943), 2: 443–45.

23. Historians and, in fact, most people speak as if there were parishes in the United States shortly after the arrival of Catholicism in Maryland. Although there were indeed communities of the faithful who received pastoral care from a resident priest and thought of themselves as parishes, these communities were, canonically, not parishes but missions with no independent identity at canon law. It was only with the promulgation of the 1917 Code of Canon Law that existing communities of the faithful with a determined territory, a resident priest as pastor, and a source of revenue to provide for the pastor's support became canonical parishes with their own juridic personality. See the decision of the Pontifical Commission for the Interpretation of the Code of Canon Law of 26 September 1921, in Letter of Apostolic Delegate to the United States, 10 November 1922: *CLD* 1: 149–51.

24. Trisco, "Bishops and Their Priests in the United States," 229.

25. See Kevin McDonough, "Beyond Bureaucracy: New Strategies for Diocesan Leadership," *CLSA Proceedings* 61 (1999): 253–55; and Robert Kealy, "Methods of Diocesan Incorporation," *CLSA Proceedings* 48 (1986): 175–76.

26. Carey, *People, Priests, and Prelates*, 43.

27. A. A. Berle and G. C. Means, *The Modern Corporation and Private Property* (New York: Simon and Schuster, 1937), 124.

28. James H. Provost, "Canonical Reflections on Select Issues in Diocesan Governance," in *The Ministry of Governance*, ed. James K. Mallet (Washington, D.C.: CLSA, 1986), 212.

29. For an illustration of the impact of the corporate culture on the funeral industry in society and the church, see Michael Budde and Robert Brimlow, "The Church and the Death Business," in *Christianity Incorporated* (Grand Rapids, Mich.: Brazos Press, 2002), 83–108.

30. Carey, *People, Priests, and Prelates*, 284.

31. See Kealy, "Methods of Diocesan Incorporation," 175–76.

32. Kevin McDonough, "Diocesan Bureaucracy," *America* 177 (11 October 1997), 11.

33. Ibid.

34. *CIC*, c. 495, §1; James Provost, "The Working Together of Consultative Bodies—Great Expectations?" *The Jurist* 40 (1980): 278.

35. National Conference of Catholic Bishops, "Fund-Raising Guidelines," *CLD* 8: 415–21. See Frederick McManus, "Solicitation of Funds and Accountability," in *The Finances of the Church*, ed. William Bassett and Peter Huizing (New York: Seabury Press, 1979), 39–47.

36. See National Conference of Catholic Bishops (NCCB), *The Implementation of the 1983 Code of Canon Law: Complementary Norms* (Washington, D.C.: NCCB, 1991), 21. See also Robert T. Kennedy, "The Temporal Goods of the Church," in Beal et al., eds., *A New Commentary*, 1478–80.

37. *CIC*, c. 1292, §4.

38. Ibid., c. 1281, §2.

39. Ibid., c. 1281, §1.

40. Ibid., c. 1284, §3.

41. Ibid., c. 493.

42. Ibid., c. 1287, §1.

43. Ibid., c. 494, §4.

44. Ibid., c. 1287, §2.

45. Andrew Greeley and William McManus, *Catholic Contributions: Sociology and Policy* (Chicago: Thomas More, 1987), 78–91.

46. See Trisco, "Bishops and Their Priests in the United States," 111–292.

47. See Council of Elvira, c. 71, in Juan Vives, ed., *Concilios Visigóticos et Hispano-Romano* (Barcelona: Consejo Superior de Investigaciones Científicas, 1963), 14.

48. Richard Helmholz, *The Spirit of Classical Canon Law* (Athens: University of Georgia Press, 1996), 284–310.

49. *CIC*, c. 1722.

50. These criticisms were originally addressed to the Charter and Norms adopted by the USCCB in June 2002; see Beal, " 'Hiding in the Thickets of the Law.' " As modified here, they remain applicable to the revised norms adopted in November 2002.

51. See Richard John Neuhaus, "Scandal Time III," *First Things*, August/September 2002, 85–93.

# TEN

## Voice and Loyalty in the Church: The People of God, Politics, and Management

### Mary Jo Bane

This is not an easy time to be a Catholic. It is an easy time to be discouraged and to withdraw from the community fully or partially, to exercise the option of "exit" in response to disillusionment with the institution. And it is a very easy time in which to exercise an angry and resentful "voice."[1] Both of these responses are understandable. Neither is a particularly constructive option, consistent with our baptismal calling or with the long-term good of the Christian community. Instead, I believe we need to be developing a loyal voice, imagining and bringing into being the church that God would have us live in, in this place, in these times.

In arguing for a loyal voice, I am not proposing a subservient or deferential voice for laity, but one consistent with the grace conferred on all of us in baptism and therefore insistent on the equal dignity of clergy, laity, and hierarchy. A loyal voice, I suggest, is attentive to revelation and respectful of tradition but also confidently prophetic and visionary and as radical as the voice of the One who lives in the church forever. It is also a voice that is educated by the human sciences of politics and management. In this chapter, I attempt to explain why the insights of those disciplines are relevant, and how they can be useful as we struggle through the crisis in our church.

### The Church as Sacrament and Communion

The church is a unique institution, both divine and human. The first chapter of *Lumen Gentium*, the Vatican II Dogmatic Constitution on the Church, describes the church as "a sacrament—a sign and instrument, that is, of communion with God and of the unity of the entire human race."[2] The church both signifies and actualizes God's redemptive love and humanity's response to that love. As God is mystery, so too the church in its essence is mystery, existing in God's grace and conferring that grace, proclaiming and inaugurating, though neither embodying nor completing, the kingdom of God.

Though we can never fully grasp the mystery of God's presence in our world, we can enhance our understanding by considering different models of or perspectives on the church, as both *Lumen Gentium* and theologians before and after the Second Vatican Council have done. Avery Dulles (now Cardinal Dulles), for example, described six models: that of institution, mystical communion, sacrament, herald, servant, and community of disciples.[3] Each of these models highlights different aspects of the life of the church and its mission. One focuses on the structure and governance of the institutional church. Others emphasize the internal spiritual, sacramental, and community life of the church. Two highlight the external mission of the church to proclaim the gospel and serve the world. Dulles's community of disciples model attempts to integrate insights from his other models around the concept of discipleship, which brings together the community for worship and instruction and sends it out for witness and service.

In his assessment of the models, Dulles says that all of the models have strengths and weaknesses, but that one of them, the institutional model, "cannot properly be taken as primary."[4] He argues that institutional structures and practices exist to serve the church in its mission as a community of grace, a sacrament, a herald, and a servant to the world. The other models all reveal the church's character as a grace-filled and spirit-inspired community, called into being and given its mission by God.

The fundamental character and mission of the church, therefore, are not for humans to create or even to fully understand; they are given to us by the mystery that is God. This might be seen to imply a uniqueness in the church that would make all analogies to human institutions inappropriate. But the church as mystery and sacrament exists in human form—in the concrete, historically situated lives of men and women who worship God in community, serve their brothers and sisters, and lead lives that proclaim the coming of God's kingdom. The church also exists in buildings, budgets, governance structures, personnel policies, schedules, and programs. In understanding this human reality of the church as institution, we can be helped, I believe, by the secular disciplines that study politics and organizations. Although secular metaphors and analogies are imperfect and inadequate, some of what humans have learned throughout history about governing polities and structuring large and complicated institutions can be helpful as we struggle to exercise a loyal voice.

In using the insights from politics and management, it is worth recognizing that although the church is unique in its God-given character and mission, it is not alone among institutions in having a mission, values, and a vision that are external to its day-to-day operations and decision making. Successful modern human polities, for example, work within a framework of written or unwritten constitutions, which both reflect and shape underlying value commitments. Successful modern organizations in all three sectors—public, profit-making, and voluntary— are governed by a powerfully articulated mission that transcends and guides day-to-day decisions and activities.[5] To any given generation of citizens or members, the constitution and the mission are given, and loyal commitment to these basic principles is a necessary virtue.

The constitution and mission of the church are given to us in a much fuller and more profound sense: they come to us from God and must compel our deepest loyalty. But just as the constitutions of polities are interpreted and developed and the missions of organizations are adapted as they are applied over time to concrete circumstances and challenges, so must we interpret and develop the polity and the institution that is the church to respond to historical times and places. Like good Supreme Court justices and executive officers of corporations, we must interpret and develop them carefully, loyal to the intent of the founders and to the history that has gone before us; like them, we look to the foundational documents and the historical records; like them, we must interpret consistently with the deep—and mostly unwritten— values that sustain the institution. Unlike Supreme Court justices and executive officers, we need not rely only on our own intellects, but have the guidance of the Spirit, who, we have been promised, is with the church forever.

I start then with the notion of the church whose mission, values, and basic constitution have been given, and whose ongoing life is guided by the Spirit. Let me turn now to deal separately with the church as a polity and as a structured institution. I will sketch a few examples of issues in the human church around which a faithful voice may be needed and of ways in which it might be exercised.

## The Polity of the People of God

Jesus has called us to be a People of God living in a community that strives to embody in its own life the values Jesus taught us—a community that is generous, forgiving, inclusive, prayerful, peaceful, respectful of the gifts of all—and that continues Jesus' mission—to bring the good news to the poor, to set the captives free, to open the eyes of the blind; to make disciples of all nations and be witnesses for Jesus to the ends of the earth.

The People of God committed to the values and mission of Jesus continually face decisions about how to live and work as faithful disciples in a constantly changing world. In making our decisions, both individually and collectively, we must continually move between what has been given to us in the deposit of faith and our call to discipleship and the concrete historical situations in which we find ourselves. Neither revelation nor authority relieves us of this obligation. Even those who would find all their answers in the Bible face the challenge of scriptural selection and interpretation. Even those most respectful of episcopal authority, including bishops themselves, recognize that the necessary expertise for making thoughtful decisions about politics and ethics seldom resides in any one person or office. Our baptismal dignity and our appreciation of the universal call to holiness imply that all believers are obligated to carry out the mission of the church to proclaim the gospel and witness to the world. All must struggle to seek answers for themselves individually and for the community to the questions posed about the concrete definition of these obligations by society and history.

As just two among many examples, the People of God today must grapple with questions such as:

- What are our obligations to those within and outside the community—for example (in these times), to the poor in the developing world and to actual and potential victims of state and nonstate violence?

- What are our privileges and obligations as recipients of God's precious gift of sexuality to both use and discipline that gift in the service of God and of each other?

As members of a community of disciples, we cannot be satisfied with leaving such questions to individual decision-making, however conscientious and discerning. As God's people, we must struggle together as we worship together. So we need mechanisms by which decisions are made in and for the community.

Here we can learn from the secular sciences. Over time, human polities have developed structures and processes for guiding collective life and making public decisions that improve upon both anarchy and autocracy, whether in the form of warlords who seize power by force or hereditary monarchies. These new procedures recognize the fundamental equality of citizens; they make use of the contributions and insights of many; and they incorporate the insight that peace, productivity, and justice require consent to the structures and practices that make such societies possible. We call these mechanisms democratic.

Now in response to assertions that the church is not and cannot be a democracy, let me state as clearly as I can that I am not suggesting that the basic mission, values, beliefs, and constitution of the church are matters for voting. They are not. They are given to us by God; they command our assent and loyalty. What I am saying is that structures modeled on monarchies, which is what we have long had in the church, are not the only possible models for collective decision making that is faithful to a heritage and mission that are not invented but given.

Especially useful, I believe, are models of "deliberative democracy."[6] These move beyond a notion of democracy in which each person votes his or her own self-interest—in which outcomes are determined by a combination of bargaining, compromise, and majority rule. "Deliberative democracy," in contrast, encourages citizens to work together to discover or create the best outcome for the polity as a whole through a process of analysis, reflection, and respectful deliberation. This is analogous, I believe, though not perfectly, to what we might call in our own tradition a process of collective discernment. If we believe that our goal is to discern the will of God concerning the various concrete actions that we take, and if we believe that the Spirit works in the community as whole, then mechanisms that are grounded in the tradition but take advantage of the insights of all are more likely than more restricted processes to reveal God's plan.

Please note that neither deliberative democracy nor collective discernment gives equal weight to all opinions. Informed and reflective insights, grounded in serious and prayerful study of the foundational documents, of history, and of current circumstances, are privileged, as are the insights and experiences of the poor, the oppressed, and the otherwise voiceless. Students of political theory and politics are developing the justifications for these models and ways to put them into practice. I suggest here that there is much to learn from them. To illustrate this, I turn to two examples, one less controversial, one probably more so.

**Obligations to the poor.** My first example has to do with obligations to the poor and their exercise both through personal charity and through state action. That compassion and care for the poor and vulnerable are integral to the life of the church seems self-evident. The scriptures speak eloquently to these issues, and the church's magisterium has, over the years, spoken clearly and powerfully through council documents, papal encyclicals, and statements by conferences of bishops.[7] The application of these principles to the lives of individuals and the public policy of nations is not, however, self-evident, and popes and bishops in modern times have generally refrained from advocating specific policies or from mandating specific individual actions.[8]

But despite the rich teachings of the church on both charity and social justice, American Catholics are no more likely than members of other denominations to give to charity, to volunteer for the needy, or to support policies advocated by their bishops (for example, a policy of increased foreign aid for poor countries).[9] I believe this results at least partly from the fact that American Catholics have not been engaged in a collective process of deliberation and discernment, a process that would explore the complicated empirical realities in the context of scripture and tradition. Such a process would require recognition of the legitimate disagreements that men and women of good will can have over specifics, of the limited capacity of clergy and hierarchy to speak to the complexities of the issues, and of the productive learning and commitment that can come from a serious process of moral dialogue. Such a process would not only enrich the lives and shape the consciences of those engaged in it, but could also become embodied in liturgy and in parish activities. It could perhaps increase the service activities of Catholic parishes and individual Catholics, another arena in which Catholics fall behind their Protestant brothers and sisters.[10]

Moreover, it could provide the foundation for official statements that speak authoritatively from and for the church. The political effectiveness of the National Conference of Catholic Bishops (NCCB) and of Catholic Charities USA is limited by the fact that they are not perceived to speak for a 60 million-member church, with a correspondingly large number of voters. And they do not, in fact, speak for grassroots Catholics, at least as evidenced by opinion poll results. A process of deliberative democracy and discernment, both in creating policy documents and in disseminating them, could make for a much more effective public voice.

I suspect that these suggestions for deliberation around social justice issues do not sound particularly radical or particularly threatening to established practices, if only because the magisterium has not spoken infallibly about social justice, written specific obligations into canon law, or defined the failure to give generously to the poor as a serious sin. But for either hierarchy or laity to conclude that obligations to the poor are not important to Christian living and because of that can be safely left to individual conscience seems to me a misreading of the gospel. I suggest both that these obligations need to be taken much more seriously, and that the actual definitions and practices of the obligations need to emerge in specific times and places from deliberation and discernment by the whole community.

**Sexual morality.** On issues of sexual morality, my second example, the magisterium has spoken both specifically and definitively and has indeed defined concrete actions, like using birth control and engaging in homosexual activity, as serious sins. On these issues, there is no ongoing process of collective discernment, not because the magisterium does not take the issue seriously but because it does. However, the effects of church teachings in the lives of Catholics are just as discrepant as in the case of obligations to the poor: the sexual morality of Catholics is virtually indistinguishable from that of the population as a whole.

I suspect most lay Catholics do not understand or appreciate the self-giving theology that lies behind recent papal statements on sexual morality, and I also suspect that the hierarchy does not understand the lives and experiences of men and women struggling to be responsible spouses and parents. And because there is no Catholic forum in which conversations on the issues can be held, there is no possibility for the development of an ethic that would incorporate both understandings (perhaps full sexual self-giving as a counsel of perfection, a stance we take with regard to full giving of possessions to the poor?) and that men and women might actually strive to live by.

I personally believe that a process of collective discernment, guided by the Spirit, would come to a different position on birth control than the one currently held officially by the church, as did the process of discernment in the commission that advised Paul VI before he issued *Humanae Vitae*. I suspect the hierarchy also believes that would be the result, and are therefore determined not to engage in the process. But do we really believe that God is pleased by a situation in which God's church officially clings to a position that defines large numbers of God's people as "serious sinners," a designation that they do not accept? Or that God is pleased by a "don't ask, don't tell" attitude among both clergy and laity that results in a situation where the crucially important issues of sexuality are not discussed in either public or private religious settings? Should we not trust that the Spirit both desires and is able to remedy the situation? And does it not make sense that the way the Spirit might do this is through the participation in deliberation of the church as a whole?

## The Church as Structured Institution

We also have much to learn, I believe, from students of large organizations, including even corporations.

Jesus' own community of disciples did not need, nor did it have, much structure. But an institution with a billion members, hundreds of thousands of paid employees, and tens of billions of dollars in financial resources clearly needs mechanisms to ensure that the organization stays faithful to its mission, values, and practices, that it conscientiously stewards the resources entrusted to it, and that it is a model of integrity and rectitude. Large human institutions have responded over time to two crucial insights: that human beings are susceptible to corruption by power and money, and that no one person or small, closed group can be as creative or as productive as a larger group whose talents and energies are mobilized in the service of the mission.

We have learned recently, and at great human and financial cost, just how much havoc can be wrecked when power and greed are unchecked in corporations or in dioceses. We have certainly learned in the corporate world that simply expecting people to behave well and exhorting them to do so does not ensure financial rectitude or basic decency. Recognizing human fallibility has led to the development of financial management and human resources practices that protect organizations and their stakeholders from some of the temptations of power. The need for such standards and procedures does not go away simply because the managers of the organization are vowed or ordained.

The importance of standards of financial accountability and transparency has been illustrated by the devastating impacts of the recent wave of corporate scandals. In the church, many dioceses have experienced sharply declining collections, at least partly due to suspicions that funds were or are being used to settle cases of clergy abuse, and that these confidential settlements contributed to the cover-up and perpetuation of the scandal. Parishes and dioceses are not required by law to disclose their financial statements, as other tax-exempt organizations must do. Some church leaders claim that financial accountability would inhibit the discretion of the bishop. But financial transparency might have prevented some of the more egregious actions of the church in protecting priests and hiding wrongdoing. And of course inhibiting the discretion of the CEO is precisely what other organizations have found it necessary to do. The church would do well to learn from the private sector both the necessity and the techniques of sound financial management.

Large organizations have also come to understand the results of human fallibility when personnel decisions are made arbitrarily by a small group of leaders—they have learned the wrongs that occur from nepotism, favoritism, and patronage. Police departments, like some other organizations, have recognized the tendencies of closed "brother-hoods" to protect their members and hide their wrongdoing, sometimes with terrible costs to the citizens they are sworn to protect. These insights have led to the development of human resources systems that include clear and public procedures for hiring and assigning staff and for assess-ing their performance. They include mechanisms for citizen complaints and for civilian review boards. Cutting-edge human resources systems include both clear criteria of performance and what is called 360 assessment—gathering feedback on performance not simply from the person's superiors but from peers and clients. All of these aspects of good personnel management have been sadly lacking in the ways priests are dealt with. None of these mechanisms work perfectly. Nonetheless, they represent a genuine improvement over systems that make their personnel decisions in secret, without input from their stakeholders and the public. Here, too, the church has much to learn from the best that secular organizations have created. Those trained and experienced in these issues can and should insist on the basic controls and processes, and help the church at all levels figure out how to institute them.

Large organizations have also learned over time not only that many hands make light work but that many brains make better work. Tightly structured command and control hierarchies with all important deci-sions made by the person at the top have given way to flatter, less centralized, more participatory organizations—and to enormous divi-dends in creativity and productivity generated in part by a more commit-ted and energized workforce. The best results come in organizations that also have a clear and compelling mission and set of values, and that simultaneously with extending participation also extend, massively, education and training. Here, too, analogies with the church, though imperfect, are both obvious and helpful. How can community worship become more welcoming and compelling? How can faith formation be more effectively carried out? How can the good news be more persua-sively communicated? How can the neighbor in need be better cared for? How can parishes make better use of the gifts of all? The answers to these questions require commitment, creativity, and innovation within the context of the character and mission of the organization. These characteristics, in turn, require structures and practices that are designed to nurture them.

Participation, freedom, and decentralization, we have learned in our human institutions, can serve the mission and increase commitment to it. Surely our God, infinitely creative and inclusive, would want us to make use of these human innovations in service of the most important mission of all.

## Bringing a New Church into Being: Parish Foundations

Envisioning a church that is both faithful to its mission and tradition and responsive to the signs of these times is an important task facing the American church as it learns from and moves beyond the scandals and struggles of the last year. The intellectual task of articulating the vision is important and difficult, since the church is a unique institution, analogous in some ways to secular institutions but very different in other ways. Bringing the vision into being is equally important and difficult, and is a task for all the baptized. Laymen and -women have much to contribute to the mission and vitality of the church, expanding the dialogue about crucial issues at the intersection of the church and the secular world, and bringing to the management of the church insights from their secular experience.

But laymen and -women cannot work effectively or faithfully independent of clergy and hierarchy. Nor should they expect the hierarchy to turn over power to the laity either on their own accord or in response to demands. Laymen and -women need to build the foundations for expanded participation carefully and patiently, respecting the roles and the expertise of clergy and hierarchy. This is best done at the parish level, where clergy and laity together can develop the skills and the practice of collective discernment and participative management. As clergy and laity learn how to do this together, they will be building more vibrant parishes, and laying the foundations for new ways of working together in dioceses and the universal church.

The foundational activities for a parish are worship, prayer, study, and service. Few parishes perform these activities with the levels of involvement and excellence that the service of God deserves. Though contemporary American Catholics are the best-educated generation of laity in the church's history, few are well educated in scripture and theology, few are practiced in prayer, and few are engaged in service or evangelization. Catholic parishes, on average, are much less active places than congregations of other denominations in educational, developmental, and service activities. Compared with both conservative and mainstream Protestant congregations of similar size, Catholic parishes have on average fewer than half as many of their members involved in adult education, choirs, or work in the community.[11] This is due at least in part to the failure of parishes to develop their capacity as organizations by mobilizing and making effective use of financial and human resources. Catholic parishes, on average, operate with only about half as many financial resources per member as similarly situated Protestant congregations, with about half the staff and about a third the number of lay leaders.

Imagine what might happen if Catholic parishes became the vibrant and effective institutions that they have the potential to be. In addition to liturgy and the religious education of young people, which many parishes do very well, they might engage a large proportion of adults in scriptural and theological study—as evangelical congregations do. They might help form individual and collective consciences through serious reflection and dialogue on moral and political issues—dialogue that welcomes disagreement and does not shy away from political or theological controversy. They might work with community partners to serve the needy in their communities and overseas—as mainstream Protestant congregations do very effectively. They might advocate effectively for public policies that are pro-life, pro-family, and pro-poor. They might train lay spiritual directors to help enhance the prayer lives of many, not just a small elite. They might become genuinely multicultural communities through effective dialogue and programming.

This cannot happen, obviously, if only priests are allowed to do the work and manage each and every aspect of activity. It cannot happen if Catholics persist in their niggardly giving habits—which are perpetuated by lack of financial accountability, by lack of meaningful participation, and by less than excellent liturgies, preaching, and programming.[12] It cannot happen if lay Catholics are encouraged to cultivate passivity and deference.[13]

Luckily, many pastors and their parishioners know that genuine partnerships are the way out of their dilemmas and recognize that adopting within the parish some of the best practices of effective polities and organizations is part of the solution.[14] They have learned that clergy and laity praying, studying, and working together at the parish level, on activities ranging from scriptural and theological study to liturgy to financial management to service in the developing world may be the best way of developing the attitudes, knowledge, and skills so necessary for trust and for productive working relationships.

Intellectually vibrant, liturgically rich, and actively mission-driven parishes are fully church in themselves. They can also provide places to which diocesan and national groups (like the NCCB and Catholic Charities) can and perhaps will feel compelled to come for broader discussion of larger issues and for mobilization of resources for larger missions. They can be both models and advocates for comparable changes in the church at higher levels. By taking full advantage of the talents of clergy and laity, the robustness of the church both locally and universally, and the guidance of the Spirit, we can indeed bring into being an even more faithful church, a church in which Jesus will feel at home.

## Notes

1. The concepts of exit, voice, and loyalty were developed by the economist Albert Hirschman in *Exit, Voice, and Loyalty: Responses to Decline in Firms, Organizations, and States* (Cambridge, Mass.: Harvard University Press, 1972).

2. Vatican Council II, *Lumen Gentium*: Dogmatic Constitution on the Church, in *Vatican Council II: The Basic Sixteen Documents*, ed. Austin Flannery, O.P. (Northport, N.Y.: Costello Publishing Co., 1995), 1.

3. Avery Dulles, *Models of the Church* (New York: Doubleday Image Books, 1987). The sixth model, that of community of disciples, was added as chapter 13 in the 1987 edition.

4. Ibid., 198.

5. For one example from the private sector management literature of the emphasis on mission and vision, see James C. Collins and Jerry I. Porras, *Built to Last: Successful Habits of Visionary Companies* (New York: Harper-Collins Publishers, 1994). From the much smaller literature on the nonprofit sector, see Christine W. Letts, William P. Ryan, et al., *High Performance Nonprofit Organizations: Managing Upstream for Greater Impacts* (New York: John Wiley and Sons, 1999).

6. For an excellent exposition of these ideas, see Amy Gutmann and Dennis Thompson, *Democracy and Disagreement* (Cambridge, Mass.: Harvard University Press, 1996). They are developed in the Christian context by David Hollenbach, S.J., *The Common Good and Christian Ethics* (Cambridge, U.K.: Cambridge University Press, 2002).

7. See, for example, John Paul II, *Centesimus Annus: On the Hundredth Anniversary of Rerum Novarum*, in *Catholic Social Thought*, ed. David

J. O'Brien and Thomas A. Shannon (Maryknoll, N.Y.: Orbis Books, 1992), 439–88; and the National Conference of Catholic Bishops, *Economic Justice for All: Pastoral Letter on Catholic Social Teaching and the U.S. Economy* (Washington, D.C.: National Conference of Catholic Bishops, 1986).

An excellent collection of the basic documents is David J. O'Brien and Thomas A. Shannon, eds., *Catholic Social Thought: The Documentary Heritage* (Maryknoll, N.Y.: Orbis Books, 1998).

8. The Catholic bishops, for example, explicitly say that the chapters in *Economic Justice for All* that make policy recommendations do not carry the same authority as the chapters on biblical and ethical foundations.

9. I have reported my own research into these issues in "The Catholic Puzzle: Parishes and Civic Life," in Mary Jo Bane, Brent Coffin, and Richard Higgins, eds., *Taking Faith Seriously: Engaging and Evaluating Religion in American Democracy* (Cambridge, Mass.: Harvard University Press, forthcoming).

10. See ibid., and Nancy T. Ammerman, "Porous Boundaries and Busy Intersections: Religious Narratives in Everyday Public Spaces," in Bane, Coffin, and Higgins, eds., *Taking Faith Seriously*.

11. These data come from Mark Chaves, *National Congregations Survey: Data File and Codebook*, available at http://saint-denis.library.arizona.edu/natcong/.

12. For good analyses of Catholic giving, see Dean R. Hoge, Charles Zech, et al., *Money Matters: Personal Giving in American Churches* (Louisville, Ky.: Westminster John Knox Press, 1996); and Charles E. Zech, Francis J. Butler, et al., *Why Catholics Don't Give . . . And What Can Be Done about It* (Huntington, Ind.: Our Sunday Visitor, 2000).

13. This argument has been made persuasively by Thomas P. Sweetser, S.J., in many books and articles; see, e.g., Thomas P. Sweetser, S.J., *The Parish as Covenant: A Call to Pastoral Partnership* (Franklin, Wisc.: Sheed and Ward, 2001).

14. For lively descriptions of some effective parishes, see Paul Wilkes, *Excellent Catholic Parishes* (Mahwah, N.J.: Paulist Press, 2001).

# ELEVEN

## Good Governance, the Domestic Church, and Religious Education

### THOMAS GROOME

I begin by locating my chapter within the overarching theme of this collection—lay participation in the oversight of the church. Let me state the obvious at the outset. It is not that the laity may or might but rather that they must participate in the governance of the church. Lay participation in the church is not something that a clerical leadership "permits" or "allows." Rather, the laity must embrace and the ordained must recognize the rights and responsibilities that come to every Christian with baptism. Nor is this the proposal of some new or liberal theology; it is as traditional as the church itself. Since the beginning, Christians have understood their baptism as initiation into the Body of Christ, commissioning every member to carry on Jesus' mission to the world. Integral to adult faith is responsibility for and to the church.

Young children are not yet considered capable of exercising their full rights and fulfilling all their responsibilities in society; adults act on their behalf. But the vision of every parent is that children grow to maturity as persons and citizens; why should it be otherwise in matters of faith? Surely the church should not treat grown adults like dependent children all their lives, doing things for them and making their decisions, even if done benevolently. The epistle to the Ephesians insists that every Christian must use his or her gifts "for building up the body of Christ" (4:12); this is required precisely "that we may no longer be infants" (4:14).

To the Corinthians, Paul explained that all the gifts are from the same Spirit and are "given for some benefit" to the life and mission of the whole community (1 Cor 12:7). Or as 1 Peter puts it: "Each one has received a gift" and should "use it to serve one another as good stewards of God's varied grace"

(4:10). Though we can differentiate the gifts within the Christian community, none should triumph over or stifle the others. Rather than a few being agents in faith and all the rest dependents, Paul proposed a deep mutuality and equality within this Body of Christ: "For in one Spirit we were all baptized into one body, whether Jew or Greek, slave or free person, and we were all given to drink of one Spirit" (1 Corinthians 12:13). In the Body of Christ, no one is any more baptized than anyone else.

Thus, to argue for lay participation in the governance of the church is only to honor the radical theology of baptism reflected in the first Christian communities. I say "radical" because those early Christians were convinced that baptism should go to the very root (*radix*) of the Christian person and community, defining their identity, commitment, and lifestyle. I would go so far as to say that clerical leaders who oppose real lay participation in the life and governance of the church are in heresy by way of a traditional theology of baptism. Either we get to participate as full members or the church should stop baptizing us.

## Theology and Legislation Already in Place

The Second Vatican Council attempted to retrieve for Catholics this theology of baptism as embraced by the first Christians, and indeed for centuries thereafter. As such, Vatican II deepened our consciousness and commitment to lay participation in the mission of the church to the world and to care for the good stewardship of the church itself. The Council taught clearly that all Christians must participate actively in the church's work of carrying on the ministry of Jesus Christ "for the life of the world" (John 6:51), and within the church itself, that we have voice in its oversight and accountability. As the Dogmatic Constitution on the Church stated forcefully, lay Christians have an obligation "to express their opinion on things which concern the good of the Church."[1]

In the Decree on the Laity, the Council stated: "Christ conferred on the apostles and their successors the duty of teaching, sanctifying, and ruling in His name and power. But the laity, too, share in the priestly, prophetic, and royal office of Christ and therefore have their own role to play in the mission of the whole People of God in the Church and in the world."[2] Note the Council's insistence that our share in Jesus' royal function brings the right and responsibility to care for good governance in the church itself, as well as in society. And the Catechism of the Catholic Church reiterates this point: "By baptism, all share in the priesthood of Christ, in his prophetic and royal mission."[3]

Vatican II went on to encourage the development of parish councils and diocesan councils in which "clergy, religious, and lay people will participate."[4] Then, in its revision of the Code of Canon Law (1983), the church put in place the canonical structures by which "lay members of the Christian faithful can cooperate in the exercise of this power" of governance.[5] Following on, the new code legislated for lay participation in diocesan synods[6] and in diocesan pastoral councils,[7] and it decreed that pastoral and financial councils be established in every parish.[8] It is true that the code sounds cautious on the limits of lay participation (e.g., the diocesan council serves only at the discretion of the bishop,[9] and a parish council "possesses a consultative vote only").[10] Yet it well establishes the principle in the law of the church: laypeople are entitled to participate in its governance.

We can say, then, that the theology and legislation are already in place. What remains to be done is implementation "on the ground." Perhaps the Holy Spirit is lending fresh impetus in our own time. Some of the good that God may draw from the current crisis might be to reengage us with this unfinished agenda of Vatican II. I summarize that agenda as reclaiming our baptism. We should not be naive, however, about the roadblocks that are still in place to the vision of the Council and its understanding of baptism. The particular impediment that I highlight and challenge here is clericalism.

### Clericalism as Pernicious to Priesthood

Let me make amply clear that I deeply cherish the sacrament of Holy Orders. An abiding commitment throughout my life has been to its renewal and reform. As Catholic Christians, the sacramental economy is core to our faith; and the quality of the church's sacramental life depends so much on its priesthood. However, I am equally convinced that the renewal of ordained priesthood can be effected only within a renewed priesthood of the laity. As we claim the rights and responsibilities of our baptism, and mature as a priestly people, we will effect the needed reforms and renewal of ordained priesthood as well. Meanwhile, we must recognize clericalism for what it is—pernicious to both ordained priesthood and to the priesthood of all believers. We must determine to root it out of our ecclesial structures and to erase it from our own consciousness.

By clericalism I mean an exclusive and elitist ideology that pedastalizes the ordained as if they are ontologically superior to other baptized Christians. Clericalism encourages a caste system, closed in upon itself and bonded to insist upon its own preference and privilege. Clericalism presumes upon a spiritual way that is far holier—preferred by God—than the ordinary path trod by all but its chosen few; in particular, it considers the married life as spiritually inferior to the celibate.

I recently heard a friend sound a note that echoed an old cultural Catholicism familiar to me; she said, "Since I was a kid, priests have been like little gods to me." She then went on to berate herself for being "so naive." I reminded her, however, that her attitude reflected how the Catechism of the Council of Trent spoke of priesthood. The Catechism of Trent, or the Roman Catechism as it was better known (first published in 1566), was how the decrees of Trent reached into the lives of ordinary people. In many cultures, priests were encouraged to draw their weekly sermon from the Roman Catechism, reviewing it over a three-year cycle. About priesthood, it declared:

> Priests and bishops are, as it were, the interpreters and messengers of God, commissioned in his name to teach men the divine law. They act in this world as the very person of God. It is evident that no office greater than theirs can be imagined. Rightly have they been called angels (Mic 2:7), even gods (Exod 22:28), holding as they do among us the very name and power of the living God.

It continues: "[T]he power of the Christian priesthood is literally heavenly; it surpasses the very power of the angels."[11]

To be fair, of course, such a statement should be read in its historical context. The more the Reformers preached a "priesthood of all believers," the more the Roman church emphasized the ontological superiority of ordained ministry. So the polemics of the time caused such exaggeration. Nevertheless, the "effective history" (Gadamer)[12] of such statements was not a balanced respect for priesthood—that indeed we should have—but a clericalism that is inimical to the vocation of ordained ministers and to the priesthood of the laity as well. On the one hand, what a hazard it is for mere mortals to enjoy such power and adulation; on the other, if they be "gods," then the laity can only "adore" them and leave everything in their anointed hands.

By contrast, authentic Christian priesthood is a servant leadership that tends to the "holy order" of a priestly people. Servant leadership—remember Jesus warning the apostles that they were never to "lord it over" or pull rank on anyone, but that "the greatest among you must be the servant of the rest" (see Mark 10:35–45; Matthew 20:20–28; Luke 22:24–26). Once, when disciples were arguing about "who is the greatest," Jesus told them that they must "become like children" to enter God's reign (see Matthew 18:1–5).

Though common parlance understands "hierarchy" as a top-down chain of command, originally *hier arche*—the opposite of *an arche*—meant "holy order." Its active meaning was to enable a community to work well together. The ministerial function of priests is still well named as "holy order," for it highlights their responsibility to nurture and engage the gifts of the whole faith community. They should be the catalysts for a community to function effectively, to work well together. Such *hier arche* would encourage the very opposite of dependency among the laity. It demands our agency in faith, encouraging this priestly people to participate with rights and responsibilities in the Christian community, working together to carry on Jesus' mission in the world.

Acting as servant leaders of holy order—this, of course, is what good priests do and struggle mightily in the effort, recently against even greater odds: embarrassment, bewilderment, discouragement, and more. Theirs, indeed, is an uphill battle—to remain good priests and not be colonized by the ideology of clericalism. Likewise, it is a struggle for the laity to embrace their responsibilities as a priestly people. There has long been a complex coalition of factors, deeply rooted in the culture of the Catholic Church, that encourage clericalism on the part of priests and the corresponding dependency on the part of laypeople. Indeed, this clericalism effectively socializes lay Catholics to treat priests as "gods"; and without a lot of self reflection and spiritual maturity, priests can be lulled into expecting as much. Pernicious!

As long as clericalism reigns, there can be no real participation by laypeople in the governance of the church. For the more we internalize dependency, the more we avoid our own agency and responsibilities in faith. Either by default or by design, we will always "leave it to them" to teach, sanctify, and govern in our place and on our behalf. If the current crisis has convinced us of anything, it should be that clericalism and the lack of lay participation in church oversight can be hazardous to the faith lives of people and to the safety of our children, and can wound the very mission of the church.

## Beginning "Close to Home"

The causes of clericalism are many and complex; analyzing them is beyond the scope of this chapter, and indeed the competence of this author. It is far more than a theological issue, and we need the help of social scientists to even begin to understand it. It should be enough to say that we must embrace the struggle to rid the church's culture of this malady. But where do we begin? Without lessening our commitment to the reform of church structures, let us begin where we can most readily begin—with our own hearts, lives, and families.

Clericalism colonizes our consciousness; it is inside of us as much as outside in the structures of the church. While we struggle on for lay participation in the oversight of the church, we can practice being a priestly people without further delay. Here I focus on how we can do so in the context of our own families and in the function of the family as religious educator. This suggestion may surprise the reader at first, but think about it: Vatican II reclaimed the ancient Christian notion of the family as "the domestic church."[13] So shouldn't our practice of good governance, free of clericalism and fulfilling our agency in faith, include our families as well as our parishes and dioceses? In fact, Vatican II's Constitution on the Church in the Modern World declared that "the Christian family . . . will manifest to all . . . the genuine nature of the Church."[14] Even if my church is still a bastion of clericalism, my family does not need to be so.

The pastoral epistles call Christians to "good governance" in their own families. In fact, people should not be chosen for governance in the public faith community—for *episcope* or oversight—unless their family life is also marked by good governance. Thus, 1 Timothy 3:2–5 says that a "bishop should be above reproach, the husband of one wife," and should "manage his own household well," for if someone "cannot manage his own household well, how can he care for God's church?" This sentiment is repeated in the epistle to Titus 1:5–11. Apart from the subversive memory that bishops should be of one spouse, there is a clear mandate here that Christians practice good governance in the domestic as well as the public church.

The emphasis on equality among the first Christian communities initially encouraged an egalitarian mode within the family as well, challenging the patriarchal order of the time. However, this sentiment was muted by the "household codes" reflected in the later deutero-Pauline and pastoral epistles; see, for example, the instructions to husbands and wives, parents and children, masters and slaves in Ephesians 5:22–6:9. Yet when contemporary scriptural scholars read such texts in the context of their time, they still insist that the Christian ecology of the family was a significant challenge to the patriarchy of the Roman household code—the dominant paradigm.[15] Good governance in the family, as in the church, did not intend for a male patriarch to lord it over the household, but called the family to function with love and mutuality as a particular instance of the Body of Christ.

### "Family" as Educator, Sadly Replaced by "School"

Throughout the Gospels, Jesus is often addressed as teacher, and teaching is the most frequent description of his work. Thus, to be a disciple—an apprentice—to Jesus demands of all Christians that they share their faith. In fact, the last great mandate that the Risen Christ gave to his community of disciples was to go teach all that he had taught (see Matthew 28:16–20). This mandate was given to all present on that hillside in Galilee—a universal commission. And it is very clear from the epistles that Christian families were to participate in the ministry of teaching the faith. That household code in Ephesians makes it clear that parents should "bring up their children with the training and instruction of the Lord" (6:4). To echo the King James translation here, parents were to "nurture" their children in Christian faith.[16]

That parents are the primary educators of their children is a wisdom of the ages, reflected throughout all ancient cultures. Here, however, we must be cautious not to hear "education" as synonymous with "schooling" and didactic teaching. The primary mode of parental education is through apprenticeship and the ethos of the home, by the enculturation and socialization that takes place through the medium of family life.

The first Christians knew well that good family governance required good religious education—within the family. However, this awareness did not survive the emergence of universal schooling. The schooling paradigm, instead of becoming a partner with family education, soon led to neglect of the latter. Today the dominant mentality—at least in Western societies—is that education is synonymous with schooling.

The notion of universal schooling emerged slowly in the Western world and represented a major breakthrough in social consciousness. Plato first made the philosophical argument that all citizens should be formally educated (though remember that "citizen" included less than 10 percent of the population in Plato's time). The first real attempt came when the emperor Charlemagne decreed (circa 800) that the monastic schools must be open to all boys of the empire, not only to those interested in becoming monks. The acknowledgment that girls should have equal access to schooling would take another thousand years.

The watershed for schooling came with the great Reformation catchcry of "sola scriptura," calling all Christians to read the Bible for themselves, thereby encouraging universal literacy. Indeed, the precise catalyst for "public" education was Luther's letter of 1524 to the German nobles urging them to establish and fund schools that would make literate every child—boys and girls. Luther, however, never intended schooling to replace family education. In that letter, he advised that boys attend school for no more than two hours each day and girls for only one, lest their schooling diminish their education at home and in the world around them.[17]

Alas, Martin's caution fell on deaf ears. Before long, the whole Western world had bought hook, line, and sinker into the "schooling paradigm," equating universal education—a fine ideal—with universal schooling. Now the school subsumed everything that could pass for education, with the parental role reduced to seeing to it that children attended a didactic process by professional teachers in an institution designed to "school" them. And though the professionalization of teaching was a social advance, the unfortunate underside was the impression that amateurs—like parents—have very little to contribute to the education of children. Though Huckleberry Finn said that he tried not to let his schooling interfere with his education, the rest of the world wasn't nearly so wise.

For education in faith, the church embraced the schooling model with equal gusto. This is not to dismiss the great catechetical work of the Confraternity for Christian Doctrine (CCD), or of parochial schools. However, the notion came to prevail that the parental role in religious education is to see to it that children attend some kind of parochial school or parish program of catechesis. Ridiculous as it sounds, we can even assume that if we "drop off" our kids for a one-hour-once-a-week parish program, we can come back later and "pick up" Christians.

There were some dissenting voices to totalizing the schooling paradigm. Writing first circa 1845, Horace Bushnell proposed that family nurture must be the primary mode of faith formation. He argued "[t]hat the child is to grow up a Christian, and never know himself as being otherwise," and was convinced that nurture in faith should be done primarily by the family.[18] In the early 1970s, Ivan Illich proposed "deschooling society" as a strategy for educational reform. Though too radical to get a hearing, Illich was trying to shift public consciousness beyond "education equals schooling," and was proposing to engage all social agencies in intentional education. In particular, he wanted parents to reclaim their role as primary educators.[19] Alas, his prophetic call was heard as utopian—read "impossible."

While the schooling paradigm triumphed in Western education—both general and religious—I am convinced that among Catholics the parental role was further discouraged by clericalism. In religious education this took the form of parents losing confidence in their own faith and their abilities to share it, and presuming that they should "leave it to Father" or "to Sister." In other words, parents lost their sense of agency as religious educators, becoming dependent on the official "experts" instead. The church even encouraged parents to assume that "they"—the experts—are the only ones who can do it well and will do it for us. I recently had a notable theologian (though not of Boston College) complain to me that his children simply don't know their faith and he blamed the local parish program. I finally said, "But why don't you teach them yourself?" It was as if I had taken the ground from under him. We then had an insightful conversation about how readily parents can expect "them" to do religious education instead of "us."

Schools are fine institutions (generally) and I am certainly not arguing against them. In catechetical education, who can deny the enormous contribution of parochial schools and Sunday schools of various types—both struggling against huge odds? I am only claiming that the schooling paradigm for educating children in faith must not be totalized, because it allows parents to forego their responsibilities; it reflects a kind of clericalism and diminishes our own priestly function. As an aspect of good governance within the domestic church, we parents must reclaim our primary function in the religious education of our children. Concretely, what might this mean?

### Reclaiming the Family as Religious Educator

Let me reiterate: for parents to be religious educators does not mean becoming more didactic in the home, buying a desk and a chalkboard and setting aside a time for regular instruction. To think this way is to remain captive to the schooling paradigm. In fact, intentional instruction in faith is probably best done in schools and parish programs. Instead, family catechesis means suffusing the whole life of the family with the values, symbols, and activities that will nurture children in Christian identity and mature the faith of parents as well. Intentionally crafting family life to educate in faith is integral to good governance in the domestic church.

By "family" I intend any and every community of domestic life. In other words, we need to shift our imaginations beyond the nuclear family of a mom, dad, and two kids, to include extended and blended families, single-, double-, and triple-parent families, straight, gay, and bent families. Family is any bonded network of domestic life and nurture. Here let me make an important parenthetical point.

I love to ask gatherings of religious educators, "How many of you grew up in a perfect family?" Invariably, no matter how big the crowd, no one ever puts up a hand. The truth is that likely 95 percent of our families are "dysfunctional" in one way or another—to use the fashionable term. But since when has God been choosy about instruments? My friend Trish is likely one of the best parents I know, with irrefutable evidence in the two wonderful children she has raised. Yet Trish has faced more social problems than most people even imagine. She came from an immigrant family and had little formal education and low earning power; she was a single parent living in poor housing; yet Trish had an extraordinary capacity to love her kids and raised them with the best of Christian values. Come to think of it, the "holy family" of Nazareth began with a teenage pregnancy out of wedlock and a great age disparity between the couple, yet look at the wonderful child they raised.

Parents should also recognize a great reciprocity between sharing faith with their children and the renewal of their own faith—what they receive in return. I have long been convinced that parents are primary religious educators to their children, but of late I am learning that children can be religious educators of their parents as well. On January 8, 2001, just four days after his birth, our wonderful little son, Theodore Thomas Griffith-Groome, now mercifully shortened to "Ted," came home to us. So, here we are, after a decidedly late start—at least for me—in the throes of young parenting. As the poet Yeats once wrote of Easter, "all changed, changed utterly, a terrible beauty is born."

Among many other learnings for me, I am recognizing how sacramental children can be to parents' lives—if we are open to God's grace working through them. I could tell a hundred stories of how Ted has nurtured my own faith; I'll tell just one here. When he was about nine months old, we were out for an early morning walk. The wind was blowing through the autumn leaves, bringing showers of them to the ground. Suddenly I became aware that Ted was mesmerized by this, I could literally "see" him listening to the wind as it rustled through the trees and being fascinated by the falling leaves. Then I, too, stopped and marveled at the wind and the beauty of the autumnal leaves—that I had not noticed before—and recognized again my own mortality. Family religious education works both ways.

## How the Domestic Church Can Educate in Faith

One way to be intentional about family religious education is to take seriously the notion of family as "domestic church." This suggests that each family should reflect within its life together all the ministries carried on by the public church, albeit with its own familial mode. Thus, the family's sacramental economy will be the feeding, caring, reconciling, serving, and so on that goes on in every Christian family, rather than setting up a mini-parish at home. This being said, I propose that all of the ministries of a Christian community can be carried on by a family, and should be done with a catechetical consciousness—should be designed to educate in faith. Precisely, the family should monitor everything about its shared life for how it nurtures the faith of its members.

We can outline the church's ministries in many ways. Since the earliest days, however, six Greek terms have had pride of place in naming the distinct functions of a Christian community:

*koinonia*—to be a life-giving community of faith, hope, and love;

*marturia*—to bear witness to Christian faith;

*leitourgia*—to worship God together;

*diakonia*—to care for human needs out of Christian conviction;

*kerygma*—to evangelize and share the Good News;

*didache*—to teach the scriptures and traditions of Christian faith.

I will summarize these functions in a fourfold schema (pairing *marturia* with *koinonia*, *didache* with *kerygma*) as the functions of *witness, worship, word,* and *welfare.* Let us imagine each being realized in the family and being done with a catechetical consciousness.

Family as witness requires that the whole life of the home be suffused with the values and perspectives of Christian faith. The members must constantly review the family's ethos and atmosphere, lifestyle and priorities, relationships and gender roles, language patterns and conversations, work and recreation—every aspect to monitor how well it reflects the convictions and commitments of Christian faith. Good governance requires that everything about a Christian family bear witness to its faith; this is how it educates most effectively in Christian identity.

Family as a worshipping community calls it to integrate shared prayer and sacred ritual into its patterns of daily life. To be effective as catechist, every Christian family needs its own "liturgy" to symbolize and celebrate its faith. I once asked a devout Jewish friend how she came by her strong Jewish identity; she immediately responded, "Oh, from the rituals in my home." Surely every Christian family can create or rediscover—old Christian cultures had plenty of them—sacred rituals for the home that will nurture the Christian identity of its members. Without family prayer and sacred symbols, the Christian home lacks good governance and is less likely to educate in faith.

Family as a community of word calls members to share their faith around scripture and tradition, among themselves and in the broader community. Even while participating in the formal programs of a parish, every Christian should be "home-schooled" in their faith. Parishes must help parents—with resources, training, suggestions, support, encouragement, expectation—to integrate God's word into the conversations of family life. In my own childhood I recall how much God-talk suffused daily conversation; phrases like "with God's help," "God willing," "God is good," and so on, were woven into our everyday speech. They can still be so in any home. By way of something more formal, I know a family that has "scripture time" every Monday night after supper. They read from the Sunday lectionary and then share what each one heard for their lives. Imagine the long-term effect on the faith of both parents and children. What an instance of good governance in the domestic church!

Family as providing human welfare requires care for the spiritual, physical, and emotional well-being of its own members, rippling outward to society and especially to the poor and those most in need. Family life must reflect love and compassion toward all, promoting justice within itself and the social values of God's reign in the world. If children grow up and adults dwell within a family that lives the values of mercy and compassion, of justice and peace, they are most likely to embrace the social responsibilities of Christian faith. Good governance in a family should include such *diakonia*; and what a powerful mode of religious education it would prove to be.

All such efforts at good governance require intentionality, especially on the part of adults in a family. Little of family catechesis "just happens," or certainly a lot more can happen if we are intentional about it. Parents can deliberately craft the environment of the home and engage all the functions of home life to educate in Christian faith. Over the long haul, what an impact such good governance will have on the life of the church and the world. It may take a generation or two, but children raised with such good governance within their domestic church will surely insist upon as much in the structural life of their public church as well.

## The Domestic Is Political

Two pressing issues that the clergy sex abuse scandal has brought to the fore for concerned Catholics are the structures of church governance and accountability, coupled with how effectively we are passing on our faith to the rising generations. These have been two of the three emphases of the Boston College initiative "Church in the Twenty-first Century: From Crisis to Renewal" (the third emphasis being issues regarding sexuality). I have coupled the two here, linking them through the family. I propose that good governance is needed in the domestic as well as the public church, and that such governance is realized to the extent that a family's shared life reflects the values and mission of a Christian community. Such domestic governance, then, is key to the family's function as religious educator.

My proposal requires at least two significant shifts in consciousness for "old" Catholics like myself: (1) when we think of participating in church governance—the right and responsibility of our baptism—we must include the domestic as well as the public church in our efforts at reform and renewal; and (2) we must break open our notion of religious education far beyond the schooling paradigm—without leaving schools or formal programs behind—and reclaim its primary location within the family and faith community. A danger in my proposal, and a worthy challenge to it, is that it could be read as diverting attention away from the need for reform in the public church, limiting our faith to the domestic arena—the shortsighted sentiment of modernity.

One of the myths foisted on Western consciousness by the Enlightenment era is that the domestic and the political belong to two different realms, one private and the other public, with religion limited to the family context and politics limited to society. But a valuable insight from contemporary feminist literature is to unmask this myth as false and misleading. In fact, the life and structures of domesticity are eminently political, with a deep reciprocity between what goes on "in the world" and what goes on "at home." We must embrace this insight as we struggle for church reform and renewal. Instead of choosing either/or in our efforts, we must choose both/and, attending to good governance in both the domestic and the public church. By God's grace, whatever success we have in either arena will have positive effects in the other.

## Notes

1. Dogmatic Constitution on the Church, no. 37, in Walter Abbott, ed., *The Documents of Vatican II* (New York: America Press, 1966), 29.

2. Decree on the Laity, no. 2, in ibid., 491.

3. *Catechism of the Catholic Church*, 2d ed. (Washington, D.C.: United States Conference of Catholic Bishops, 2000), no. 1268, p. 323.

4. Decree on Bishops, no. 2, in Abbott, ed., *Documents of Vatican II*, 397.

5. *Code of Canon Law*, English translation by the Canon Law Society of America (Washington, D.C.: Canon Law Society of America, 1983), canon 129:2.

6. Ibid., canon 463.

7. Ibid., canon 512.

8. Ibid., canons 536 and 537.

9. Ibid., canon 514.

10. Ibid., canon 536:2.

11. *The Roman Catechism* (Boston: Daughters of St. Paul, 1985), 308 and 312.

12. See Hans-Georg Gadamer, *Truth and Method* (New York: Crossroad, 1990), 301–2.

13. Dogmatic Constitution on the Church, no. 11, in Abbott, ed., *Documents of Vatican II*, 29.

14. Constitution on the Church in the Modern World, no. 48, in Abbott, ed., *Documents of Vatican II*, 252.

15. See, for example, Elisabeth Schüssler Fiorenza, *Bread Not Stone* (Boston: Beacon Press, 1984), esp. ch. 4.

16. This became the flagship text for the classic work of Horace Bushnell promoting family-centered religious education, titled *Christian Nurture* and first published in 1860.

17. See Martin Luther, "To the Councilmen of All Cities in Germany That They Establish and Maintain Christian Schools," in Kendig Cully, ed., *Basic Writings in Christian Education* (Philadelphia: Westminster Press, 1960), 137–49.

18. Horace Bushnell, *Christian Nurture* (New Haven, Conn.: Yale University Press, 1947), 4.

19. See Ivan Illich, *Deschooling Society* (New York: Harper and Row, 1971).

# TWELVE

## The Emerging Role of the Catholic Laity: Lessons from Voice of the Faithful

### JAMES E. POST

The Catholic Church entered the twenty-first century with a host of administrative, policy, and doctrinal problems. The complexity of the church's administration, plus an intense conflict between Vatican-led advocates of centralized authority and proponents of decentralized authority, made some form of administrative crisis predictable. Unforeseen by most observers, however, was the emergence of a scandal surrounding clergy sexual abuse of children that would form the specific context in which these pressures would erupt. The results, in the view of observers, have been nothing less than catastrophic.[1]

The sexual abuse of children by members of the clergy was thrust into the public arena by two uniquely American institutional forces: the courts and the media. The courts provided the forum for hearing the criminal and civil charges against priests, and the media covered the scandal, asking questions about causality and complicity, and exploring the sinecures of church power that safeguarded predator priests for decades.

Clergy sexual abuse occurred in churches, schools, and religious programs because the relationship between adults, who were ordained to a religious life that emphasizes morality, and children, who were young and compliant with the commands of authority figures, fostered trust and dependency between child and adult. That the adult was a priest made it easier for the child to trust and more shattering when that trust was violated. The court orders that eventually forced church officials to release personnel records of priests accused of abuse, and the media's commitment to publishing such correspondence, provided the American public with an incomparable window into the inner workings of church administration. Many laity did not like what they saw. The result was a public outcry of the sort not heard in Catholicism for hundreds of years. The role of the laity came to be redefined through this crisis of Catholicism.

Two themes resonate throughout the story of the clergy sexual abuse scandal. The first involves the clash of two *-isms*: secularism and clericalism. The problems of the secular world—power, sex, gratification, consumption, and self-absorption—converged with the problems of the clerical world, including power, privilege, and secrecy. Both worlds invite excesses and abuse of authority: the Enron Corporation and the Catholic Church have more in common than either business leaders or bishops would like to admit. Moral integrity is a casualty of both secularism and clericalism, and it is lost at both the individual and the institutional level. For the Catholic Church, the convergence of secularism and clericalism in the sexual abuse scandal confirmed the worst fears of those who believe that the church has either forsaken fidelity to gospel teachings, or, alternatively, that church leaders have embraced the rituals of "ultramontanism" in lieu of faithfulness to gospel values.[2]

The second theme that resonates throughout the sexual abuse crisis is the gap between the prevailing administrative practices of the church and the modern theory and practice of management. Managing complex institutions has become a sophisticated profession in the past fifty years, with more highly educated executives in every sphere of organizational life. A sea change has taken place in the governance, guidance, and management of public, private, and nonprofit entities in recent times.

One area of importance is the creation of new tools to promote institutional accountability. The search for effective remedies to the abuse of power and weak governance has led scholars and public officials to redesign governance structures and systems in ways that favor openness, transparency, and accountability in business, government, and nonprofit organizations. The sexual abuse crisis raised the question, Why does the Catholic Church ignore the lessons of good practice drawn from the business, governmental, and nonprofit sectors?

Crises often spur organizations to action. The responses may take personal, organizational, or institutional form, and very often, all three types of change transpire. As the sexual abuse crisis escalated and the gap between public expectations and institutional performance widened, pressure mounted on bishops, priests, laity, and the community to "do something." Individuals felt compelled to speak out and take action "in good conscience"; new organizations, such as Voice of the Faithful and Voice of the Ordained, were created. Existing institutions struggled to cope with criticism, and the new realities of American Catholicism emerged for the public—Catholic and non-Catholic alike—to see. The result was a swirl of ideas about causes and symptoms, remedies and solutions. These ideas produced a vigorous and unusually public debate about the strengths and the failings of the structures, processes, and culture of the Catholic Church.

To many, this public conversation about the behavior of the Catholic Church was a gust of fresh air blowing through a musty institution. To some observers, the crisis pointed to an urgent need to correct aspects of a system that had failed to protect children and defend Catholic values.[3] To others, the crisis drew attention to the need for reform-oriented leaders, rejection of authoritarian behavior, and attention to institutional decline. Mostly, however, the numerous calls for change encouraged practical people to think in practical ways about fixing a system that had not protected children from the moral depravity of pedophile priests.

Virtually no one defended the status quo. But not everyone welcomed "fresh air" into the church. Some saw the crisis as a serious threat to an established order—a system of faith, action, and authority. Their message seemed to be, "Respond, yes; change, no."[4] As a result, the pressures for changing the church contested with pressures for defending traditional administrative ways. The tension was both creative and destructive. And at its center was the question of what role the Catholic laity could—and *should*—play in the Catholic Church of the twenty-first century.

## History of a Crisis

Historians and scholarly observers of the Catholic Church have argued that the clergy sexual abuse scandal precipitated the worst crisis in the church's entire 500-year history in North America. The sexual abuse crisis had deep roots, but was not a highly visible controversy until 2002. Although a number of high-profile cases took place in the United States between 1985 and 2000 (e.g., the criminal case against Fr. James Porter in Fall River, Massachusetts), they did not command public attention or generate widespread public pressure for reform. Things began to change on January 6, 2002, when the *Boston Globe* published the first of a series of special "Spotlight Team" investigative reports regarding the administrative handling of Fr. John Geoghan, a Catholic priest who had molested more than 100 children over the course of nearly thirty years. The *Globe* reported on a collection of church documents that Massachusetts judge Constance Sweeney had ordered the Archdiocese of Boston to release to plaintiffs (Geoghan victims) as part of a pretrial discovery process. The *Globe* had requested court permission to review the records; Judge Sweeney approved the request.[5]

Church records revealed that Fr. Geoghan had been transferred from one parish to another, despite numerous allegations of sexual abuse. The records showed that Geoghan had been sent to various medical facilities for treatment of his "illness" over the course of several decades, but always returned to ministry despite the misgiving of therapists and physicians. The pattern of relocation and concealment was guided by an administrative policy of the Archdiocese of Boston, headed by Cardinal Bernard F. Law, the Archbishop of Boston.

The *Globe*'s investigative work started in August 2001, when sources convinced the editorial staff that the Geoghan trial would "blow the lid off" the long-rumored story of widespread clergy sexual abuse. The secrets surrounding pedophilia and child abuse that had been so successfully kept out of public sight were about to become very public knowledge.

### A Great Awakening

The Geoghan disclosures launched a painful period of awakening for Catholics in Boston and elsewhere. For one year, the story of clergy sexual misconduct provided daily front-page stories for newspaper and television audiences. Geoghan was the first of a series of priests whom the world would come to know as sexual predators.

In April 2002, another wave of sensational charges occurred when a Massachusetts court ordered the Archdiocese of Boston to turn over the personnel records of Fr. Paul Shanley to plaintiffs' attorneys. These files revealed a pattern of sexual abuse and manipulation that appeared even more depraved and scandalous than that of Fr. Geoghan. Fr. Shanley was a charismatic priest, whose strong personality and commitment to working with "street kids" made him a local hero in Boston. Unfortunately, his actions also involved the alleged rape and abuse of countless vulnerable children and teens. Inexplicably, the Archdiocese of Boston's administrators never "pulled the plug" on Shanley by withdrawing him from these ministries. Instead, he too was transferred from parish to parish. His assignments continued to provide access to children. He was reported to have attended meetings of the National Man-Boy Love Association (NAMBLA) and to have publicly stated that there was nothing wrong when an adult engaged in sexual relations with a child.

These revelations fanned the flames of public outrage. People were shocked at reports of Shanley's behavior and aghast at the cover-up and concealment by various bishops of the archdiocese. Public speculation focused on whether Shanley was blackmailing officials of the archdiocese. "How else," people wondered, "could he have remained free for so many years?" Officials of the Archdiocese of Boston even wrote recommendation letters to the bishop of San Bernardino, California, claiming that they knew of no reason Shanley could not be assigned to work in that diocese. The public disclosures prompted Shanley, who relocated to California in the late 1990s, to go into hiding. He was apprehended on a fugitive warrant in May 2002 and returned to Massachusetts to be tried on criminal charges of child rape.

The Geoghan and Shanley revelations were major turning points in the scandal and produced a wave of public relations responses from officials of the Catholic Church. On March 9, 2002, Cardinal Law met with 3,000 lay leaders from the parishes of the Archdiocese of Boston. The program for this "convocation" was radically restructured in the weeks before to include major listening sessions in which members of the laity could share their views of the crisis with the cardinal and auxiliary bishops. The media also attended (but was not permitted into the hall), and news coverage of the event was extensive. The event provided the first public forum at which members of Voice of the Faithful stated their mission, goals, and agenda.

In April 2002, the Vatican summoned the American Catholic prelates (including Cardinals Bevilaqua, Dulles, Egan, George, Keeler, Law, Mahoney, and McCarrick) and Bishop Wilton Gregory, president of the United States Conference of Catholic Bishops (USCCB), to Rome for a meeting with Pope John Paul II. The news media intensified their coverage and provided major network coverage of the Vatican meetings and the papal statement that decried the scandal.

It was reported that Cardinal Law had offered his resignation to the Holy Father during a private meeting. The alleged resignation was declined, however, and Cardinal Law was instructed to stay the course in Boston. He returned to the city amidst charges that the archdiocese was facing financial and moral bankruptcy. The anger of local Catholics in Boston was palpable.

In June 2002, Catholic bishops assembled in Dallas for their semiannual meeting. The agenda was dominated by the sexual abuse scandal. Under Bishop Wilton Gregory's leadership, the USCCB had crafted a statement of principles (Charter) that would guide the church's substantive response to the crisis. A policy of "zero tolerance" for child abuse was announced. But the bishops provided little substantive evidence of a willingness to discuss publicly the mounting crisis. Media coverage was intense, and reporters spoke at length with the many victims of abuse, academic experts, and representatives of Catholic laity groups, including Voice of the Faithful, in attendance.

During the summer, the conflict simmered. Voice of the Faithful (VOTF), which had been formed in the months immediately following the Geoghan and Shanley disclosures, organized an "international convention" and drew an overflow crowd of 4,200 people to Boston in July. The group also created a philanthropic fund, the Voice of Compassion (VOC) Fund, to attract donations from people who would not give to the annual Cardinal's Appeal because of its lack of transparency (or because of anger directed at Cardinal Law). The VOC fund was intended to function as a "mirror image" of the Cardinal's Appeal, the archdiocese's largest fundraising venture, with requirements for disclosure of how the money was to be used. (It was said that this would prevent diversion of funds to secret settlements and legal fees associated with the scandal, a major concern among Catholic donors.)

The VOC fund challenged traditional giving patterns in the Catholic Church, and on July 22, only two days after the VOTF convention, Cardinal Law issued a press release publicly refusing to accept funds from the group. VOTF shot back that the Cardinal's own behavior was compromising services to Catholics throughout the archdiocese and amounted to "Cardinal Law's $10 Million Mistake."

As the summer wore on, rhetorical skirmishes between VOTF and bishops intensified. In August, bishops from Bridgeport, Connecticut, and Rockville Centre, New York, issued orders banning Voice of the Faithful members from using church property for meetings. The bishops claimed that VOTF had a "hidden agenda" based on the appearance of several controversial speakers at the July convention. VOTF responded with charges that the bishops were forsaking their spiritual and pastoral responsibilities by condemning the laity for the bishops' own failings.

### The Grassroots

The conflict percolated through September and October 2002, with several more bishops (Camden, New Jersey; Newark, New Jersey; Brooklyn-Queens, New York) banning VOTF from using church facilities. Still, the group's membership continued to grow. VOTF claimed 1,000 members in the spring of 2002. By June, the number exceeded

13,000. In July, at the time of the convention, the number was 19,000. By October, the group reported more than 25,000 supporters, with most connected through its internet website www.votf.org.

VOTF local groups, known as "affiliates," also provided a source of growth. Organized at the parish level, these "Parish Voice" (PV) groups ranged in size from a few dozen members to several hundred per affiliate. Because the issue of clergy sexual abuse was so volatile, some pastors sought to block VOTF affiliates from forming in their parishes. But others were supportive and acknowledged the need for what one called a "public cleansing." By October, more than forty-two Parish Voice groups existed in the Archdiocese of Boston, and more than 100 existed throughout the United States.

The inability to use church facilities for meetings was an impediment to the functioning of these PV groups. Local affiliates issued strong calls to remove the bans. In October, Cardinal Law rescinded a ban that had been imposed by one of his auxiliary bishops on a VOTF affiliate in North Andover, Massachusetts. The North Andover community had vigorously challenged the ban, and the letter of the auxiliary bishop was widely published and challenged as unfounded. On October 13, Law overturned the ban for all existing VOTF affiliates in the archdiocese, but left in place a ban on the use of church property by any newly formed VOTF group. VOTF's national leaders continued to oppose Cardinal Law and other bishops over banning orders, claiming that they were divisive and fundamentally immoral, denying the very parishioners who bought and paid for these churches the right to use the space for discussing how to respond to a great crisis. The bishops were unmoved.

### Priests Awaken

Priests also became empowered through the events of 2002. Originally formed in the summer of 2001 as a forum for discussing the challenges of being a priest in the modern church, the Boston Priests' Forum (BPF) became a vehicle for priests to express their concerns and dissatisfaction with the archbishop, Cardinal Law. As the months dragged on, the Boston Priests' Forum developed greater cohesiveness and a more coherent voice. Finally, in December 2002, after the third wave of clergy sexual abuse revelations, fifty-eight Boston area priests, led by individual members of the Forum, signed a letter calling on Cardinal Law to resign. This unprecedented act, less an act of revolution than a cry of pain, proved to be the shock that stirred the Vatican to finally accept Law's resignation.

In New York City, a group of priests calling themselves Voice of the Ordained (VOTO) organized a meeting of more than 700 priests to discuss the crisis and their concerns about issues such as due process and fair treatment for those against whom allegations were made. The mere existence of the group and the holding of their meeting generated extensive media coverage.

## The Archbishop Resigns

Cardinal Bernard F. Law was considered by many observers to be the most powerful bishop (archbishop) in the American Catholic Church at the beginning of the twenty-first century. By many standards, he was one of the outstanding prelates of the worldwide church. During 2002, however, his credibility steadily eroded as the scandal unfolded. His decisions in the Fr. Geoghan case showed him to be complicit in the reassignment decisions, with evidence that he personally knew of Geoghan's extensive history of child abuse allegations. In the case of Fr. Paul Shanley, Law had actually written to the bishop of San Bernardino, California, that Shanley was a priest in good standing.

On November 26, 2002, Cardinal Law held his first face-to-face meeting with Voice of the Faithful leaders. He made various representations about the effectiveness of archdiocesan policies to protect children and several times reiterated his personal commitment that justice would be done to resolve old cases, as well as protect against future harms. One week later, however, on December 3, 2002, documents were publicly released from the more than 10,000 pages of records the archdiocese had turned over to plaintiffs' attorneys under court order. The disclosures were devastating and marked the third great turning point in the scandal.

The records revealed shocking accounts of more priests abusing boys, girls, young women, and adults. They added a new dimension to the scandal; the documents showed that Cardinal Law and his auxiliary bishops had, since 1984, engaged in a pervasive pattern of administrative concealment and cover-up. Unlike the Geoghan and Shanley cases, where the evidence was confined to the actions surrounding a single priest, the new documents revealed a wider and more persistent pattern of cover-up. The calls for Cardinal Law's resignation escalated. Within a ten-day period, unprecedented actions took place to convince the Vatican that Cardinal Law could no longer lead the nation's fourth largest diocese. Law's days seemed numbered.

The cardinal traveled to Rome on December 9, ostensibly to present a plan to Vatican officials that would have the Archdiocese of Boston voluntarily declare bankruptcy under Chapter 11 of the U.S. bankruptcy law. Such an action would place all claimants into a single pool and force movement toward a so-called global settlement of hundreds of pending lawsuits. The Vatican provided no official opinion on the proposal, but newspaper accounts suggested that officials were greatly troubled by the potential precedent-setting effects of such an action.

Behind the scenes, other decisions were being made. Cardinal Law huddled with a variety of Vatican insiders. Early in the week, it seemed that he might survive the pressure to resign. By midweek, however, momentum had shifted and papal acceptance of the resignation was secured. On Friday, December 13, 2002, Pope John Paul II personally accepted Cardinal Law's resignation in a public ceremony. Bishop Richard G. Lennon, an auxiliary bishop in Boston, was named Apostolic Administrator to oversee the affairs of the archdiocese. The news spread around the world: America's most prominent Catholic Church leader had been forced to step down because of his mishandling of the sexual abuse crisis. The crisis had reached its most dramatic and public moment. The ripple effects would continue for years to come.

## From Social Movement to Action Organization

The crisis raised a number of profound and difficult questions about the future of the Catholic Church. Three overarching questions have dominated academic and practical discussions of the outlook for the church:

- First, can an institution that is founded on a moral purpose successfully respond to a deep moral crisis and avoid a loss of the legitimacy that is essential to its place in society?

- Second, will the Catholic Church survive a growing divide between bishops and laity that began in 2002–2003?

- Third, will the church accommodate a more expansive role for the laity within its existing structures and processes?

Each of these issues touches on fundamental principles of modern management theory. For example, theory and practice demonstrate that all organizations are open systems that both affect, and are affected by, their environment. Thus, organizations must adapt to their environments if they are to survive. In modern thinking, an organization's stakeholders—defined as those who benefit from, or assume some risk because of, the organization—have a legitimate interest in the decisions, processes, and effects of the organization and its activities.

**Table 12.1.**   *Timeline, January 2002–January 2003*

| | |
|---|---|
| January 2002 | ▪ 1/6/02 *Boston Globe* publishes first story on Fr. John Geoghan and cover-up. *Globe* articles follow, providing extensive detail on cover-up by bishops of the Archdiocese of Boston. |
| February | ▪ 2/11/02 Parishioners at St. John the Evangelist parish in Wellesley, Massachusetts, hold initial meeting to discuss the crisis. |
| | ▪ 2/25/02 "Voice of the Faithful" name is adopted by group. |
| March | ▪ 3/9/02 Archdiocesan Convocation brings together 3,000 lay leaders to address crisis in listening sessions with bishops. |
| | ▪ First round of VOTF elections. |
| April | ▪ 4/9/02 Cardinal Law flies to Rome to offer his resignation. It is declined. Public outrage greets Law upon his return to Boston. |
| | ▪ U.S. Cardinals summoned to the Vatican to meet with John Paul II. |
| | ▪ 4/9/02 The archdiocesan records of Fr. Paul Shanley are released under court order and reveal a record of abuse and rape charges. Cardinal Law recommended Shanley to San Bernardino, California, diocese as a priest in good standing. |
| | ▪ Second round of VOTF internal elections. |
| May | ▪ Intense media interest and coverage of Voice of the Faithful. |
| June | ▪ Third round of VOTF internal elections. |
| July | ▪ 7/20/02 "Response of the Faithful" convention draws 4,200 to VOTF's first international event. |
| | ▪ 7/22/02 Cardinal Law issues press release turning down funds from the VOTF-sponsored Voice of Compassion–Boston Fund. |
| August | ▪ First bans on use of church property are confirmed (Bridgeport, Connecticut, and Rockville Centre, New York). |
| September | ▪ Bans are confirmed in Archdiocese of Boston |
| October | ▪ Cardinal Law ends bans on VOTF affiliate groups formed before October 13, 2002; bans remain on groups formed after that date. |
| November | ▪ 11/26/02 Cardinal Law meets with VOTF leadership delegation. |
| December | ▪ 12/3/02 Ten thousand pages of personnel records are released by the Archdiocese of Boston and reveal an extensive pattern of administrative cover-up and concealment. |
| | ▪ 12/9/02 Cardinal Law travels to Rome to discuss bankruptcy proposal and his future with Vatican officials. |
| | ▪ 12/11/02 VOTF's Council formally calls on Cardinal Law to resign. |
| | ▪ 12/13/02 Cardinal Law's resignation is accepted by John Paul II. Bishop Richard G. Lennon is appointed Apostolic Administrator. |
| January 2003 | ▪ Fourth round of VOTF internal elections (president, vice president, treasurer, and secretary are elected for one-year terms). |

These maxims suggest that the Catholic Church had critical stake-holders—bishops, clergy, laity—whose interests were so vitally affected as to reshape the environment in which the church exists. Under such conditions, the church is required to adapt to new realities in its operating environment, adjusting policies, processes, or practices to meet the legitimate expectations of vital stakeholders.

Management theory must contend, however, with other truths and realities. Democratic processes, openness, and accountability are not embraced in all institutions. Participatory principles are not effective in every institution or in all societies. It is argued that "oil and water do not mix." During 2002 and 2003, the Catholic Church in the United States provided a unique opportunity to consider whether democratic principles such as openness, accountability, and participation could be introduced into one of the world's longest-operating institutions, an institution whose authoritarianism is legendary. In the face of a host of new realities, is the Catholic Church fit to survive in the twenty-first century as a more open system, adaptive to its environment, in ways that incorporate the interests of all its stakeholders?

### Role of the Laity: Voice of the Faithful

The emergence of a group of shocked, angry, and outraged Catholics is, by itself, not surprising. The disclosures and revelations of 2002 stunned people of many religious faiths. Editorials in local newspapers hinted at the disbelief of people of all religious orientations at the meltdown of the Catholic Church's moral integrity. What proved surprising, in retrospect, however, was the rapid development of Voice of the Faithful as a social movement and its subsequent development into an action-oriented organization with a strategic focus.

VOTF is a social movement that began as a public phenomenon. The movement drew people who wanted to be part of a powerful experience taking place in 2002. The experience began as an event—the weekly meetings that attracted hundreds of Catholics who wanted to express their feelings, to be heard and respected, and to believe that they could—together—make a difference in the behavior of the Catholic Church. The emotional fuel that energized these meetings changed over time—first, anger and outrage; second, determination; third, commitment.

VOTF was a social movement before it became an organization. An emotional magnet drew people together. The shock, outrage, and anger provoked by the disclosures of clergy sexual abuse and administrative cover-up provided a unifying force.

The early organizational challenges involved planning meetings, co-ordination of speakers, and the increasingly complicated logistics of space, parking, and distribution of materials. The basement of St. John the Evangelist Roman Catholic Church in Wellesley, Massachusetts, had a capacity of about 180. By the fourth weekly meeting, the room was too small. The meetings moved across the parking lot to the school basement, named "Philbin Hall" in honor of the previous pastor, Msgr. John Philbin. (Philbin, eighty-four, was in residence at St. John's during 2002, and counseled many of the parishioners who founded VOTF. He preached powerful homilies calling for an end to secrecy and articulating the pain of priests as the disclosures continued. As one VOTF founder said, lovingly, "Fr. John walked with us every step of the way.") The capacity of Philbin Hall was 350 people; the meetings stretched the facility to its limits. By April, the weekly meetings were drawing crowds of more than 500 people and simultaneous meetings were held in the school and church halls, with speakers rushing across the parking lot from one building to the other. Attendees came from as far away as Maine, New Hampshire, Connecticut, New York, New Jersey, Pennsylvania, and Maryland.

The appeal was more than emotional energy. As media coverage expanded, local newspaper and television reporting included network television (ABC, CNN, CBS, NBC, Fox), wire services (Reuters, Associated Press, Bloomberg), national newspapers (USA Today; Los Angeles Times; Christian Science Monitor; New York Times), and the international press (Irish Times, London Times, Swedish TV, Netherlands TV, Spanish radio). The presence of a large media corps helped guarantee that the experience was "exciting" as well as informative. Hundreds of faces were visible in those television news clips.

People were excited to be present, to participate, and to become part of the VOTF movement. The emotional energy that fueled the early meetings began to give way to a different kind of energy—the sense that something significant was taking place, and that these people and their organization could make a difference. It was the excitement of being a Catholic in 2002. The Catholic Church was in crisis, but people were ready to fight for it.

The emotional "peak" was reached on July 20, 2002. VOTF held a convention, called "Response of the Faithful," at the Hynes Convention Center in Boston. VOTF's "first international conference" drew more than 4,200 participants (the Hynes Center's official capacity). Remarkably, every aspect of the convention was organized entirely by volunteers. The galvanizing genius behind this effort was a passionate, talented businessman named Paul Baier.

A software entrepreneur in his late thirties and father of a nine-year-old daughter, Baier became a critical player in the evolution of VOTF. He was a smart, hands-on manager with a "can-do" attitude. He quickly created a website for the organization and facilitated internal communication, posting of minutes, and more. The excitement of having a website "that actually worked" (as one happy member said) had an unintended benefit—it enabled people from other locations to follow what was happening in Wellesley. This proved invaluable in providing information about the group's mission, goals, and meetings. The media used the site as a resource for background information and updated schedules of events. Technology would prove to be a critical element in the development of VOTF.

Baier conceived and financed the fledgling organization's convention. In classic entrepreneurial style, he worked tirelessly to organize, coordinate, and energize hundreds of volunteers. His weekly e-bulletins to the membership provided an important update of events, plans, and critical needs. The updates energized members in Boston and elsewhere. On the day of the convention, representatives from dozens of states and foreign nations participated. The program, also arranged by volunteers, included prominent Catholic speakers. They, too, wanted to be part of the shared VOTF experience.

The convention marked an emotional highpoint for VOTF as a social movement. But the euphoria of the convention was quickly followed by a declared state of conflict between VOTF, Cardinal Law, and other bishops who imposed bans on the group's use of church property for meetings. It took some time for VOTF leaders to grasp what had happened, but when they did, it was clear that VOTF was no longer a social movement. It had become an organized threat to an established clerical order that throughout history has marshaled every resource to crush opposition. VOTF became an organization because it had to become one—and had to function strategically—if its mission and goals were to be achieved.

### Strategy and Organizational Design
Strategy—the idea of purposeful action designed to accomplish goals—involves choices. All organizations reflect choices through their behavior—through what is done and what is not done. Thus, organizations manifest their strategies, even when they are not fully intentional.

As VOTF emerged in 2002, the process of decision making became increasingly strategic and focused on purposeful actions designed to achieve major goals. Critical administrative, governance, and policy decisions were thrust on the organization throughout the first year. The number of decisions, and the speed at which they had to be made, led to some actions that failed, while others succeeded beyond expectations. Overall, VOTF made extraordinary progress in a short period of time because of the wide-ranging expertise of its leaders and members.

The scope of activities, and the unprecedented demands that public visibility generated, forced critical decisions involving activities, systems, and accountability. Because the group's members had a "bias for action" to influence the behavior of church leaders, governance often seemed to be a step behind its actions. From the earliest days, VOTF conducted its meetings in plenary sessions, supplemented by the formation of working groups to focus energy and attention on specific topics. Within two months, it became evident that a steering committee was needed to coordinate activities, plan plenary session programs, and anticipate needs. A proactive approach emerged as individuals and working groups infused imagination into media relations, program planning, and organizational concepts such as the Parish Voice system of affiliates and the Voice of Compassion charitable fund.

Discussion of appropriate governance led to formal adoption (at a plenary meeting) of an organizational design involving elected officers. The terms for such officers were quite short at the outset (one month, three months, and six months in the first three elections). It was not until January 2003 that officers were elected for a full one-year term of office. Representative governance has been a living concept in VOTF. As the membership and locus of activity shifted away from Boston, efforts were made to develop more representative structures. Although geography is a limiting factor, a number of electronic conferencing experiments have been tried with varying degrees of success. In 2003, the Representative Council (successor to the plenary meeting) adopted a motion designed to improve the "voice" of regions around the U.S. in charting national policy.

One of the most important actions taken by VOTF leaders was the establishment of an office to serve as "world headquarters" for VOTF activities. The office was sublet from a VOTF member and provided the physical space needed to coordinate convention plans in June and July 2002. Symbolically, the office also served as a tangible expression of the group's determination to continue developing its national and global presence. The selection of an acting executive director provided management expertise to the entire operation. In the six months following the convention, the VOTF staff of paid and volunteer members grew, and a fund-raising operation evolved to support the organization's expanding activities.

Funding of VOTF activities evolved rapidly. From January to June 2002, nearly all activities were funded through a "pass-the-hat" system of voluntary donations. The convention involved the sale of tickets as well as donations, with total expenses exceeding $60,000. In June 2002, VOTF was incorporated as a nonprofit corporation in Massachusetts. An application for a section 501c3 tax-exempt designation was filed with the Internal Revenue Service to enable donors to claim tax deductions for their contributions. The designation was granted in December 2002, a fact that enabled the organization to achieve ambitious fund-raising goals in its first year.

The most demanding decisions, without question, involved the development of policy positions on the issues that affected lay Catholics. It was decided early on that VOTF represented middle-of-the-road Catholics who loved the church and were determined to reclaim its moral integrity. There was a consensus that the organization should pursue a centrist philosophy and avoid "hot-button" issues that divided the church, including ordination of women, priestly celibacy, and homosexual priests. VOTF spokespersons repeatedly emphasized the primacy of the group's mission—to provide a significant role for the laity in the governance and guidance of the Catholic Church—and its three goals— to support survivors of clergy sexual abuse; to support priests of integrity; and to shape structural change to ensure that such problems do not recur.

Each goal generated extensive discussion by working groups and officers to ensure that the actions taken were consistent with the core values shared by VOTF members. In supporting survivors, for example, much effort was given to building credibility with survivors through coalitions with survivor organizations such as Survivors' Network of those Abused by Priests (SNAP) and The Linkup. In supporting priests of integrity, VOTF encountered questions from priests and laity who questioned the definition of "integrity"—e.g., must a priest support VOTF to be considered a "priest of integrity?"

The most challenging discussion involved the third goal: to shape structural change. The intention was to ensure that the systems and structures that facilitated clergy sexual abuse and its cover-up were changed. Secrecy, concealment, and deception had to become practices of the past. VOTF's Structural Change Working Group worked with canon lawyers, theologians, and church historians to define a practical approach to structural change. The document became the basis for dialogue with bishops about the meaning of VOTF's controversial slogan, "Keep the Faith. Change the Church."[6]

## Going Forward

Throughout 2002, Catholics created their voice, expressed outrage, and challenged leaders who enabled the sexual abuse to occur. VOTF became the means for many Catholics to stand up and say, "No! This is not what our church stands for."

A powerful linkage was formed with survivors of clergy sexual abuse. VOTF members responded in many ways to the injustice that survivors suffered. The laity stood with survivors at vigils, protests, and public events; helped raise funds to assist those in need; pressed dioceses to provide therapeutic programs; lobbied for suspension of statute of limitations laws that prevented cases from being brought to trial; and participated in workshops, meetings, and conferences. They saw the "face of Christ" in those who suffered, respected survivors' stories, and supported survivors' organizations (e.g., SNAP and The Linkup).

The laity also learned that achieving structural and cultural change in the Catholic Church would be "a marathon, not a sprint." Consciousness was raised, to be sure, but the systems, structures, and culture that produced the crisis were not quickly transformed. Other lay leaders also encountered significant levels of resistance from some bishops. Kathleen McChesney, head of the Office of Child and Youth Protection, and Governor Frank Keating, chairman of the National Review Board, both faced opposition from some bishops who refused to vigorously implement their own Charter and Norms. Some dioceses were slow to undertake the audits that the bishops had promised. As 2003 drew to a close, the forces of change were still pitted against the forces of resistance. Healing still seemed a distant hope.

## The Emerging Role of the Catholic Laity

The Catholic laity still faces a long, difficult road to reforms that will open the church to sunlight and accountability. VOTF has helped galvanize pressure for the reforms that Vatican II promised to all Catholics. The laity remains on the margins of decision making in the Catholic Church, its role in the governance and guidance of the church dispropor-

tionately small relative to its education and talents. The future will
continue to be a story of struggle to introduce a more balanced form
of power and authority into the Catholic Church.

## Challenges Ahead

VOTF faces several challenges as it begins its third year of activity. It
must grow its membership and increase the effectiveness of its affiliates.
It must vigorously promote self-education initiatives among lay Catholics. The organization must patiently and steadfastly challenge the entrenched resistance to change that is the unfortunate hallmark and legacy
of the clerical culture.

Conceptually, VOTF is challenged to continue addressing its goals
and dealing with its constituent groups. It must support survivors
through active outreach to survivors' groups and to individuals and
must urge civic authorities (district attorneys and attorneys general) to
use their investigative and grand jury powers to subpoena records, take
depositions, and file criminal cases against abusers and accessories to
their crimes.

VOTF must also continue reaching out to priests and discussing their
needs, expectations, and ideas for healing. It is important to support
the due process rights of priests under codes of civil and canon law. It
is necessary to defend the right of priests to act according to their
conscience in matters related to the administration of the diocese in
which they reside. There is a need to support and celebrate the courage,
integrity, and pastoral commitment of priests (and all religious) as the
church responds to this great crisis.

Dialogue with bishops at the diocesan, national, and international
levels of the church is essential. VOTF must not give up on the bishops,
even as it presses to hold bishops accountable for their actions.

The Catholic laity must continue to advocate for the implementation
of the Charter and Norms for protection of children, and it must urge
bishops to create, implement, and support vigorous systems of lay
involvement in diocesan governance and administration.

Every diocese must be challenged to introduce transparency and
disclosure into its annual fund-raising appeals. The sources and uses of
money must be disclosed; administrative fees, overhead, development,
and expenses must be disclosed; publicly audited annual reports must
be available on the diocesan website. Catholic donors—large or small—
must value disclosure and hold their dioceses accountable for
disclosure.

## Conclusion

The events that brought lay Catholics together in 2002 involved the realization that a great social injustice—the sexual abuse of children by clergy—was being perpetrated inside the Catholic Church. Thousands of members of the Catholic laity were moved from emotional shock and outrage to the moral conviction that the church must change and the abuse must stop. Today, there is a broad consensus among all stakeholders—bishops, clergy, and laity—that the church must cleanse itself of abuse and the culture of secrecy and concealment—what Garry Wills has termed "structures of deceit"—that permitted this evil to continue for decades.[7]

For more than two years, thousands of Catholic laywomen and -men have asked—with fresh enthusiasm—what does it mean to be Catholic, to be members, citizens, of the Catholic Church? VOTF provided a means for thousands to stand up, speak out, and address deep flaws in the church. The result may be a "revolution of the middle," rooted in Vatican II, where personal stewardship for the well-being of the church is described as a baptismal responsibility of every Catholic, not only clergy and bishops. As David J. O'Brien observed thirty years ago, "The present ferment in the church has its roots both in the dramatic changes in Catholic life and culture initiated by Pope John XXIII and the Second Vatican Council and in the tumultuous events that have punctuated American society in the last decade."[8] Perhaps today's "revolution of the middle" is the transformational change that Vatican II promised.

By most measures, VOTF is still a short story. Now in its third year, the organization is establishing stronger national and international representation through Parish Voice affiliates and strategies for growth and action. The organization has provided a reason for thousands of Catholics to stay in the church. It has absorbed anger and frustration and has channeled it into a force for positive change. Yet no one believes the job is done. Catholic laypersons, clergy, survivors, and bishops must work together to restore and renew a wounded church.

Fr. Donald Cozzens has stated: "This is the laity's moment." VOTF has evolved as an action-oriented means for the Catholic laity to embrace this moment in time and encourage all Catholics to join the movement and fulfill their baptismal responsibility to participate in the governance and guidance of the Catholic Church.

David Gibson has recently argued that three types of change are taking place in the U.S. Catholic Church today. Structures, policies, and attitudes are changing. The laity is the pivotal actor in effecting such change, and "voice" is the means to accomplish this end.[9]

The crisis in the Catholic Church is too deep and profound to be resolved without undertaking significant change in the structures, systems, and culture that produced it. On February 27, 2004, the National Review Board released the results of a study of clergy sexual abuse from 1950 to 2002. The results are devastating: more than 4,430 priests were alleged to have abused minors; 10,667 victims of abuse were documented; and more than $572 million was expended to treat priests, compensate lawyers, and achieve settlements with survivors of abuse.[10] Many experts believe the data are still underreported, and that the actual number of victims is substantially higher. The case for change is greater today than anyone imagined in January 2002 when the Geoghan case was first disclosed.

The emerging role of the Catholic laity is one of voice. By creating a voice, and using that voice to call for, and shape, the change process, the laity will participate in the governance and guidance of the church. Through its voice, the laity can fulfill its baptismal responsibility to be stewards of the church. For this moment in time, VOTF is a catalyst for the change the Catholic Church needs.

## Notes

1. See, for example, Peter Steinfels, *A People Adrift: The Crisis of the Roman Catholic Church in America* (New York: Simon and Schuster, 2003); and David Gibson, *The Coming Catholic Church: How the Faithful Are Shaping a New American Catholicism* (New York: HarperCollins, 2003). These authors analyze underlying conditions that threaten the church, including human sexuality, reduced numbers of priests, the role of laity in the church, the role of women, sweeping demographic changes, and intrahierarchical squabbles for power and influence. Steinfels opens with this sentence: "Today the Roman Catholic Church in the United States is on the verge of either an irreversible decline or a thoroughgoing transformation" (1). Gibson's first sentence reads: "Little more than a year into the third millennium of Christianity, a milestone that Pope John Paul II heralded as the occasion for a rebirth of faith, the Catholic Church found itself plunged into a crisis over sexual abuse by priests that left historians reaching back centuries for comparisons. Many cited the French Revolution or the Protestant Reformation; others, the Inquisition and even the Holocaust" (1).

2. See John T. McGreevy, *Catholicism and American Freedom: A History* (New York: W. W. Norton, 2003), 12.

3. See Gibson, *The Coming Catholic Church*. See also Jay P. Dolan, *In Search of an American Catholicism: A History of Religion and Culture in Tension* (New York: Oxford University Press, 2002), 257–59.

4. Throughout 2002, defenders of the existing order tried to minimize the scope and consequence of the scandal. George Weigel, whose syndicated columns are popular in the diocesan Catholic papers, and Deal Hudson, editor of *Crisis*, a conservative magazine (www.crisismagazine.com), were among those who sought to apply damage control to the crisis in 2002.

5. The *Boston Globe* maintains an extensive collection of published articles, relevant documents, and photos on its website, www.BostonGlobe.com.

6. James E. Muller and Charles Kenney, *Keep the Faith, Change the Church* (New York: Rodale Press, 2004).

7. Garry Wills, *Papal Sins* (New York: Doubleday, 2002), 7–9.

8. David J. O'Brien, *The Renewal of American Catholicism* (New York: Oxford University Press and the Paulist Press, 1972), 26.

9. See Gibson, *The Coming Catholic Church*, 342–50.

10. "The Nature and Scope of Sexual Abuse of Minors by Catholic Priests and Deacons in the United States, 1950–2002," a research study conducted by the John Jay College of Criminal Justice, The City University of New York, February 2004, for the United States Conference of Catholic Bishops. See also "A Report on the Crisis in the Catholic Church in the United States," The National Review Board for the Protection of Children and Young People, 27 February 2004.

# THIRTEEN

## The Church of the Third Millennium: In Praise of *Communio*

### LADISLAS ORSY, S.J.

The title of this chapter reflects an ambitious project. The underlying question—*What is the church going to be in the third millennium?*—reaches into a future that is well beyond our horizon. Surely, we cannot see that far—well into the third millennium. The question, however, is deceptive. It is not about the future: it concerns the present. Let me reformulate it: *As we perceive and experience various movements in the church today, do we find any that has the potential to mark and shape the life of the community in the coming centuries?*

Once our query is put into such terms, it makes sense. The search for the answer must be a process of discovery not so much about what-is-to-come as about what-is-now in our midst. History—the well-known *magistra vitae*, "teacher of life"— encourages us to undertake such a task. After all, how could Christians not be curious about the forces that agitate the community? Their duty is clearly to be alert in searching for them, insightful in understanding them, and fair and wise in judging them. This duty is all the more pressing in that we know from the past that some movements have contained powerful energies that have given a new direction to the life of the community for centuries.

Such change in direction occurred at the end of the eleventh century: Pope Gregory VII liberated the Western church from an all-pervading secular influence. He performed a needed and salutary operation, but by doing so, he also initiated a movement in the "Patriarchate of the West" toward an increasing centralization. The trend received a new impetus in the period of the Counter Reformation and reached its peak in the nineteenth and twentieth centuries. Parallel with it, in the same West, the traditional Catholic doctrine of "communion" was gradually lost from sight and waned in practice. The Eastern churches did not follow suit, and the two branches of the same tree kept growing in different directions. Such a "growing apart from each other" has probably contributed more to the mutual alienation of the two churches than the ill-conceived excommunication (in 1054) of Patriarch Cerularius by the imprudent papal legate Humbert. (There is a lesson of history: the reunion of the two churches does not depend on dialogues by select committees alone; the people of both sides must enter into a vital process of "growing together," a process that is bound to take a long time before they can give each other the "kiss of peace" of full communion.)[1]

Since such a great change occurred before, it makes sense to raise the question in our age full of changes: *Are we at the threshold of a new era in the church's history?* Or, to put it another way: *Is an ecclesiastical culture of some nine hundred years coming to an end, and is a new one emerging?* Let me stress: I am querying about a change in ecclesiastical culture, which is of human creation—even if it belongs to a community of divine foundation.

## The Church Is at a Turning Point in History

Karl Rahner stated that through Vatican Council II the church has become a worldwide church—not only in scope and ambition but effectively. The bishops at the Council came close to representing every part of our planet's territory. They made the concerns of the human family their own, especially in the "Pastoral Constitution on the Church" and the "Declaration on Religious Liberty." Such proclamations were well timed; after the horrors of two world wars, the nations were starved for good news.

To go to the nations is the task of the church: "Go into all the world and proclaim the good news to the whole creation" (Mark 16:15). The church should not just wait for the nations to come, the church must go out to meet them. It must bring them, in words and in deeds, the Good News with its liberating strength—in a language they can understand and through signs and symbols that attract them. These are basic principles of communication.

That is not all, however. From the dawn of the modern age, our Western civilization has undergone a deep transformation: new forms of political order have emerged. Admittedly, some innovations had their dark sides and caused immense tragedies, but others led to the practice of new virtues that no Christians can reject. Responsible governments were created, and the citizens learned the art of intelligent and responsible participation in political life. In the midst of such enlightened changes, the proclamations of the church—more often than not composed in an archaic style—became less and less intelligible. The manner of its operations, inspired to an extent by the courts of absolute monarchies, became less and less attractive to outsiders—even if, at home, many kept delighting in it.

If the church wants to be at home among the nations, it must reflect the new social virtues in its own pattern of speaking and manner of living. A cultural communion on a human level is the best preparation for a communion in the good news.[2]

## Images in Contrast

Today, the church is known through contrasting images. On the one hand, it offers a strong image of well-being. The Roman Catholic community is recognized the world over; especially through the activities of the papacy, it has gained respect to a degree not seen before. The Holy See is present in international assemblies, even if its voice may be a cry in the wilderness. The See of Rome has built up a tightly knit administrative organization that enables it to supervise the local communities and to intervene with authority whenever it judges necessary.

On the other hand, local churches in many parts of the world are displaying the symptoms of deeply embedded internal weaknesses. They celebrate the Eucharist less and less: for lack of priests, the source of life is drying up. The sacrament of forgiveness and healing is in abeyance in countless places—in this age that surely needs the reconciling power of grace. The numerous cases of abuses of minors have revealed an organism that lacks a vigorous self-protective system; corruption was able to penetrate the body and spread far and wide before any remedial action was taken. In the West, people, especially young people, keep drifting away from the "institutional church" (as they say it), hardly realizing that they cannot distance themselves from the visible body of the church without eventually losing touch with its soul, the life-giving Spirit of Christ.

What is happening? The contrasting images cannot be explained in any other way than by conflicting currents in the community, that is, in the minds and hearts of the people. And the result of such conflicts is turbulence. If the Kingdom of God is at hand, there is turbulence in the Kingdom. Indeed, "turbulence" may be the appropriate image to describe the state of the church: it means swirling and threatening waters. But let us have no mistake: turbulence speaks also of life and energy;

strong currents are needed to create it. It is usually a preliminary play to a new equilibrium, which is a river of quiet and powerful flow. Let us keep this parable in mind.

But what are the colliding currents? One is for upholding the order of a highly centralized administration; another is for creating a new order according to the demands of communion. One current comes from a distant past. From the end of the eleventh century and then through the second millennium, an ideological and practical trend developed. The church was increasingly understood, in places high and low, as a rigidly hierarchical institution where divine gifts (except those conferred by the sacraments) were descending on the community by the mediation of the popes, bishops, and clergy. Structures and practices were introduced accordingly, and doctrinal positions were developed to justify them. All good things were seen as channeled from above. The rights of the superiors were to instruct and to command; the duties of the subjects were to listen and to obey. Much of the God-given intelligence and energy "in the provinces" remained unused.

The other current is of recent origin. Pope John XXIII reversed the old trend by calling an ecumenical council. He was aware that a new order was needed (he called it *aggiornamento*, "updating"), and he let the reform come, not from himself as one who was placed above, but from the bishops "in the provinces"—that is, from below. Through four sessions in so many years, and through painful struggles, the Second Vatican Council offered a new vision and called for new practices. It perceived the church as a "communion," *communio*, of persons in a deep and unique sense: they are bonded into a unity by the Spirit of Christ who distributes his gifts directly to individual persons—for the welfare of the whole. The task of the hierarchy is not so much to mediate gifts as to coordinate them for the good of the whole. Thus, in the Dogmatic Constitution on the Church, prime place was given the People of God: they precede the hierarchy. (To stress this vision and to emphasize that I am writing about a unique theological reality, from now on I shall use the Latin term *communio*. Although it can be translated as "communion," its derivative in English does not have the rich content that the Latin has accumulated in its Christian use.)

## Vatican II: A Seminal Council

Vatican Council II was a seminal council, perhaps much more than any other in history. For this reason, to comprehend it and apply it to the everyday life of the church may take longer than was the case for any other council. It set a new course for the church, a course that will take centuries to unfold. It professed an "ecclesiology of *communio*" of which we see the first manifestations only. Through its fresh insights, the Council has released an immense amount of energy that is conflicting with an old current.

In this conflict of currents, the church is stretched, but we should not worry. If the impetus for the Council came from the Spirit, the Spirit will grant the needed strength to the people to cope with troubles. Let us remember that the Council did proclaim with its full authority that its work *placuit Spiritui sancto et nobis*—"it pleased the Holy Spirit and us."

With that encouragement, we can read the signs of the times. One sign is certainly emerging: at the very center of the conciliar event is the declaration that the church is a *communio* of persons. It appears that we are entering a new millennium in which the church will become more and more a *communio* of persons, not only internally but also in its external organization and operation. Thus, it will be a sign to our fragmented human family, a powerful sign of the gospel message of peace. It may take a long time for the faithful to see all the implications of this vision; it might take even longer to see the vision translated into practice. But the Council is more than an event to contemplate: it is a powerful voice mandating future generations, individuals and communities, to implement the demands of *communio*. Conceivably, our present generation will see only the first movements of this process.

## What Is *Communio*?

Although we often hear the expression "ecclesiology of *communio*," rarely do we get an explanation of its theological reality. Those who invoke it, turn easily to secular models, which may be useful but are not enough. Others, after a brief reference to some doctrine, turn to the issue of its application, be it pastorally or canonically—which is laudable but may lack a sound theoretical foundation.

For correct practice, we need a well-grounded theological understanding: we must get as close as we can to the mystery, that is, to the internal reality of *communio*. Of course, around a mystery we can see only with the eyes of faith—but through them we have a perception that we can articulate. Thus, in the inner life of God we discover *communio*: he is one in divinity and three in persons. In him, there is unity in diversity, or diversity in unity. We can say "In the beginning" (cf. John 1:1) there was an indivisible One, and in the One there were three persons, unique and divers.

This eternal pattern speaks of the very nature of *communio*: it tells us that no person can exist without being in unity with other persons. In the divine "model," mysterious as it is, we find the clue for achieving some understanding of what *communio* among human beings ought to be—in particular in God's fledgling Kingdom that is the church.

The German theologian Heribert Mühlen, well inspired by the Council, described the church as "one person in many persons." The one Spirit of Christ is holding many individuals together.[3] *This is—briefly but substantially—the theological meaning of* communio. But among human beings, composed of spirit and matter, the internal reality needs external expression. Without it, in our created order, we would have only a ghost of a church. Hence the question, and still a substantial one: In the church, what are, what can be, the external structures and norms needed to express and to sustain *communio*? The answer may not come easily because our experience is confined to a highly centralized community. But we should not be discouraged: if the council mandates us to build *communio*, it calls on us, as a first step, to use our imagination—and for a holy purpose!

## Adventure in Imagination

In our Catholic tradition, we have a splendid example of an "adventure in imagination" in the famous work of St. Thomas More on Utopia, or to give its full title: "On the Best State of a Commonwealth and on the New Island of Utopia"—that is, at Noplace, which existed only in Thomas's fantasy.[4] The aim of the writer was not to give a lesson in geography or history; as one of his contemporaries put it, it was to provide "a truly golden handbook *"nec minus salutaris quam festivus"* ("no less salutary than festive"; or, loosely translated, "no less life-giving than celebrating").[5]

This is what an adventure in imagination can accomplish: it can seek out life-giving features and celebrate them in a festive manner. The aim of such an approach is not a scholarly report, still less an aggressive demand. It simply throws a broad light on what appears fair, just, and beautiful—and leaves it at that, hoping that from a flight of fancy future generations will create a life-giving reality. (Indeed, Thomas discovered the life-giving nature of religious freedom and celebrated it on the pages of *Utopia*. His contemporaries did not listen; they were busy waging wars of religion. But some four hundred years later, Vatican Council II accepted the message; the gentle vision of an artist became the hard policy of the church.) On a modest scale then, *mutatis mutandis*, I intend that my chapter on the external features of the church as *communio* should be taken as a discourse that is "life-giving and celebrating," as a piece "in praise of *communio*"—using artistic liberties and fair excesses that are fitting for a festive occasion.

Before I embark on the project, some further clarifications are in order. *First*, throughout the exposition that follows we must keep in mind that the church is a structured *communio*; in it, diversity in unity exists in various degrees and with varying intensities. Initially, through the sacraments of initiation and the reception of God's word, all the faithful are united in a mysterious way. Then, within this fundamental unity, through the sacrament of orders another *communio* emerges, that of the servant-leaders who are given the privilege to be qualified witnesses of God's revelation and to serve and govern with power the people. Finally, from early times a special type of *communio* emerged in the church, that of "religious" or "consecrated" communities. While their origins are not in a sacrament, they are the fruits of the Spirit.

*Second*, in "imagining" the "best state" and "better functioning" of these divers units, my aim is to search for good and proper balances among the vital forces in the social body of the church. My intention is not to hurt or destroy any permanent value. My proposals are rooted in tradition—even when they seem to be new. Several of them are suggestions to revive ancient practices.

*Third*, before I turn to concrete solutions, I focus on their theoretical foundations. This is the only sound method: we need a correct vision before we can undertake a prudent action—if we do otherwise, we shall end up in an erratic process. We must know our theological values before we create practical norms to serve them.

*Fourth*, a good deal of the external structures and norms serving *communio* ought to be of human creation. Hence, it is not enough for any person, any community to long for the golden days of a new era; each and all have to work for it and build it. We are mandated to use our ingenuity to bring it about.

## Communio of the Baptized Believers

The sacraments of initiation are visible signs of invisible events that only the eyes of faith can perceive: individual persons are assumed into a *communio* of persons—into a unity created and sustained by the Spirit of Christ who as one person is holding many persons and distributes his gifts among them. This unity in the Spirit is more foundational than any difference that may emerge from the divers gifts. At this level there are no superiors and no inferiors: all belong to God's people. There is the source of the dignity and of the rights and duties of the Christian people—they all belong to the *communio* of saints—so we profess in the Apostolic Creed.

This *communio* is a theological reality that no human power can take away. After the Second Vatican Council, however, ecclesiastical authorities introduced a new policy that is bound to reduce its potential: they have excluded nonordained persons from any effective participation in decision-making processes. True, the Council held that the bishops receive their power to govern, *potestas regiminis*, through the sacrament of orders—which was to revive an early tradition. After the Council, however, some theologians and canon lawyers drew from this teaching an unwarranted conclusion—one that was hardly traditional. They asserted that the episcopal power to govern is so exclusive and indivisible that a nonordained person cannot effectively share in it. This position found its way into the Code of Canon Law of 1983, which states: "Those who have received sacred orders are qualified . . . for the power of governance." The code continues: "Lay members of the Christian faithful *(christifideles laici)* can *cooperate* in the exercise of the same power." In other terms, nonordained persons are not qualified to "participate" in the "power of governance . . . also called the power of jurisdiction," which in practice means that they are excluded from any active voice in deliberative processes that could be regarded as an exercise of the bishop's jurisdiction.[6] The capacity for "cooperation," although ill defined in theory, in practice has been interpreted as rendering the laity "qualified to be consulted" or "able to help with the implementation of a decision."[7]

Historical precedents do not support this new policy: they offer ample evidence against it. The most striking examples of laypersons participating in the power of governance are the convocations of nine ecumenical councils by the Byzantine emperors and empresses, and the active participation, in the West, of nonordained persons in universal (later recognized as ecumenical) and ecumenical councils.[8] A further instance is in the governing of "quasi dioceses" by abbesses (surely not ordained!), a situation upheld as correct by the Holy See from the Middle Ages well into the nineteenth century. Such instances (and many more could be adduced) should be enough to induce serious doubt about the validity of the present policy.

A participation of the nonordained in the episcopal power should not be regarded as somehow destructive of the bishop's jurisdiction, partly because there is a dogmatic limit to participation (there cannot be any participation in the bishop's sacramental capacity to consecrate and to ordain), and partly because the participation in any given case would be subject at some point to an episcopal judgment. Yet to take part in deliberations and effectively contribute to a final decision would strengthen the bond of *communio* between the bishop and his people; it could bring significant help to the bishop and would make good use of the wisdom and responsibility of the nonordained. As it is now, many of the talents and energies of the nonordained are condemned to lie fallow.

*Communio* does not exclude authority, but it demands new manners in exercising it. Peremptory orders are alien to it, because obedience is perceived as a virtue rooted in intelligence and freedom, a "reasonable sacrifice." *Communio* demands firm laws and compliance, but legislation and administration must be performed as humble service. In such a climate, the laws are well received and observed.

*Communio* postulates an "open government": a rigid wall of secrecy would destroy all partnership between the governed and the governors. In a climate of openness, there is mutual accountability, not in a legal but in a moral sense. The hierarchy must recognize that they cannot govern well unless they ask for and accept contributions from the people. Bishops (including the Bishop of Rome) have a need (and hence a duty) to consult in both doctrinal and prudential matters. They need counsel even more in doctrinal matters because the revelation is preserved in the memory of the universal church (cf. Vatican I and II); they need it in prudential matters because the hierarchy has no gift of unfailing prudence. There is a marked difference between the promised assistance of the Spirit to the church in matters doctrinal and matters practical—a difference that is rarely attended to. Yet few distinctions are more important for the correct understanding of the operations of the hierarchy in general and the papacy in particular. In matters of doctrine, the divine guarantee is absolute: historical events and human opinions will not prevail over the revealed truth; the message of salvation is as fresh today as it was when first announced; the church is eternally young. In prudential matters, however, the officials acting "in the name of the church" hold no divine promise to assure that their actions will represent the highest degree of prudence—or that those actions will be prudent at all. The consequences of this traditional and sound distinction are far-reaching. The response of the people to a doctrinal definition cannot but be an assent of faith, "I believe"; the response of the same people to a practical determination can be justifiably critical.

In a church of *communio*, the social manners ought to be simple: courtly titles and senatorial robes do not fit in well. The official language cannot but be straightforward—according to the gospel your speech should consist in yes and no.

Does this mean that the church of *communio* is a democracy in the political sense? Absolutely not. The People of God believe that the mandate "feed my flock" comes from the Redeemer; it is a power from above, with its specific content as it was articulated by the two Vatican councils. But they believe also that each person—justified and sanctified—is endowed with a sense of faith, intelligence, and moral sensitivity. Accordingly, those in charge must honor the people by being open and transparent with them not only concerning the general policies of their administration but about the use of the church's material assets. They must also provide swift justice in cases of distress. Such manners generate mutual trust that cements the social body together more than any strict ordinance.

The reader may have noticed that I am not using the word *laity*: it is an ambivalent term. In the early centuries, it referred to all the members of the church; in modern usage, it designates the nonordained. Admittedly, we hear a great deal about the charism of the laity, but a critical question cannot be avoided: How could a charism emerge from the fact that a person has not received the sacrament of orders—from a nonevent? What would it add to the universal charism of the baptized believers?

A theology that claims "The laity has the special task to sanctify the secular *but is not mandated to build the church from the inside*" is a truncated theory. Similarly, to assert that the business of the clergy is to build the church from the inside and not to improve the world would be faulty theology. St. Catherine of Siena was a layperson and worked to restore the integrity of the internal structures of the church; Pope St. Gregory the Great was a bishop and in a time of distress assumed much of the civil administration of the city of Rome. The nonordained can certainly be incorporated into decision-making processes in the church—provided, of course, that they have living faith and charity.

Vatican Council II called the church a "hierarchical *communio*"—a venerable expression since it comes from a council, but it needs explanation. "Hierarchical" is an adjective: it indicates that "by divine ordination" (cf. Council of Trent, canon 6, *de ordine*) the organism is structured. While there is a fundamental equality among the members, there are also real differences (not merely functional) in the tasks and offices allotted to each. To speak of "hierarchical *communio*" is to tell the truth but not the full truth: the expression does not speak of "service." To call the church a "structured *communio*" might be a better way of speaking.[9]

## *Communio* among Ordained Persons: A Particular *Communio* within the Universal *Communio*

What is the sacrament of orders? What happens in an ordination? Normally, we think of ordination as the receiving of a gift through the imposition of hands with the appropriate prayers accompanying it. In our imagination we see this event as a grace descending from above on the candidate. This perception reverses the true dynamics of the sacrament. Ordination is an act of the Spirit: he lifts up a person and incorporates him into the particular *communio* of the "servant shepherds," to serve *and* lead the community.

The *communio* among the ordained is structured in a particular way: there are bishops, presbyters, and deacons. Yet this structure is not built on a military pattern, so that the highest in rank commands and the lower ones merely obey. They must function as of one mind and of one heart: they all need each other. This internal unity of the clergy needs to be manifest in all canonical rules dealing with the clergy. This simple statement is pregnant with practical consequences. It means that none of the three orders have the full intelligence and prudence required for taking care of a local church (a diocese): they must work together, and canon law must set the framework for their work. The bishop alone cannot govern the diocese.

## *Communio* of Bishops and Presbyters in the Local Churches

In the invisible world of charisms, the bishop and the presbyters are members of one organic "sacerdotal" body; it follows that on the external level there must be an organ representing this unity; hence, there must be an effectively functioning *presbyterium* presided over by the bishop. To have a priests' council is not a concession; it is a theological necessity.

The promise of obedience that is demanded from the priest at the time of his ordination must be understood in the context of the existing sacramental *communio*: it is a one-sided expression of a sacred covenant between the bishop and the priest. A future reform of the rite may well include a promise on the part of the bishop to be faithful to the priest and respect his intelligence and legitimate freedom. Our canon law, as it is now, puts the emphasis more on a "superior-inferior relationship" between the bishop and the priests than on their *communio*, which is to say that a priority has been given to what is hierarchical over what is *communio*—a reversing of the good order.

Although ordinarily we speak of the bishop and "his priests," in truth, they are God's priests. The priests, like the bishops, receive their "power to feed the flock" not from any human superior but directly from God through the sacrament of ordination. The role of the bishop is to insert the priests "anointed by the Spirit" into the visible structure of the diocese.

### *Communio* in Local Churches between the Deacons and the Priests (Sacerdotes: Presbyters and Bishops)

Although recently the diaconate has been restored, overall, the deacons have not assumed their ancient task—allotted to them in the early centuries. Their traditional task was twofold: to administer the physical and material possessions of the church (so that the bishops and presbyters would be free to proclaim the word), and to take care of the indigents, of the orphans, the homeless, and—in more general terms—those whose lives were broken.

Such an enrichment of the deacons' task (called to proclaim the charity of the church), need not take away or diminish their participation in the liturgy; rather, it would incorporate them more intensively into the daily life of the community. It opens the possibility of having not only "permanent" deacons but also full-time deacons.

Let me mention here that the ordination of women to the diaconate definitely remains a "disputed" question, and hence an open one. The historical evidence that in the Eastern church, for several centuries, women were called to "serve" the needs of the community, and that they were consecrated by prayer and imposition of hands, is not in doubt.

### *Communio* among the Bishops: The Bishops' College

The theological opinions about the nature of the bishops' college are far from being settled. All agree that it is a structured *communio*: the pope is the head of the college; the bishops are the members.

One school, however, sees the pope as having two offices: he is the Vicar of Christ endowed individually with the plenitude of power, *and* he is the head of the episcopal college participating in the collective power of the college. To illustrate this view: When an ecumenical council is in session, the pope shares—in a privileged way; he is the head—the power of the college. However, should anything go wrong with the council's deliberations, he can simply assume his office of Vicar of Christ and, well, dissolve the council.

Another school sees the power of the college as one and undivided, and sees the college as not divisible. Peter's successor has one office: the Vicar of Peter who is the head of the college. The rock on which the church is built is intimately united with the edifice; it is never a piece alone. Admittedly, we are dealing with a complex and complicated issue, but a theology of *communio* could hardly admit the theory of "two offices."[10]

*Communio* of bishops contains a complex set of rights and duties. The bishops together have the task of taking care of the universal church: the principal instrument for this purpose has been and remains their gathering in a universal council. It is the prime manifestation of the "episcopal collegiality."

Legitimate partial gatherings, however, are also authentic expressions of the bishops' unity; historically, these gatherings have been a way of taking care of a group of local churches within the same cultural or political region. Right from the beginning the church honored such partial assemblies and listened to their voice. It follows that regional synods—or for that matter, the episcopal conferences—have a life of their own and share in the power of the episcopal college. The theological *communio* of the bishops—apart from the celebration of an ecumenical council—is not expressed in our *ius vigens*, the presently valid canon law.

## Communio between the See of Rome and the Local Churches: The Exercise of Primacy

Pope John Paul II in his encyclical *Ut Unum Sint (That They May Be One)* made an extraordinary request:

> I insistently pray the Holy Spirit to shine his light upon us, enlightening all the Pastors as theologians of our churches, that we may seek—together, of course—the forms in which this ministry may accomplish a service of love recognized by all concerned. . . . This is an immense task, which we cannot refuse and which I cannot carry out by myself.[11]

We saw numerous responses published in articles and books. The authors deserve attention, but most if not all of them failed to realize the extent of the problem. They focused on the office of the pope—as the encyclical did—and offered various modifications in order to make it more attractive to Christian churches and communities—so as to promote the cause of ecumenism. But the papacy does not exist alone, it is an organic part of the *communio*. There is no way of finding "forms in which this ministry may accomplish a service of love recognized by all concerned" without a radical conversion of the whole church— communities and individuals—in their attitude toward the papacy. If the papacy ought to change, the community needs to change with it. Reform can be obtained only through coordinated dialectical movements.[12]

It follows that any proposal concerning the reform of the exercise of the primacy must be done with the understanding that changes in the papal office are possible only if they are balanced by *corresponding transformations within the community at large*—and those transformations might be more difficult to obtain than revisions to the exercise of the papal office. If the pope is willing to transfer some responsibility, another organ must accept it.

Let us see, then, how the church could move from a highly centralized administration toward a *communio*-oriented operation—without harming our traditions.

1. The change must begin in a reformed understanding of the Petrine office; it must be a perception that honors the "determinations" of the two Vatican Councils but does not amplify them. We have good directions from Vatican Council II: one of the prime tasks of the pope is to coordinate with divinely given authority God's gifts in the community. His duty is to discover and recognize in the churches God's particular gifts in their multiplicity; he must be alert to them. He must surely "confirm them in their faith," but he must also be listening to them— consistently.[13]

2. Further, the pope is divinely commissioned (and assisted by the Spirit) to be a privileged witness to our tradition, the tradition that lives in the whole church. He must be careful not to impose his personal theological or philosophical opinions on the faithful. The distinction may not be easy, but it ought to be honored, nonetheless. The discreet and restrained attitudes of popes John XXIII and Paul VI during the Second Vatican Council set an example. Also, the pope must make sure that his subordinates observe the same rule scrupulously.[14]

3. As the pope is free to exercise his "rights," he is free to use *restraint* in the use of the same rights. Such restraint can help the development of a church of *communio*. An example illuminates this principle better than any explanation. The pope has the right to appoint bishops. In the first millennium, he exercised this right in emergencies or necessities. In the second millennium, the right became "ordinary practice." The input of the local faithful has been reduced to a bare minimum. A return to the earlier practice would enable the people to contribute more to the church's governance, and the *communio* between the Holy See and the people could increase greatly.

4. There is a need to honor the principle of subsidiarity. Recently, officials for the Holy See have repeatedly voiced the idea that there is no room for subsidiarity in the church: the pope cannot be subsidiary to the bishops. The problem, however, is more with the name than with the substance and intent of the principle. To honor the role of a lower organ before the higher ones come into play is equivalent to honoring the nature and purpose of every organ; if the lower one is functioning well, an undue intervention from above can provoke only stagnation and paralysis.

5. Intense *communio* between the head of the episcopal college and its members cannot flourish if communication remains on the level of occasional consultations; those who are one in the episcopal order must have an effective share in the acts of teaching and in the processes of decision making. Such participation can only strengthen the primacy.

The papacy does not exist in isolation. The Bishop of Rome is part of the episcopal college—its head, surely, but still a member. Vatican Council II asserted an internal "ontological" collegiality sustained by the Spirit (one Spirit in many bishops!), from which the works of collegiality must flow; if it exists, it must become effective. For this intent of the Council a pale imitation was substituted and called affective collegiality. What is the force of a collegial *affectus* if it does not spring from a Spirit given internal reality?

Episcopal conferences today are hardly more than the gathering of the bishops with the task of executing orders and directions coming from Rome. National and regional conferences have potentials in creativity that they should be able to use to good effect. There is a need for giving life to the Roman Synod that gathers the representatives of episcopal conferences. It needs to be lifted up so the members can use their intelligence freely to identify problems of the church and to propose remedies.

6. The reform of the exercise of the primacy cannot be accomplished without the reform of the Roman Curia, since so much of that exercise consists in the operations of the Curia. To put the issue in its proper context, we should recall that the offices and officials of the Curia have no power of their own. Granted, canon law speaks of their "ordinary" power, but in reality the pope lends them power. In matters of doctrine, of course, not even the pope can delegate them any power because the assistance of the Spirit to Peter's successor is a personal privilege that he cannot share with anyone.

Problems usually arise from the fact that the Roman Curia is in the service of the whole Catholic *communio*, that is, in the service of the faithful at large and in particular of the bishops, but it is hardly in dialogue with them. The lack of constitutional channels for any such communication is often justified by saying "the Curia is subject to the pope only."

Could anything be done without in any way diminishing the rights of the papacy? Admitting that the issue is complex and that a lot of reflection is needed to find new "forms in which this ministry [that is, of the Curia] may accomplish a service of love recognized by all concerned," a beginning could be made without much difficulty.

The same pope who appoints the Curia could certainly appoint an international episcopal committee with the mandate to "visit" the Curia and evaluate its operations—say every five years—with the duty to report to the pope in person. This would in no way hurt the primacy; it would be a striking manifestation of episcopal collegiality. Such a procedure would help everybody all around: the Curia would benefit since its accomplishments could be recognized and its weaknesses identified; the pope would benefit because he would get an independent report from his brother bishops (those not involved directly in his administration); and finally, in the long run, the universal episcopate as well as the faithful at large would get improved service. This is a modest proposal: it is no more than an attempt to apply to the Roman Curia the rule *ecclesia semper reformanda*, which is applicable to all human structures inside the church—and the Curia is a human institution.

## Religious Communities in a Church of *Communio*

Here I use the expression "religious communities" in a general and popular sense to cover the great variety of "specially dedicated" associations, officially called "institutes of consecrated or apostolic life." No matter what their structures and norms are, if they wish to flourish in the third millennium, they must appropriate the essential elements of *communio*; they must do it within their own household and in their relationships with the local and universal church. For some, mainly those who have their origins in the first millennium, this will be easier: the Rule of Benedict for his monasteries remains an authentic guide for building small "cities of God" where *communio* reigns supreme. Orders founded in the second millennium may have to undertake more reflection and adapt themselves more extensively if they were designed in keeping with the modes and manners of a highly centralized church. To seek the reforms needed is not infidelity to their original charism; it is fidelity to the ever-evolving charismatic life of the universal church. To cling stubbornly to structures and norms that the church is leaving behind would be to choose stagnation and demise.

No more need to be said on this matter, because the ways and means of a new life ought to be created by the communities themselves: the seed for such sensible transformation is in the original charism. The Spirit who once inspired the founding members is not dead or absent: his life-giving generosity is ever present. Excessive fidelity to the structures that worked well in the past can be a radical apostasy from the life-giving present.

## Communio and Ecumenism

Here I can only indicate the nature of the "ecumenical movement" in the existing matrix of the *communio*—stressing the need for both an ongoing study of the issue and a practice consistently improved by experience.

The restoration of the unity among Christian churches and communities is essentially a work toward expanding and perfecting an already existing *communio*. Such a basic *communio* is present whenever there is a unity in their profession of faith and in their possession of the sacraments.

No universally applicable law exists as to how the unity could be expanded and perfected: in the concrete order, it is always a healing process between various units that by Christ's intent should be one, but that by human failures became separated.

This healing process is complex because it involves the conversion of the minds and hearts of communities and immensely numerous persons. Throughout the process, we should keep in mind that the starting point cannot be to "bring back to Christ" a group of "schismatics" or "heretics" but to find a common understanding of the Word of God with another community that has also surrendered to Christ by receiving his word and/or his sacrament.

This perception also shows why this healing process can never consist only in doctrinal dialogues—indispensable as they are. An agreement not backed and sustained by the community at large cannot create unity: the aftermath of the Councils of Lyon (1245) and Florence (1439–45) should prove that much abundantly. If today we hear that the dialogues among the churches are not producing the expected results, the response is that often enough expectations were misplaced. Time has come for a more realistic approach: Christians praying together and practicing charity jointly can advance the union of churches as much or more than learned dialogues. A conception that places too much hope in the agreements among the leaders of the churches is not a conception that flows from the understanding of the church as *communio*.

So much for seminal thoughts: they need to unfold and be put into practice. They have the potential for hundredfold fruits.

## Conclusion: Looking into the Future

Vatican Council II ended on the feast of the Immaculate Conception in 1965. After the solemn Mass at St. Peter's, Yves Congar, who contributed so much to the success of the Council, wrote in his diary: "Today, the church is sent to the world: *ad gentes, ad populos. Incipiendo, non a Ierosolyma sed a Roma* [to the nations, to the peoples. Starting not in Jerusalem but from Rome]. The Council will have an explosive force [*va éclater*] in the world. The moment of Pentecost that John XXIII has foretold has become a reality today."[15]

Some forty years later, we look back. Was Congar right? Has the Council become an explosive force among the nations? Do the peoples of the earth see the church coming to them in a new robe and speaking a new message? It seems, it appears, that the opposite has happened. While in some ways the church has become more visible than ever, in other ways it has revealed immense internal weaknesses and the nations are hardly listening. Did Congar misread the signs of the times and—in the exultation of the last session of the Council—fall into a false prophecy?

Not so. Congar saw right. He had sharp sight and good perception. Yet—as happened even to biblical prophets before him—he perceived well what was coming, but misjudged the distance of the coming. He saw a faraway event as if it were present. Maybe, in the exultation of singing the great hymn of thanksgiving *Te Deum*, he failed to realize how much time will be needed to move from insights to practices— from vision to legislation. He was so enticed by the magnificence of the conciliar decisions that he did not notice the obstacles on the way to their implementation. Today the dynamics that dominated the debates of the Council are active again in the universal church; the Council is replayed in the community at large. The currents from the second millennium favoring strong centralization are here and working, but the currents promoting *communio* (for the third millennium?) are also present and operating.

At the Council, a strong minority wanted no changes from the post-Tridentine church: they found allies among the faithful after the Council. At the same Council, a majority wanted to renew the church by taking their inspiration from biblical and patristic sources: they found dedicated followers after the great meeting. And—just as it happened forty years ago—the two currents keep colliding.

In our church of today, there is a fair amount of hidden dissent from the Council, mostly in the form of reinterpreting it to the point where it becomes insignificant and irrelevant. Yet, throughout the church, there is also an immense desire for the implementation of the Council's decisions.

How will it all end? The church is in God's hands. But while we try to look into the future and we ask, *What is to come?*, it is right and just to recall again the statement used by ecumenical councils: *"placuit Spiritui sancto et nobis"*—"it pleased the Holy Spirit and us."

The key to the future is there. Whatever has pleased the Spirit has an intrinsic force that will not get lost in history. What God has initiated, he will bring to a good end. In God's own time, the Council will emerge in all the splendor and with the radical exigencies that Yves Congar perceived so well. Gregory VII is remembered for having initiated a movement toward a strong centralized government. Perhaps a millennium from now, John XXIII will be remembered for having changed the course of events and set the church on the path for experiencing increasingly the goodness of *communio*. Blessed be his name.

Toward the end of the Council, when the outcome was already certain, Congar wrote in his diary: *"vidimus—videbimus mirabilia* (we see—we shall see wonders)."[16] The correct answer to our original question—"What will the future hold?"—should be: In God's own time, *vidimus—videbimus mirabilia*: "we see—we shall see wonders."

## Notes

1. For a detailed historical account of the origins of this centralizing policy, see Friedrich Kempf, "Primitiale und episcopal-synodale Struktur der Kirche

vor der gregorianischen Reform," *Archivium Historiae Pontificae* 16 (1978): 22–66. I quote the summary preceding the article (my translation from the original Latin "Summarium"):

> In antiquity the *episcopal* synodal structures were of great importance; they prevailed over the primatial structures. In the Carolingian and Ottonian times, however, they lost their strength while the primitial structures increasingly prevailed. [These changes] transformed the relations between bishops and metropolitans, between metropolitans and the Holy See, between the Holy See and the episcopate. There is no doubt that the Latin church by choosing its own way separated itself *[se alienaverit]* from the Greek church which preserved much better the episcopal synodal structures. This alienation went so far as to make their schism inevitable. (Ibid., 27)

See also Kempf, "Die Eingliederung der überdiözesanen Hierarchie in das Papalsystem des kanonischen Reacts von der gregorianischen Reform bis zu Innocenz III," *Archivium Historiae Pontificae* 18 (1980): 57–96. "Summarium" in translation:

> The metropolitans, primates, and patriarchs who in early times enjoyed a relative autonomy, in the Code of Canon Law are listed among the persons whose power consists in a participation in the power of the Roman primacy. The Latin church alone holds this conception; it evolved gradually from the Carolingian times; it was forcefully applied by the popes of the Gregorian reform, then somewhat loosely by the contemporary canonists; more firmly by Gratian. Finally, it was firmly established by the Decretists and the Decretalists, also by Innocent III, and it became prevalent for the following seven centuries. To this long historical period the ecclesiological doctrine of Vatican Council II put an end. (Ibid., 57)

Kempf remarks in the conclusion of this second article: "In any case, the attitude [of the Latin church] to the Eastern churches has been substantially changed" (ibid., 96).

2. A remark by a contemporary bishop is to the point: "Above all, Vatican Council II was looking for a sincere opening to the world and to the modern culture. After the Council of Trent, and during the whole period of the counter reformation, our church withdrew more and more into itself and became locked into an attitude against modernity. On the long run, this mentality proved itself to be sterile and fruitless. The church's manner of presenting itself and announcing its message contributed greatly to the emergence of times and of a culture that was not ours anymore. For this reason John XXIII proposed his program of *aggiornamento*." Jozef De Kesel, Auxiliary Bishop of Mechelen-Brussels, "Annoncer l'Evangile aujourd'hui," *Nouvelle Revue Théologique* 126 (2004): 3–4.

3. Heribert Mühlen, *Una mystica persona: Eine Person in vielen Personen* (München: Schöningh, 1967).

4. For this method of "doing theology" by "imagination," I wish to give credit to Ghislain Lafont, monk of the Monastery of Pierre-qui-vire in France and former professor of theology at the Ateneo Sant'Anselmo in Rome; see his book *Imaginer l'Eglise catholique* (Paris: Cerf, 1995), available in English translation: *Imagining the Catholic Church* (Collegeville, Minn.: Liturgical Press, 2000). The method is analogous to that of Einstein's thought experiments; it is as simple as it is productive. There is ample field for its application in canon law. In fact, this chapter could be considered an introduction to a massive undertaking: imagining a new code of canon law (with all its canons) grounded in the theology of *communio*.

5. *De optimo reipublicae statu deque nova insula Utopia. Libellus vere aureus, nec minus salutaris quam festivus, clarissimi disertissimique viri THOMAE MORI inclitae civitatis Londinensis civis et Vicecomitis* ("On the Best State of a Commonwealth and on the New Island of Utopia: A Truly golden Handbook, No Less Beneficial than Entertaining, by the Most Distinguished and Eloquent Author THOMAS MORE, Citizen and Undersheriff of the Famous City of London"). See *Utopia by Thomas More*, ed. George Logan et al. (Cambridge: Cambridge University Press, 1999), 3.

6. *Code of Canon Law*, English translation by the Canon Law Society of America (Washington, D.C.: Canon Law Society of America, 1998), canon 129, sections 1 and 2 (emphasis added).

7. Canon 1421, section 2, at a first reading, seems to allow genuine "participation" of laypersons in the power of jurisdiction, and it is often quoted as a proof that in principle they are not excluded. It reads: "The conference of bishops can also permit the appointment of lay persons as judges; when it is necessary, one of them can be selected to form a college." A closer examination, however, of the text and context, and some reflection on the intent of the legislator, suggest the opposite: the canon determines how far "cooperation" may go; it makes no concession in the matter of participation. It uses the term "judge" in a restricted sense. A lay "judge" is never judge in a normal full sense: a lay judge may never function alone; several lay judges may not form a college; a single lay judge can be given a place within a college provided all the others are in orders. To conclude from such minimal concessions that the legislator *intended* to reverse or weaken his doctrinal statements in paragraphs 1 and 2 of canon 129 can hardly be a balanced—and correct—interpretation. The fact that nowhere in the code or in the subsequent practice of the Holy See can we ever find a clear instance of laypersons being permitted to "participate" in the power of jurisdiction indicates strongly that there is no such concession in canon 1421 section 2 either.

8. "The oldest [Nicea] of these assemblies [ecumenical councils] have this in common with the most recent one [Vatican Council II] that they were purely episcopal councils. In between there is a widening of the circle of participants in favor of abbots ... ; of the representatives of ecclesiastical bodies,

cathedral chapters and universities, and finally even in favor of the representatives of the secular power. In the councils of the central period of the Middle Ages not only the Church but Christendom, both ecclesiastical and lay, were represented." Hubert Jedin, *Ecumenical Councils in the Catholic Church* (New York: Herder and Herder, 1960), 230–31.

9. Alexander Carter, former bishop of Sault Sainte Marie, Ontario, Canada, reports an impromptu exhortation addressed in 1939 by Pope Pius XI to the students of the Canadian College in Rome, on the fiftieth anniversary of their college. Carter was one of the students present.

> You are the young priests who have come to Rome. You are going back to Canada and will continue to build the Church there. I do not place any limits on the providence of God, but I am sure that my life expectancy is very short. I want you to take this message away with you. The church, the mystical body of Christ, has become a monstrosity. The head is very large, but the body is shrunken. You the priests, must rebuild that body of the church and the only way that you can rebuild it is to mobilize the lay people. You must call upon the lay people to become, along with you, the witnesses of Christ. You must call them especially to bring Christ back to the workplace, to the marketplace.

Carter comments: "This powerful message was like a Last Will and Testament of the Pope. As a matter of fact that was his last public audience. All audiences were cancelled the following day and he died not long afterward." Alex Carter, *A Canadian Bishop's Memoirs* (North Bay, Ontario: Tomiko Publications, 1994), 50–51.

10. The expression "Vicar of Christ" for the pope entered into use around the twelfth century; earlier, "Vicar of Peter" was current. The title "Vicar of Christ" was born out of devotion and became hallowed through its constant usage by the faithful. It was never meant to be a precise theological or canonical statement; if it were taken literally, it would raise enormous problems. Vatican Council II tried to balance its one-sided use for the pope by repeatedly insisting that every bishop was a vicar of Christ in his diocese, which is essentially an assertion that there is one episcopate and all who received the sacrament share in it. The pope receives no higher gift in his ordination than the other bishops, but he is given a much broader field for the exercise of his sacramental power. See "Titles, Papal," in *The Papacy: An Encyclopedia* (New York: Routledge, 2002), 3:1494–95.

11. John Paul II, *Ut Unum Sint* (25 May 1995), no. 96.

12. An example makes this clear: Assume a political community that has been governed by a philosopher king (your can think of Plato's Republic), where the citizens have been educated to expect all enlightenment and initiative as coming from above. Such a society lives by one vision and is used to concerted obedience. If you ever want to change their way of life, it

cannot be done by bringing modifications into the office of the philosopher king alone.

13. The often voiced distinction between *ecclesia docens* and *ecclesia discens*, "the teaching and learning church," can be misleading and even damaging if it is applied literally. The ongoing duty of the hierarchy is to learn about and to obey the tradition that lives in the whole church; in the witnessing of this tradition, however, the hierarchy holds a privileged position, *sacred principatum*, "holy priority."

14. The well-known silencing of theologians in the years before Vatican Council II was due to an excess in Rome: they were condemned because they did not follow the theological opinions prevailing in Roman offices and universities. They were quietly rehabilitated by the Council.

15. Yves Congar, *Mon journal du Concile* (Paris: Cerf, 2002), vol. II, 515.

16. Ibid., 503.

# Acknowledgments

Some of the chapters of this book were initially written in the form of lectures or panel presentations as part of Boston College's "The Church in the Twenty-First Century" initiative. Other contributions from scholars from a variety of fields were commissioned to provide a more complete discussion of this subject matter. Special thanks are due to all the contributors to this volume.

# Contributors

R. Scott Appleby is professor of history at the University of Notre Dame, where he also serves as the John M. Regan, Jr. Director of the Joan B. Kroc Institute for International Peace Studies. He has directed Notre Dame's Cushwa Center for the Study of American Catholicism and codirected the Fundamentalism Project, an international public policy study. A historian of religion who earned a Ph.D. from the University of Chicago (1985), Appleby is the author of *The Ambivalence of the Sacred: Religion, Violence, and Reconciliation* and *Church and Age Unite! The Modernist Impulse in American Catholicism.* He is a coauthor, with Gabriel Almond and Emmanuel Sivan, of *Strong Religion: The Rise of Fundamentalisms around the World* and *Transforming Parish Ministry: The Changing Roles of Clergy, Laity, and Women Religious.*

Mary Jo Bane is Thornton Bradshaw Professor of Public Policy and Management at Harvard University's Kennedy School of Government. She was assistant secretary for families and children at the U.S. Department of Health and Human Services from 1993 to 1996, and cochair of President Clinton's Working Group on Welfare Reform, resigning after the president signed the 1996 welfare bill. She is the author of *Here to Stay: American Families in the Twentieth Century* and, with David T. Ellwood, *Welfare Realities: From Rhetoric to Reform.* With Brent Coffin and Ronald Thiemann, she edited *Who Will Provide? The Changing Role of Religion in American Social Welfare.* Bane is a graduate of the Foreign Service School of Georgetown University and has a master's degree in teaching and a Ph.D. in education from the Harvard Graduate School of Education.

John Beal was ordained for the presbyterate of the Diocese of Erie (Pennsylvania) in 1974 after theological studies at the Catholic University of Leuven in Belgium. In 1985 he received his JCD from The Catholic University of America, and in 1992 he joined the faculty of the Department (now School) of Canon Law at The Catholic University, where he is now associate professor of canon law. He has published numerous articles in *The Jurist, Studia Canonica, Monitor Ecclesiasticus, Concilium, The New Theology Review,* and other scholarly publications, and is coeditor of and a contributor to *A New Commentary on the Code of Canon Law,* sponsored by the Canon Law Society of America.

**Michael J. Buckley, S.J.,** is professor of theology at Boston College. He completed his doctoral studies at the University of Chicago, and his dissertation was subsequently published as *Motion and Motion's God.* Before joining Boston College in 1992, he was rector of the Jesuit School of Theology at Berkeley, where he taught for eighteen years; visiting professor at the Pontifical Gregorian University in Rome; executive director of the Committee on Doctrine for the United States Bishops; and a professor at the University of Notre Dame. In 2001, he delivered the D'Arcy Lectures at Oxford University. He is the author of numerous scholarly articles and books.

**Lisa Sowle Cahill** is J. Donald Monan, S.J., Professor at Boston College, where she has taught theology since 1976. She is a past president of the Catholic Theological Society of America, has served as a theological consultant to the U.S. bishops in preparation for the 1987 Synod on the Laity, and is a member of the Catholic Common Ground Initiative Committee, established by Cardinal Joseph Bernardin to improve dialogue in the church. Cahill's most recent book is *Family: A Christian Social Perspective.* Her Santa Clara Lecture, "On Being a Catholic Feminist," was published by the University of Santa Clara in 2003.

**Francine Cardman** is associate professor of historical theology at Weston Jesuit School of Theology in Cambridge, Massachusetts. She holds a Ph.D. in historical theology from Yale University. Cardman has been a member of the Eastern Orthodox–Roman Catholic Consultation in the United States, is a past president of the North American Academy of Ecumenists, has served on the board of directors of Network, the Catholic social justice lobby in Washington, D.C., and is a founding member of the Women's Theological Center in Boston. Her teaching and research interests include the history and theology of early Christianity, early Christian ethics, the history of Christian spirituality, feminist theology, and ecumenism. She has translated Augustine's commentary on the Sermon on the Mount and has published articles and essays on early Christian theology and the development of doctrine; praxis and ecclesiology in early Christianity; women's ministry in the early church; Vatican II; and issues in ecumenical theology.

**Thomas Groome** is professor of theology and religious education at Boston College. He holds a Ph.D. in theology and education from Union Theological Seminary and Columbia Teacher's College. His most recent book is *What Makes Us Catholic: Eight Gifts for Life*, and he is also the author of Sadlier's *Coming to Faith* religion curriculum (K–8 grades), the most widely used catechetical series throughout American Catholic schools and parishes.

**S. Mark Heim** is the Samuel Abbot Professor of Christian Theology at Andover Newton Theological School in Newton Centre, Massachusetts. He has been deeply involved in issues of religious pluralism and Christian ecumenism. An ordained American Baptist minister, he represents his denomination on the Faith and Order Commission of the National Council and World Council of Churches. In addition to the theology of religions and ecumenical theology, his research interests include science and theology, Baptist history, and global Christianity. His writings on topics from comparative theology to Baptist identity appear frequently in professional and scholarly journals. He is the author of *Is Christ the Only Way?*; *Salvations: Truth and Difference in Religion*; and *The Depth of the Riches: A Trinitarian Theology of Religious Ends*.

**Terence L. Nichols** is associate professor of theology and chair of the theology department at the University of St. Thomas, St. Paul, Minnesota. He is the author of *That All May Be One: Hierarchy and Participation in the Church* and *The Sacred Cosmos: Christian Faith and the Challenge of Naturalism*, as well as of various articles in *Pro Ecclesia, Gregorianum, International Philosophical Quarterly, Zygon*, and other journals.

**Ladislas Orsy, S.J.,** studied philosophy and canon law at the Gregorian University in Rome, theology at the Faculté de Théologie St. Albert de Louvain, Belgium, and civil law at Oxford University in England. He taught at the Gregorian University, Fordham University, and The Catholic University of America, and he is presently professor of law at Georgetown University Law Center. Orsy is the author of several books and numerous articles, among them "Lonergan's Cognitional Theory and

Foundational Issues in Canon Law: Method, Philosophy and Law, Theology and Canon Law" in *Studia Canonica*; *From Vision to Legislation: From the Council to a Code of Laws*; *The Church: Learning and Teaching: Magisterium, Assent, Dissent, Academic Freedom*; and *Theology and Canon Law: New Horizons for Legislation and Interpretation*.

**Pheme Perkins** is a professor of New Testament at Boston College. She has served as president of the Catholic Biblical Association of America and is an associate editor of the *New Oxford Annotated Bible*. She holds a Ph.D. from Harvard University and is the author of over twenty books on the New Testament and early Christianity, including the commentaries on John and the Johannine Epistles in the *New Jerome Biblical Commentary*; *Peter, Apostle for the Whole Church*; *Jesus as Teacher*; and *Reading the New Testament*.

**Stephen J. Pope** is an associate professor in the theology department of Boston College, where he teaches social ethics and theological ethics. He received his Ph.D. in theological ethics from the University of Chicago in 1988. Pope has also taught at the Saint Paul Seminary in St. Paul, Minnesota. He participates in a faculty summer seminar at Wycliffe Hall, Oxford University, on the relationship between science and Christianity. Among his publications are *The Evolution of Altruism and the Ordering of Love* and the edited book *The Ethics of Aquinas*.

**James E. Post** is president and a cofounder of Voice of the Faithful and professor of management at Boston University, where he teaches strategic management of nonprofits, business ethics, and corporate public affairs. Among his fifteen books are the award-winning *Private Management and Public Policy* (with Lee Preston) and *Redefining the Corporation* (with Lee Preston and Sybille Sachs). He has been a consultant to the World Health Organization, the U.S. Agency for International Development, the President's Commission on Sustainable Development, and the Nestle Audit Commission, an independent commission monitoring that company's business and marketing practices in developing nations.

**Francis A. Sullivan, S.J.,** entered the novitiate of the New England Province of the Society of Jesus after graduating from high school. During the course of studies, he obtained a master's degree in philosophy at Boston College in 1945, a master's degree in classics at Fordham

University in 1948, and an STL at Weston College in 1952. After ordination to the priesthood, he was sent to Rome for further study at the Gregorian University, where, after obtaining the STD in 1956, he was appointed to the faculty of theology and taught ecclesiology for the next thirty-six years. Since becoming an emeritus faculty member in 1992, he has joined Boston College as an adjunct professor of theology.

# index